Communicating Food in Korea

Korean Communities across the World

Series Editor: Joong-Hwan Oh, Hunter College, CUNY

Korean Communities across the World publishes works that address aspects of (a) the Korean American community, (b) Korean society, (c) the Korean communities in other foreign lands, or (d) transnational Korean communities. In the field of (a) the Korean American community, this series welcomes contributions involving concepts such as Americanization, pluralism, social mobility, migration/immigration, social networks, social institutions, social capital, racism/discrimination, settlement, identity, or politics, as well as a specific topic related to family/marriage, gender roles, generations, work, education, culture, citizenship, health, ethnic community, housing, ethnic identity, racial relations, social justice, social policy, and political views, among others. In the field of (b) Korean society, this series embraces scholarship on current issues such as gender roles, age/aging, low fertility, immigration, urbanization, gentrification, economic inequality, high youth unemployment, sexuality, democracy, political power, social injustice, the nation's educational problems, social welfare, capitalism, consumerism, labor, health, housing, crime, environmental degradation, and the social life in the digital age and its impacts, among others. Contributors in the field of (c) Korean communities in other foreign lands are encouraged to submit works that expand our understanding about the formation, vicissitudes, and major issues of an ethnic Korean community outside of South Korea and the Unites States, such as cultural or linguistic retention, ethnic identity, assimilation, settlement patterns, citizenship, economic activities, family relations, social mobility, and racism/discrimination. Lastly, contributions relating to (d) transnational Korean communities may touch upon transnational connectivity in family, economy/finance, politics, culture, technology, social institutions, and people.

Pachappa Camp: The First Koreatown in the United States, by Edward T. Chang

Communicating Food in Korea, edited by Jaehyeon Jeong and Joong-Hwan Oh

Korean Digital Diaspora: Transnational Social Movements and Diaspora Identity, by Hojeong Lee

Korean Food Television and the Korean Nation, by Jaehyeon Jeong

The 1.5 Generation Korean Diaspora: A Comparative Understanding of Identity, Transnationalism, and Culture, edited by Jane Yeonjae Lee and Minjin Kim

Newcomers and Global Migration in Contemporary South Korea: Across National Boundaries, edited by Sung-Choon Park and Joong-Hwan Oh

Health Disparities in Contemporary Korean Society: Issues and Subpopulations, edited by Sou Hyun Jang and Joong-Hwan Oh

Koreatowns: Exploring the Economics, Politics, and Identities of Korean Spatial Formation, by Jinwon Kim, Soo Mee Kim, and Stephen Suh

Korean International Students and the Making of Racialized Transnational Elites, by Sung-Choon Park

Transnational Mobility and Identity in and out of Korea, edited by Yonson Ahn

Korean Diaspora across the World: Homeland in History, Memory, Imagination, Media and Reality, edited by Eun-Jeong Han, Min Wha Han, and JongHwa Lee

Mediatized Transient Migrants: Korean Visa-Status Migrants' Transnational Everyday Lives and Media Use, by Claire Shinhea Lee

LA Rising: Korean Relations with Blacks and Latinos after Civil Unrest, by Kyeyoung Park

Communicating Food in Korea

Edited by
Jaehyeon Jeong and Joong-Hwan Oh

LEXINGTON BOOKS
Lanham • Boulder • New York • London

Published by Lexington Books
An imprint of The Rowman & Littlefield Publishing Group, Inc.
4501 Forbes Boulevard, Suite 200, Lanham, Maryland 20706
www.rowman.com

6 Tinworth Street, London SE11 5AL, United Kingdom

British Library Cataloguing in Publication Information Available

Library of Congress Cataloging-in-Publication Data

Names: Jeong, Jaehyeon, editor. | Oh, Joong-Hwan, editor.
Title: Communicating food in Korea / edited by Jaehyeon Jeong and Joong-Hwan Oh.
Description: Lanham : Lexington Books, [2021] | Series: Korean communities across the world | Includes bibliographical references and index. | Summary: "An in-depth investigation of the complex relationships among food, culture, and society in Korea, Communicating Food in Korea presents diverse interpretations of food's economic, political, and sociocultural relevance. Grounded in a variety of disciplines, the chapters research the ways food intersects with social issues in Korean society"—Provided by publisher.
Identifiers: LCCN 2020056263 | ISBN 9781793642257 (cloth ; permanent paper) | ISBN 9781793642264 (epub) | ISBN 9781793642271 (pbk)
Subjects: LCSH: Nutrition policy—Korea (South) | Food—Social aspects—Korea (South) | Food security—Korea (South) | Food in popular culture—Korea (South)
Classification: LCC TX360.K6 C66 2021 | DDC 394.1/2095195—dc23
LC record available at https://lccn.loc.gov/2020056263

Contents

Acknowledgments

The purpose of this edited volume is to introduce the scholarship of food studies, which focuses on the central themes and issues of how food is communicated in contemporary Korea. This work is intended for international readers who are less familiar with the development of this research field in Korean academia, and those readers who are also interested in academic work on food, culture, and society. We would like to thank Julie E. Kirsch, senior vice president and publisher at Rowman & Littlefield Publishing Group, Inc., and Courtney Morales, editor at Lexington Books, for their support in this project. We also acknowledge the support and assistance from staff members at Lexington Books who helped us with the publication process.

This edited volume of food studies in the Korean case addresses a wide variety of topics, such as colonialism, food symbolism, food safety, gastronationalism, Buddhist temple food, counterculture, cultural policy, multiculturalism, halal food, food tourism, food security, and food crisis. In this light, it will offer the readers a multidimensional account of the ways in which food communicates with diverse social and cultural issues in Korea. We would like to give special thanks to each author who permitted us to include his or her scholarly work in this edited volume. Finally, we would like to express our deepest gratitude to the Korea-based publishers who generously allowed us to include their published works. Without their support, this edited volume would not have been able to be shared with the world.

Introduction

Jaehyeon Jeong and Joong-Hwan Oh

Despite its mundane position in our lives, food is a key means of social communication and cultural signification. Food features as a marker of social distinction, a domain of customs and beliefs, and a system of symbolic value-creation, often intersecting with issues of social imagery, power relations, public policy, and cultural identities (Barthes 1979; DeSoucey 2010; Mintz 1985; Parasecoli 2008; Sutton 2010; Wright and Annes 2013). As a pervasive social phenomenon, our foodways—what we eat, where we eat, when we eat, how we eat, and with whom we eat, for example—are also germane to the organization of social life and reveal economic, political, ideological, and emotional relationships between people (Cwiertka and Walraven 2001).

Due to its central role in human relations and its sociocultural relevance, food has been an important focus of research across diverse disciplines in humanities and social sciences, from history to anthropology, sociology, cultural studies, political economy, and communication studies. Specifically, scholars have explored food's complex relationships with intersectional identities, the politics of representation, (post-)colonialism, neoliberalism, lifestyles, cultural capital, counterculture, social activism, sovereignty, and sustainability, among others (Adema 2000; Bower 2004; Collins; 2009; Cramer, Greene, and Walters 2011; Cwiertak 2012, 2014; de Solier 2005; Kelly 2017; Ketchum 2005; Oren 2013; Parasecoli 2008, 2013). Not surprisingly, there has been a noticeable growth of peer-reviewed journals that have provided interdisciplinary discussions on food, culture, and society, including *Anthropology of Food, Appetite, Digest: A Journal of Foodways & Culture, Food, Culture & Society, Food and Foodways, Food & History, Food Studies: An Interdisciplinary Journal*, and *Gastronomica*, to name a few.

While the increasing number of high standards of research has examined a wide range of topics as to food and foodways, much of academic attention has been given to the North American and European contexts. Of course, some Asian food cultures that have established a global profile, such as Chinese, Japanese, and Indian cuisines, have gained scholars' interests grounded in the fields of history, anthropology, ethnic studies, multicultural studies, and globalization studies (Appadurai 1981; Cwiertka 2006; Cwiertka and Walraven 2001; Hiroko 2008; Lu and Fine 1995; Ohnuki-Tierney 1993; Palat 2015). Notwithstanding the growing international recognition, Korean food culture, however, has remained outside of academic discussion; and, it has been narrated from the Western perspective, if at all. It is not to say that Western scholars' understanding of Korean food culture has been prejudiced or misinforming. Rather, those studies have paved the way for Korean food studies by providing historically deep and geopolitically balanced interpretations, as demonstrated by Cwiertka's works (2012; 2014). Yet, Korean food and foodways are still suffering from a lack of diverse voices and cross-disciplinary interrogations in comparison to the Asian counterparts. On the one hand, the lack of academic conversation might have come from a relatively low cultural status of Korean food in the United States. On the other hand, it should be noted that much of discussion has been inaccessible to American readers as it has been written by Korean scholars in Korean.

As food cultures have been more diversified and sophisticated in accordance with economic and sociocultural developments, there has been a growing social interest in food matters in Korea over the past decades: for example, food has become a major element of the Korean entertainment industry, a cultural signifier of lifestyles, a powerful marker of self-identification, a popular segment of tourism, and a major means of national branding. This changing role of food has led to the rise of food-related research, especially from the perspective of humanities and social sciences, which, in turn, has contributed to the cultural legitimacy of food in Korea. Although many Korean scholars have engaged with academic dialogue across disciplines, their perspectives have hardly been introduced to foreign audiences because of language barrier, as mentioned earlier, as well as a limited accessibility to Korean journal database. The current book is designed to bring Korean scholars' voices to English-speaking readers, to shed light on how food is communicated in contemporary Korea, and more broadly, to enrich the scholarship of food studies. In order to provide a comprehensive understanding of Korean food's economic, cultural, and political relevance, thirteen Korean journal articles published in English have been collected from diverse disciplines, encompassing economics, political science, literature studies, communication studies, international studies, area studies, geography, nutrition research, culinary/hospitality research, and tourism research.

Here, it is important to note the significance of the Korean case in exploring the complex relationships between food and communication. Like other national cuisines, *hansik* (Korean cuisine) is a modern construct: Japanese colonialists coined the term *Joseon eumsik* (food of the Joseon Dynasty) in order to distinguish it from their mainland food, and the term was replaced by *hansik* for administrative purposes when the modern form of Korean nation-state was established (Joo 2011). As the origin of the term *hansik* tells, Korean food culture has evolved through constant interactions with social, political, and economic circumstances, as well as with other culinary cultures. In the 1960s, the food-focused US foreign assistance, also known as PL-480, had great impacts on Korean dietary culture by promoting the consumption of wheat and corn and by compelling American nutritional science (Office of the Historian n.d.). The 1986 Seoul Asian Game and the 1988 Seoul Olympics, along with the Trade Liberalization of Foreign Processed Food in 1987 and the Liberalization of Overseas Trip in 1989, made globalization close to the surface of Koreans' daily diet, which ironically led to the prevalence of statist discourse of Korean culinary *tradition*. The global force of market opening in the 1990s pushed the Korean agricultural industry into the global economy system, and a large influx of foreign labor forces accelerated by the 1997 Asian Financial Crisis changed the landscape of the Korean food service industry and eating-out culture in a significant way. From the mid-2000s on, the Korean government has promoted Korean cuisine to carve out its global position by implementing such cultural policies as "Creative Korea," "Han-Style," and "Korean Food Globalization" projects; and, these national projects have reconfigured the Korean food industry and have made gastronationalism visible in both public and private sectors (Jeong 2020).

As these examples demonstrate, the history of Korean food and foodways embodies diverse social issues, including (post-)colonialism, globalization, neoliberalism, nationalism, cultural hybridity, social construction of traditions, social identities, and cultural economy, which have been the major research focus of (food) scholars from different disciplines, but are still in need for in-depth investigation. Admittedly, food's intersection with these social issues is not a Korea-specific phenomenon and can be found in different cultural contexts. However, given the history of Japanese colonialism and the Korean War, the rapid economic development and sociocultural transformations, the prevalent myth of *pure* national cuisine, and the recent efforts to promote national cuisine both domestically and globally, the Korean case will provide abundant discursive resources for the understanding of the intersection between food, culture, and society. Combining thirteen peer-reviewed journal articles from a variety of disciplines, this edited book will offer a multidimensional account of the ways in which food communicates with diverse social issues in Korea.

The current volume is organized primarily in four parts: (I) From Colonialism and Hunger to Food Sovereignty, (II) National Cuisine in the Era of Globalization, (III) Food Practices in Multicultural Korea, and (IV) Food Tourism and Food Crisis. Chapters in part I present historically and thematically diverse analyses of food matters in Korea. In accordance with major social transformations that the Korean society has undergone, main themes of food-related discourses have largely changed, ranging from rice production and poverty to food sovereignty and food security. The reclamation projects during the colonial period changed the natural environment of the Korean Peninsula so as to develop agricultural areas, and thus, to support a stable food supply within the Japanese Empire and the formation of a colonial landlord system. By analyzing articles on reclamation projects from the *Official Gazette* of the Japanese Government-General of Korea, chapter 1 illustrates the development of reclamation projects and business entities during Korea's colonial period. With the rich historical data, the author demonstrates how the quality agricultural land was developed due to the relatively low cost of the projects and how the additional rice, produced by the expansion of agricultural land, was exported to Japan. In addition, the author reveals that the reclamation projects were geared toward increasing business profit in the Japanese Empire even if their goal was to distribute food within the Japanese Empire and stabilize Japanese immigration.

In the chaotic time after the Korean War, Koreans suffered a full-scale destruction of the economic system and the psychological and cultural deficiency led by violent modernization. By analyzing the symbolism of food that appeared in modern Korean novels, chapter 2 vividly describes key characteristics of modern Korea. Focusing on the formation novels written in the 1960s and the 1970s, such as Lee Mun-Gu's *Gwan Chon Essay* and Lee Dong-Ha's *Toy City*, the author aptly presents what meanings were carried by the symbols of food and eating, which were expressed in the novels as a combination of various aspects of *parole*, including concrete situations, characters, and contexts. Through a careful semiotic analysis of food symbols, the author interprets the postwar Korea in terms of hunger society (both physically and psychologically), traumatic modernization armed with individualism and monetary economy, the collapse of the mutually benefiting community, placelessness, and the epic of self-discovery. Since the democratization movement of the 1980s, there have been ongoing debates on the revision of the constitution in Korea, and the debates have always involved such topics as the value of agriculture and the rights of peasants. Specifically controversial have been the questions of what agricultural values should be included in the constitution and of what should be meant by sustainable agriculture based on such values. Chapter 3 outlines the implications of the UN Declaration on the Rights of Peasants as a direction for a sustainable agriculture model that can suggest alternatives to the global agri-food system to be included in Korea's new constitution. To this end, the chapter analyzes historical changes in the food security regime and international agri-food policies and also traces the transformation of Korean agriculture correlated with changes to the international regime. Consequently, it demonstrates the important contribution on discussions regarding the rights of peasants in the UN to proliferate alternative discourses on contemporary agri-food systems both at global and national level.

As demonstrated by many studies, national cuisine functions as a strong way of preserving national identity, as well as a powerful signifier of intranational sameness, common history and ancestry, and national competitiveness. Based within qualitative inquiry, chapters in part II critically examine how national cuisine has been narrated, (re)invented, and promoted in contemporary Korea. *Kimchi* represents a distinctive flavor and basic food of Korean cuisine; accordingly, it has been at the center of the public discourse of Korean food, global promotion of Korean culinary culture, and food-related international conflicts (especially, with Japan and China). Considering *kimchi* as a representative symbol of Korean foodways and Korean everyday life, chapter 4 identifies three historical phases in which *kimchi* has emerged as a national symbol: (1) declaration of independence in taste, (2) promotion of national food, and (3) international conflicts over national food. In addition, the author discusses the major characteristics of each historical period as follows: the liberation from symbolic domination of imported foreign food, the large social mobilization surrounding national food as well as the scientific institutionalization and industrialization, and the standardization of national food and the increasing international trade, respectively. This chapter broadly contributes to the scholarship of food and nationalism by addressing food as an entry point for exploring cultural nationalism, state intervention, international labor division, and globalization.

In Korea, temple food has gained growing attention since the mid-1990s. Chapter 5 examines the cultural politics of Buddhist temple food in contemporary Korea. Particularly, it analyzes the complex interplay between popular concerns for health and economic security and the converging and diverging interests of the state, business, and the Buddhist establishment. In the chapter, the author argues that the reinvention of temple food as tradition serves not only to reaffirm the national identity and ease a collective anxiety about rapid social change but also to promote national competitiveness in the global market. The author's findings also allow us to reexamine the postcolonial view of agency in that they demonstrate the significance of health and economic security in popular agency over the pleasure of consumption. Moreover, this chapter elucidates how public concerns, sociocultural mobilization, and collective identity are appropriated or mediated by the institutionalized actors, such as government, business, and the Buddhist establishment. Within a similar context, chapter 6 investigates how Buddhist cuisine and Andong food have been (re)invented as traditional Korean cuisine. Specifically, the chapter focuses on how a sense of nostalgia is capitalized and how a particular food practice is commodified through decontextualization. Chapter 6 is in parallel with chapter 5 in that it perceives the recent development of Buddhist cuisine (and Andong food) as an outcome of both the public's demand for healthy food and the Korean society's attempt to carve out its position in the globalized world. Interestingly, the author interprets the rise of traditional cuisine (i.e., Buddhist temple food and Andong food) as a potential sign of people's desire to form a counter-culinary culture. However, the author concludes that consumers end up with taking part in the self-expanding capitalist market rather than forging a genuine counterculture.

In 2008, the Korean government announced the globalization of *hansik* as a national project and declared 2008 the "Year of Korean Food Globalization." Since then, the government and its associated organizations have fostered a large number of discussions on Korean food, using public announcements, festivals, exhibitions, forums, and media outlets. Understanding the growth of governmental discourse of national cuisine as a struggle for nation-ness, chapter 7 examines how the Korean government utilizes national cuisine to narrate the Korean nation and sustain the binding force of the nation-state in the face of open-market structures. Through an analysis of news articles about Korean food globalization published before and during the early Lee MyungBak administration, this chapter reveals that the Korean government's growing interest in Korean cuisine was initiated not only by its awareness of the increasing size of the global food industry, but also by its efforts to maintain the national unity of the Korean society, which would be weakened by the KORUS FTA. Also, the author's analysis of *The Taste of Korea*—an online newsletter of the Korean Food Foundation—presents the recurring themes of governmental discourses on Korean cuisine and their implications on Koreanness.

The economic crisis across East Asia in 1997 made Korea undergo a brutal neoliberal globalization. Due to the increasing need for a cheap labor force, the Korean society experienced a large influx of migrant workers from northeast China, the Philippines, and other Southeast Asian countries. In addition, the growth of international marriage, mainly caused by a massive domestic migration of young Korean women from rural to urban areas, greatly affected the ethnoscape of Korea. This demographic shift led to the social transformation from a monoracial Korea to a multicultural and global Korea in a relatively short period (Ahn 2013). Chapters in part III address diverse issues observed within a multiracial and multicultural Korea. With the increase of Muslim workers, Muslim food culture has gradually developed in the ethnic enclave of migrant workers since the 1990s. Chapter 9 explores the change of Muslim food culture in Korea and discusses how the Korean food industry and government have adopted halal certification system to promote Korean food exports and brand values. By reviewing the Korean government's halal food policies, the authors trace how the Korean government has endeavored to enter the increasing global halal market, even if they admit the fact that the Korean halal market emerged in the 1990s apart from the government's intervention. They argue that the interplay among the Korean government, Korean food companies, and the Korean Wave has made it possible for domestic agricultural products to be halal certified and has enhanced the competitiveness of Korean food in the global halal market.

As demonstrated by the enactment of the "Multicultural Families Support Act" in 2008, the quality of life of multicultural family became an important social agenda in Korea, generating a variety of questions to be answered. Given the significance of dietary life in managing multicultural family's stable living, chapters 9 and 10 seek to identify major culinary patterns or issues found within multicultural family. In particular, chapter 9 investigates the food insecurity among intermarried couples and intrahousehold discrepancy between Vietnamese wives and Korean husbands. Drawing on a cross-sectional analysis of the "Cohort of Intermarried Women in Korea" study, which involved eighty-four intermarried couples, the authors discover the marked discrepancy in food insecurity between Vietnamese wives and Korean husbands that are mainly caused by financial issues and a lack of Korean foods palatable to Vietnamese taste. Chapter 10 examines the immigrant wives' food practices with regard to Korean cuisine and dietary patterns. Through the extensive survey of 600 immigrant wives from thirty-seven multicultural centers of the nationwide YWCA, the authors identify diverse factors that affect the degree to which immigrant wives adapt to Korean food culture, including the country of origin, the length of residence in Korea, and the level of education in Korean culinary culture. Taken together, chapters 9 and 10 demonstrate the significance of subsequent studies and policy developments in relation to multicultural family's food practices and food insecurity.

Food not only occupies a mundane position in our daily lives but also is an important element of leisure and tourism. As shown by the recent tourism literature, food provides tourists with an easy opportunity to experience *authentic* local cultures; and, tourists' gastronomic experience is strongly associated with their travel satisfaction and revisit intention. Within this context, food tourism has become a serious agenda among cultural policy makers in Korea since the late 2000s, and the Korean tourism industry has aggressively utilized Korean food to attract both domestic and foreign tourists. Focusing on global tourists' travel experience in Korea, chapter 11 explores the complex relationships among tourists' demographic characteristics, food satisfaction, revisit intention, and word-of-mouth intention. More specifically, it examines (1) the influence of tourists' demographic characteristics (i.e., cultural background, gender, and education) on food satisfaction; (2) the influence of tourists' food satisfaction on revisit intention; and (3) the influence of tourists' food satisfaction on word-of-mouth intention. From domestic tourists' perspectives, chapter 12 assesses how perceived value and nutrition information are associated with behavioral intention for domestic food tourism. Through a case study of the city of Busan and a quantitative analysis of the self-reported surveys, this chapter presents different roles played by tourists' learned nutrition information and their gastronomic values in food tourism. The authors also suggest perceived value and nutrition information as a determinant of revisit intention in domestic tourism.

While food features as a vital component of the tourism experience, food security and food crisis are ongoing global issues that require continuous attention. Korea is no exception. Specifically, since the 8th Multilateral Trade Negotiations (the Uruguay Round) forced market opening of agricultural products, a sustainable agriculture model has been hotly debated in Korea. Prior to the 2007–2008 rice crisis, individual countries in East Asia took full responsibility for their own food security problems and felt obliged to consider self-sufficiency the only option to ensure food security. Yet, the 2007–2008 rice crisis in East Asia revealed that food security threats could originate from unexpected sources and that individual country's unilateral approach could not properly deal with food security problems. Accordingly, the leaders of East Asian countries took the initiative to establish a capable regional mechanism to ensure food security. Chapter 13 discusses the issue of food security at the regional level, interprets the institutionalization of the ASEAN Plus Three Emergency Rice Reserve (APTERR) as an encouraging movement, and suggests regional cooperation as a viable option for the future of food security in East Asia. Given the uncertainty of the scheme's sustainability, the shifting nature of food security concerns, and each country's different approach to food security, however, the author claims that it is premature to celebrate what has been accomplished. Instead, the author calls for the necessity of a gradual approach with a long-term perspective, which could propel East Asian regional integration and community building, and which, in turn, would reduce the current gridlock surrounding the future of regional food security.

REFERENCES

Adema, P. (2000). Vicarious consumption: Food, television and the ambiguity of modernity. *The Journal of American & Comparative Cultures, 23*(3), 113–123.

Ahn, J. (2013). Visualizing Race: Neoliberal Multiculturalism and the Struggle for Koreanness in Contemporary South Korean Television (doctoral dissertation). Retrieved from https://repositories.lib.utexas.edu/handle/2152/21558.

Appadurai, A. (1981). Gastro-politics in Hindu South Asia. *American Ethnologist, 8*(3), 494–511.

Barthes, R. (1979). Toward a psychosociology of food consumption. In R. Forster & O. Ranum (Eds.), *Food and Drink in History* (pp. 166–173). Baltimore, MD: Johns Hopkins University Press.

Bower, A. (Ed.). (2004). *Reel Food: Essays on Food and Film.* New York: Routledge.

Collins, K. (2009). *Watching What We Eat: The Evolution of Television Cooking Shows.* New York: Continuum.

Cramer, J., Greene, C., & Walters, L. (Eds.). (2011). *Food as Communication-Communication as Food.* New York: Peter Lang Publishing, Inc.

Cwiertka, K. (2006). *Modern Japanese Cuisine: Food, Power and National Identity.* London: Reaktion Books.

Cwiertka, K. (2012). *Cuisine, Colonialism and Cold War: Food in Twentieth-Century Korea.* London: Reaktion Books.

Cwiertka, K. (2014). The global hansik campaign and the commodification of Korean cuisine. In K. Kim & Y. Choe (Eds.), *The Korean Popular Culture Reader* (pp. 363–380). Durham: Duke University Press.

Cwiertka, K., & Walraven, B. (Eds.). (2001). *Asian Food: The Global and the Local.* Honolulu: University of Hawaii Press.

de Solier, I. (2005). TV dinners: Culinary television, education and distinction. *Journal of Media & Cultural Studies, 19*(4), 465–481.

DeSoucey, M. (2010). Gastronationalism: Food traditions and authenticity politics in the European Union. *American Sociological Review, 75*(3), 432–455.

Hiroko, T. (2008). Delicious food in a beautiful country: Nationhood and nationalism in discourses on food in contemporary Japan. *Studies in Ethnicity and Nationalism, 8*(1), 5–30.

Jeong, J. (2020). *Korean Food TV and the Korean Nation.* Lanham, MD: Lexington Books.

Joo, Y. (2011). 음식인문학: 음식으로 본 한국의 역사와 문화 [Food Humanities: Korean History and Culture from the Perspective of Food]. Seoul: Humanist.

Kelly, C. (2017). *Food Television and Otherness in the Age of Globalization.* Lanham, MD: Lexington Books.

Ketchum, C. (2005). The essence of cooking shows: How the Food Network constructs consumer fantasies. *Journal of Communication Inquiry, 29*(3), 217–234.

Lu, S., & Fine, G. (1995). The presentation of ethnic authenticity: Chinese food as a social accomplishment. *The Sociological Quarterly, 36*(3), 535–553.

Mintz, S. (1985). *Sweetness and Power: The Place of Sugar in Modern History.* New York: Penguin.

Office of the Historian. (n.d.). USAID and PL – 480, 1961-1969. Retrieved from https://history.state.gov/milestones/1961-1968/pl-480.

Ohnuki-Tierney, E. (1993). *Rice as Self: Japanese Identities through Time.* Princeton, NJ: Princeton University Press.

Oren, T. (2013). On the line: Format, cooking and competition as television values. *Critical Studies in Television, 8*(2), 20–35.

Palat, R. (2015). Empire, food and the diaspora: Indian restaurants in Britain. *South Asia: Journal of South Asian Studies, 38*(2), 171–186.

Parasecoli, F. (2008). *Bite Me: Food in Popular Culture.* Oxford: Berg.

Parasecoli, F. (2013). Food, cultural studies, and popular culture. In K. Albala (Ed.), *International Handbook of Food Studies* (pp. 274–281). New York: Routledge.

Sutton, D. (2010). Food and the senses. *Annual Review of Anthropology, 39*, 209–223.

Wright, W., & Annes, A. (2013). Halal on the menu?: Contested food politics and French identity in fast-food. *Journal of Rural Studies, 32*, 388–399.

Part I

FROM COLONIALISM AND HUNGER TO FOOD SOVEREIGNTY

Chapter 1

Reclamation Projects and Development of Agricultural Land in Colonial Korea

Chaisung Lim

The[1] purpose of this study is to estimate the statistics of colonial reclamation using data from articles from the *Official Gazette* of the Japanese Government-General of Korea and elucidate how reclamation projects were ethnically promoted by business entity and region. This study shows that modern large-scale reclamation projects in the colonial period changed the natural environment of beaches at ebb tide, and that ethnic Koreans also participated in small-scale reclamation projects.

Various goals, for example, sufficient water supply, traffic improvement, and tourism income through the land development of coastal areas have been cited as reasons reclamation was necessary (Lim 1988, 1–2). The primary significance of the reclamation projects in colonial Korea can be found as the solution to Japan's food shortages, ultimately by increasing the supply of food with the expansion of farmlands. Korea, which is geographically close to and strongly influenced by Japan, was responsible for supplying food to Japan. Because Taiwan had both rice and sugar industries, it was able to choose between rice and sugar according to market trends. However, Korea could only plant and harvest rice due to its climate.[2] Therefore, reclamation projects, which significantly expanded farmlands and the degree of land intensification, gained attention in the early days of the colonial rule.

Another key function of the reclamation projects in colonial Korea was that they represented a way to facilitate the immigration process from Japan to Korea. Agricultural immigration of Japanese farmers to farmlands pushed existing Korean farmers from their land, causing social tensions. However, over the long term, Japanese immigrants, contrary to their earlier intentions, moved away from rural areas, engaged in lending and commerce, and became absentee landowners who entered into contracts with Koreans as tenant farmers. In this regard, the reclamation projects were very important in that they

13

faithfully guaranteed Japanese immigrant farming without causing confrontation with existing Korean farmers (Fujii 1924).

In this respect, the colonial rule of the Japanese Empire may be said to have benefited colonial development on an economic level (Matsumoto 1992). The development, in turn, had institutional aspects, such as the denial of the existing order and the establishment of a new market economy, along with the quantitative aspects of economic growth and per capita GNP increase. The development was a process in which the improvement of the welfare of the locals was not primarily made but the interests of the mother country were carried out. Huh (2011) argued for *development without development* for locals with colonial modernization writers, such as Kim Naknyeon and Cha Myungsoo (Cha and Hwang 2015; Huh 2011, 2014; Kim 2006; Park 2015; Rhee 2012a, 2012b; Woo 2015). Nevertheless, the colonial rule of the Japanese Empire brought about an irreversible change in colonial Korea.

The reclamation projects brought about environmental change to the land and secured farmland, which became the basis for food production. In addition, the ethnic Koreans actively participated in reclamation projects of government-owned land as a business opportunity. The creation of such opportunities cannot be explained only through the lens of invasion and colonization. An ethnic disparity should be pointed out; the reclamation projects were an opportunity for ethnic Koreans to become businesspeople in the agricultural sector who overcame the difficulties of long-term investment of fixed capital and of construction. The process of modernization in colonial Korea meant colonial modernization propelled by the Japanese Empire.

Despite their significance, the reclamation projects in the colonial period have not received much attention in previous studies. While Park and Oh (2004) explained the development process, technology, and utilization of reclamation projects in the Joseon Dynasty period, it is still difficult to grasp the scale of the reclamation projects as a whole. Yang (2010) introduced some cases confined to the late Joseon Dynasty and recognized that the reclamation technology from the seventeenth century to the 1960s was continuous in terms of the use of human labor. However, she ignored the fact that modern design technology, such as civil engineering works using bogies and rails, was introduced during the colonial period, and that local constructors did not conscript workers as overlords but rather paid them as employers for the reclamation projects.

Even though Park (1989) examined the ethnic distribution of the reclamation projects in the colonial period using the *Chosen Land Improvement Booklet* (1940), he could not fully elucidate the situation of the reclamation projects before the 1920s and after the end of the Chosen Rice Production Increase Plan (CRPIP).[3] From a geographical point of view, Namgung (1991) examined the evolution of residents' settlements in reclamation areas through surveys of the Mangyeong River and Dongjin River. In addition, Oh (2009), Koh (2009), and Huh (2011) introduced the colonial reclamation projects based on Lim's (1995) research achievements.[4]

TIDELANDS OF THE KOREAN PENINSULA
AND THE ADMINISTRATIVE SYSTEM
OF RECLAMATION PROJECTS

Reclamation projects aimed to build dikes, block tide, exclude internal water, and obtain farmland for various purposes on tidal flats formed by factors such as materials supplied from the upstream, tidal tributaries, indented shorelines, waves, and geological structures. Even though the progress of reclamation projects was directly influenced by the accumulation of land capital, the degree of technological development, and socioeconomic demand, it was basically defined by how much tideland existed.[5]

The west and south coasts of the Korean Peninsula have estuaries rich in sediments supplied by the many rivers. The coastline is also a complicated ria coast that has a winding outline and many islands. In addition, the tidal ranges can reach global levels, with the peak in Incheon. Korean tidal ranges that have a direct relationship with tideland development are listed in table 1.1 (Tochi kairyōbu 1929).

The average tidal range of the east coast is small, whereas those of the west and south coasts are significantly larger. Among Korean cites, Incheon has the largest tidal range, which is about 9.5 meters. The tidal range gradually decreases from the peak of Incheon in the northern area toward the center of the city, but the tidal range increases toward the Pyeonganbuk-do area. The

Table 1.1   Tidal Range in the Korean Peninsula (Unit: Meter)

Geographical Location	High Tidal Range	Low Tidal Range
Dasa Island, Pyeonganbuk-do	7	4.9
Seok Island, Hwanghae-do	5.5	3.7
Daecheong Island, Hwanghae-do	3.9	2.5
Jumun Island, Gyeonggi-do	8.7	6.1
Jemulpo, Gyeonggi-do	9.5	6.5
Sajangpo, Chungcheongnam-do	7.4	5.2
Gunsan Port, Jeollabuk-do	7.6	5.3
Mokpo, Jeollanam-do	4.4	3
Yeosu, Jeollanam-do	3.6	2.3
Jinhae Bay, Gyeongsangnam-do	2.3	1.4
Busan Port, Gyeongsangnam-do	1.3	0.9
Yeong-il Bay, Gyeongsangbuk-do	0.2	0.2
Wonsan Port, Hamgyeongnam-do	0.5	0.4

Source: Adapted from Yamaguchi (1910, 101–104).

tidal range of the southern area of Incheon also gradually decreases closer to the southern part of the Korean Peninsula. In the south coast, the Jeollanam-do coastal area has a large tidal range, and the tidal range decreases toward the Gyeongsangnam-do coast. The tidelands are distributed according to these differences in tidal range.

Tidelands, which have economic significance, naturally change with the situation of the times, and this situation is determined by capital and technological development (Nongeochon jinheung gongsa 1979, 4). As technology advanced, reclamation projects moved from shallow water to deeper water. Therefore, the reclamation methods progressed from surrounding the sea exposed at low tide with a seawall to obtain farmland to blocking an estuary or an entrance of a bay, including the part of the sea not exposed at low tide, to construct a freshwater lake, build an internal waterproof dike, and develop tideland with natural or mechanical drainage. In the economic sense, tidelands can be defined more broadly.

The bedrock of the west and south coasts is composed mostly of granite, granite gneiss, and crystalline gneiss (Geonseolbu 1979, 101). These rocks are usually covered with a thick weathered layer, and they protrude from the sea in various places, forming marine cliffs and wave-cut platforms. The soil of the tideland is composed mainly of fine sand, silt, and clay, which are rich in organic matter, as diluvial and alluvial soil carried by rivers and seawater are deposited there. The tideland from Gyeonggi-do to Jeollanam-do can be classified as clayey tideland because it has a lot of clay soil, whereas the tideland north of Hwanghae-do is known as sandy tideland because it has a lot of sand soil (Tochi kairyōbu 1929, 101).[6] Approximately 1 million ha of tidelands on the Korean Peninsula cover 5 percent of the nation's land area (Ban 1977, 235) (figure 1.1).

The reclamation projects during the colonial period were carried out based on the National Uncultivated Land Utilization Law (1907) from September 1907 to July 1924 and the Chosen Public Waters Reclamation Act (1923) since August 1924. First, those who wished to participate in reclamation projects needed to submit a series of documents and drawings, including the application form to the governor-general.[7] Next, the governor-general decided whether or not to grant a reclamation license through an appropriate examination, and give the license to the applicant if approved.

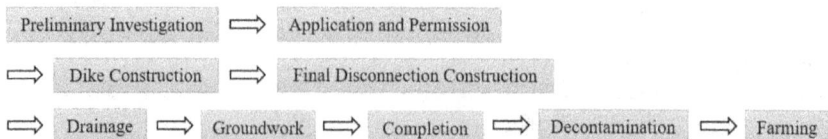

Preliminary Investigation ⇨ Application and Permission

⇨ Dike Construction ⇨ Final Disconnection Construction

⇨ Drainage ⇨ Groundwork ⇨ Completion ⇨ Decontamination ⇨ Farming

Figure 1.1   Reclamation Project Process.

When the applicant obtained a reclamation license, he or she became a licensee and paid the license fee to the governor-general and addressed the difficulties presented by the circumstances to help ensure the success of the project within the term of the license. The most important construction step in a reclamation project was the construction of a seawall, which required a lot of sand, stone, and concrete. The critical moment of the embankment construction was the final disconnection or terminal blocking, during which the speed of the tidal current was so fast because of the difference between the inside and outside water levels, which could cause the loss of the seawall. Normally, the workforce and equipment were intensively mobilized to complete seawall construction during the low tidal season each year (Kang 1993, 190). It usually took two to three years to build such a seawall in the colonial period (Tochi kairyōbu 1929, 36) (table 1.2).

After the ground construction was completed and the land category was identified, the reclamation licensee needed to fill out an application form for completion and submit it to the governor-general with a completion report, ground plans of the actual survey, and mensuration. When the completion was authorized, the ownership of the reclaimed land was confirmed.[8] Reclamation projects were one of the most labor-intensive forms of capital-to-land conversion because they first required building a seawall, breaking off the tide, excluding internal water, and in the case of farmlands, establishing various irrigation facilities. It required a long term of seven or eight to ten years to complete decontamination work, crop harvests, and capital withdrawal after beginning the construction. In the case of rice farming, direct planting was carried out until the second year after crops were harvested because direct planting was better when the farmland contained salt, and the transplantation of rice seedlings was carried out from the third year after desalting. The nitrogen level in tideland soil was very low, only 38 percent of that in normal rice paddy soil. For this reason, nitrogen fertilizer like ammonium nitrate was considered ideal (Nongjigwanliguk 1958, 23–24). Due to fertilization, the soil of reclaimed land contained more nitrogen than that of uncultivated land.

Table 1.2 Soil Nitrogen Content (Unit: Millionth in a Cubic Centimeter of Dry Fine Soil)

Soil	Nitrogen	Percentage
Rice Paddy	600	38
Uncultivated Land	465	30
Subsoil	273	18
Ordinary Rice Paddy	1569	100

Source: Adapted from Misu (1944, 54).

ADVANTAGE OF RECLAMATION
PROJECTS IN COLONIAL KOREA

Reclamation projects were considered a means of helping settle both agricultural immigrants from Japan and independent farmers in Korea. If the state transferred unemployed rural people to reclaimed land acquired through reclamation and sold arable land under twenty-five-year installment payment contracts, an immigrant could become an independent farmer on the condition that the state would subsidize 50 percent of the net construction cost. This effort produced benefits, such as unemployment relief, land expansion, food increase, and equitable land distribution (Matsumura 1929, 3).

Fujii (1924, 19–20), who was called "King of Irrigation in Korea" at that time, said, "It is no surprise that land reclamation in Korea is the most important thing for the industrial development and the rule of the Japanese Government-General of Korea. In other words, for the sake of true harmony between ethnic Japanese and ethnic Koreans and the Japanization of ethnic Koreans, at least millions of ethnic Japanese should immigrate and ethnic Koreans must be sent to Japan inland and the distinction between Japan inland and Korea should be eliminated." This Japanese immigration had many side effects, the most serious of which was driving out Korean farmers from their means of production, that is, the land.

Fujii continued to point out: "In addition to receiving the antipathy consciously, even though the Japanese immigrant worked hard at first, he later accustomed himself to Korean customs; he stood on the ridges between rice paddies only to supervise farming and took a strong dislike to carrying the manure himself, as he was the landowner. As a result, the real immigration business fell into a dead end. It is an urgent issue for me to concentrate my efforts on the reclamation of uncultivated land as much as possible as a method of immigration to Korea, which is a serious problem in national policy." Reclamation was emphasized as a precondition for the promotion of large-scale Japanese immigration. Though Fujii (1924) himself promoted the reclamation projects as a means of Japanese immigration, the scale of immigration was limited.

In terms of individual capitalists and businessmen, these reclamation projects were practically not carried out at the national level but through the calculation of business profit and opportunity cost.

As for a person who actually inspected the reclamation of tidal land, construction expense per *tanbu* (approximately one-tenth ha) is 50 yen. . . . Farmlands were fertile soil. . . . Harvest from successfully reclaimed land usually amounted to 4 *koku* (180.39 l) of unhulled rice per *tanbu*. It was not surprising

that the harvest of 5-6 *koku* of unhulled rice per tanbu from previously successfully reclaimed land was also considerable. . . . Whereas the price of 1 *tanbu*
of paddy was over 400 yen in Japan inland and especially the price of a good
paddy was over 1,000 yen because of many purchase applicants, it is obviously
possible to purchase the best paddy for 140 yen in today's Korea. However,
it was hard to buy more than a dozen *chobu* (approximately 1 ha), and it was
never an easy business to manage scattered farmlands. And the average harvest
from a mature paddy was . . . 2 *koku* per *tanbu*, even from hundreds of *chobu* of
farmlands. . . . The farming of a mature paddy yielded profit at the moment of
the purchase, but the reclamation of tidal land could not earn a full income for
5 years. (Yamane 1918, 14–15)

Although the article by Yamane was written in 1918 and therefore it
would have been impossible to determine reclamation project costs during
the entire colonial period, it shows the reason many people were involved in
the reclamation projects despite the risks of long-term fixed capital investment and business failure. The ratio of the market value of the best paddy
in Korea to that of a mature paddy in Japan per *tanbu* was only 35 percent,
and the ratio of the market value of the reclamation project cost to that of a
mature paddy in Japan was about 10 percent. Therefore, it was much more
advantageous to carry out a reclamation project in Korea than to invest capital in Japan inland. In addition, because the reclaimed land contained a large
amount of organic matter,[9] if proper decontamination and fertilization were
carried out, it was usually possible to harvest four *koku* of unhulled rice per
tanbu.[10] Therefore, reclamation projects had a relative advantage in terms of
cost and harvest.[11]

The Japanese Government-General of Korea, in contrast to the Government
of Japan, referred to the advantages of the reclamation projects due to the natural characteristics of Korea as follows (Tochi kairyō-bu 1928, 73–74). First,
the seawall length of the Korean reclamation project was shorter than that of
the Japanese reclamation project because the tidal flats in Korea had a lot of
indentation. A seawall of about 21 meters was needed for the reclamation of
an area of 1 *chobu* in Japan, but a seawall of six meters was enough in the
case of Korea. Second, tidal flats in Korea were higher, and storm invasion
was less severe than that in Japan, so the seawall was low and the structure
was relatively simple.[12] Third, owing to the aforementioned two reasons, it
was enough to pay about 43 yen per *chobu* in Korea, compared to 210 yen
in Japan inland.[13] Fourth, reclamation in Korea was relatively convenient for
business management under the support of the Japanese Government-General
of Korea. Fifth, as 44 percent of farm households in Korea were purely tenant
farmers, it was easy to secure farmers (table 1.3).

Table 1.3   Seawall Extension and Construction Costs in Korea and Japan (Unit: *Chobu*, m, *Yen*)

Licensee	Cultivating Area	Seawall Length	Seawall Construction Cost	Construction Cost[a]	Seawall Length[a]
Sakae Reclamation Work, Yatsushiro County, Kumamoto Prefecture	1,020	16,165	1,919,995	188	16
Ryusei Village Arable Land Readjustment Association, Kishima County, Saga Prefecture	13	1,333	84,071	609	103
Taiho Village Arable Land Readjustment Association, Saga Prefecture	99	4,305	330,660	435	43
Gyuya Village Arable Land Readjustment Association, Saga Prefecture	57	3,596	162,147	284	63
Subtotal (Japan)	1,189	25,400	2,496,873	210	21
Estate Company, Young-am County, Jeollanam-do	653	1,609	204,372	31.3	2
Hori Farm, Younggwang County, Jeollanam-do	300	2,284	216,901	72.3	7
Fuji Farm, Okku County, Jeollanam-do	1,800	13,327	732,729	40.71	7
Tada Farm, Chungcheongnam-do	61	485	59,752	97.95	8
Subtotal (Korea)	2,814	17,705	1,213,754	43	6

Source: Adapted from Ayata (1922, 351).
Note[a]: Construction cost is the seawall construction cost per *tanbu*, and seawall length is the seawall length per *chobu*.

HISTORICAL TRENDS OF RECLAMATION PROJECTS AND RECLAMATION DECISION FACTOR ANALYSIS

The statistical tables presented in this paper are based on "the disposal of national uncultivated land" and "the disposal of the public water reclamation for agricultural purposes" that appeared in the *Official Gazette* in the Korean Empire period and the Japanese colonial period. The terms used in this paper are *license*, *completion*, *transfer*, *extinguishment*, and *recovery*.

License means permission for a reclamation application, while "completion" indicates permission of a licensee of reclamation to complete the project after the successful establishment of the project. *Transfer* refers to both an inheritance and handling of a reclamation right, while *extinguishment* means a loss, return to the government, and cancellation of a reclamation right. Finally, *recovery* refers to the revival of a reclamation right that has lost its legal effect from exceeding the license date. The data from the *Official Gazette* include information such as land address, land area, original land category, license land category, name and address of licensee, the person who attained the completion of project, transferor, transferee, and number of participants. The data give more detailed information than any other type of data about the reclamation project.

These statistics may be questionable in terms of the accuracy or reliability of the numerical values, in that they were related to the number of reclamation subprojects indicated in the *Official Gazette*. This information can be compared with other available data. There are some official statistics on colonial reclamation projects, but they do not cover the whole reclamation period. Among them, the "survey on public water disposal for agriculture" of the *Chosen Land Improvement Booklet* (1941) shows the trend up to 1941. These statistics cover 65 percent of reclamation licenses, 99 percent of completion districts, 106 percent of completion rice paddies, and 47 percent of extinguishments. The completion area is almost the same between the data from the *Official Gazette* and the *Chosen Land Improvement Booklet*, but the license and extinguishment data are very different. This result was largely because a reclamation subproject with an area of more than 3 *chobu* was considered significant under the jurisdiction of the Japanese Government-General of Korea, and a subproject with an area of less than 3 *chobu* was considered significant under the jurisdiction of an individual province. Reclamation projects with an area of less than 3 *chobu* were unlikely to succeed. Nevertheless, these statistics suggest a variety of information by ethnic group, business entity, and region.

Applications for a license, which indicated a desire to invest in a reclamation project, seemed robust from the start and grew significantly with the rapid increases in rice prices and land value from the late 1910s to the 1920s. Since then, even though the number of license applications slightly reduced compared to the previous period, the number of license applications achieved a stable state later, until finally, it sharply declined with the closure of the CRPIP in 1934. Licenses somewhat increased from 1936 and extremely regressed when wartime controlled the economy after the outbreak of the Pacific War. The gross number and area of reclamation licenses under the disposal of the governor-general of Korea were 1,438 cases and 201,318 *chobu*, respectively (Jeollanam-do: 330 cases, 45,036.46 *chobu*; Hwanghae-do: 176

cases, 43,507.1 *chobu*; Chungcheongnam-do: 326 cases, 37,859.12 *chobu*; Gyeonggi-do: 217 cases, 21,212.92 *chobu*; Jeollabuk-do: 70 cases, 19,416.45 *chobu*; Pyeongannam-do: 86 cases, 14,175.48 *chobu*; Pyeonganbuk-do: 124 cases, 13,052.13 *chobu*), during the entire colonial period. Reclamation rights were licensed mostly on the west coast, such as in Jeollanam-do, Hwanghae-do, Chungcheongnam-do, Jeollabuk-do, Pyeongannam-do, and Pyeonganbuk-do. The average area per case was 140 *chobu*, which was considered a large-scale project. Based on this average area, the ratios of the individual provinces were 198 for Jeollabuk-do, 168 for Gyeongsangbuk-do, 176 for Hwanghae-do, and 118 for Pyeongannam-do respectively. The reclamation scale of these areas was relatively large (figures 1.2 and 1.3).

There was no guarantee that a licensee would succeed in a project because a reclamation project generally required a minimum of seven to ten years for an incubation period between the initial investment and the first harvest from the reclaimed farmland. Therefore, reclaimed land rights were constantly

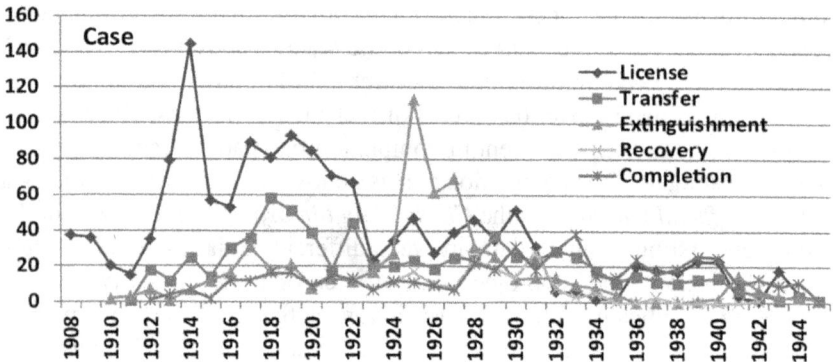

Figure 1.2　License, Transfer, Extinguishment, Recovery, and Completion of Reclamation (Unit: Number of Projects).

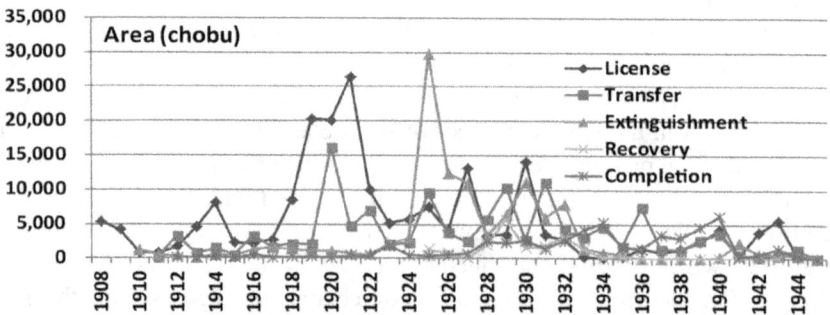

Figure 1.3　License, Transfer, Extinguishment, Recovery, and Completion of Reclamation (Unit: *Chobu* of Projects)

transferred during the reclamation period. The total number of transfers was 731, and the total area was 126,178.9 *chobu*, which accounted for about 51 percent and about 63 percent of the licenses, respectively. As can be seen from the ratio of the area, which was about 10 percent larger, the average area per case was 172.61 *chobu*; in turn, this area was 30 *chobu* larger compared to the average area of licensed projects. Transfers occurred mostly in large-scale projects than in small-scale projects and most actively in Jeollanam-do, Chungcheongnam-do, Gyeonggi-do, Hwanghae-do, and Pyonganbuk-do, which corresponded to the license. Jeollbuk-do was the largest province with an average area of 455.74 *chobu*, followed by Hwanghae-do, Jeollanam-do, Pyeongannam-do, and Pyeonganbuk-do. In addition, extinguished reclamation rights, which meant failure of a project, represented 591 cases and an area of 110,384.7 *chobu*, which accounted for 41.1 percent and 54.97 percent of licenses, respectively. It was also possible to recover a previously extinguished reclamation right; such recoveries of rights represented 151 cases and an area of 18,108.29 *chobu*.

The successful completion of a reclamation project was authorized by the Japanese Government-General of Korea. Even though the completion area did not increase significantly from the second half of the 1910s to the first half of the 1920s, the number of such cases steadily increased. This outcome was a result of the small size of completed projects during the reclamation period. Since the mid-1920s, particularly 1928, reclamation projects made great achievements. Wages and material prices plummeted, resulting in cost reduction during the Great Depression. Regardless of the brief stagnation in 1935, shortly after the end of the CRPIP, which guaranteed up to 50 percent in government subsidies for major reclamation construction costs, this trend continued until 1940.[14] However, reclamation projects rapidly recessed because of the material and labor shortages in the controlled economy during the Pacific War, which began in 1941 (figure 1.4).

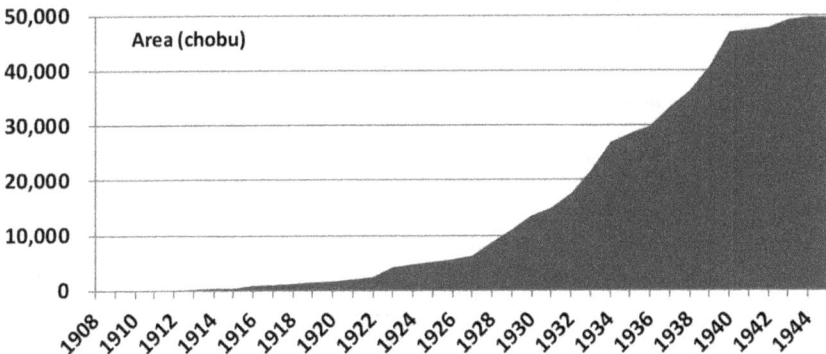

Figure 1.4   Cumulative Area of Reclamation Completion in Colonial Korea.

Completed projects represented 492 cases and an area of 49,596.1 *chobu* during the colonial period. This is equivalent to about 34 percent of the total cases and about 25 percent of the total reclamation licenses, excluding a few projects that were continued at the time of liberation from Japanese rule. Although some reclamation projects were under construction at the time of liberation, only 30 percent of the licensees succeeded. The average area per completed project was 100.8 *chobu*, which was reduced by 40 *chobu* compared to the total number of licenses. By province, Jeollanam-do had the largest production with 129 cases and an area of 14,786.3 *chobu*, followed by Hwanghae-do with 53 cases and an area of 7,977.2 *chobu*, Jeollabuk-do with 33 cases and an area of 7,232.2 *chobu*, and Pyonganbuk-do with 48 cases and an area of 6,686.0 *chobu*. It is worthwhile to note that the reclamation area in Chungcheongnam-do was only 4,637.5 *chobu* in spite of the province's 93 cases, while the reclamation area in Jeollabuk-do amounted to 7,232.2 *chobu* in spite of the province's 33 cases. This outcome shows the difference in project scale between provinces.

To examine the causes of these reclamation projects, this study performed a regression analysis on the license and completion areas of the reclamation projects, the results of which are shown in table 1.4. The explanatory variables were rice price, paddy land price, interest rate, and policy dummy (CRPIP year = 1, not CRPIP year = 0).[15] Since the multicollinearity between rice price and paddy land price is obvious, the respective analysis models are different. The signs of the explanatory variables are expected to be: rice price (+), paddy land price (+), interest rate (-), and policy dummy (+). The results

Table 1.4 Analysis of Table Reclamation Project Decision Factors (OLS White Hetero-skedasticity-Consistent Standard Errors & Covariance)[a]

		License Model		Completion Model	
		①	②	①	②
Constant	coefficient	−2	−7	12.62	13.705******
Term	*t*-value	−1	−1	5.563	4.484
Rice Price	coefficient	2.037**[b]		−0.637	
	t-value	3		−1.097	
Paddy Land	coefficient		2.093**		−0.517
Price	*t*-value		2		−1.01
Interest Rate	coefficient	0.329**	0.467**	−0.455***	−0.523***
	t-value	2.729	2	−5.36	−5.335
Policy	coefficient	0	0	1.746***	1.680***
Dummy[c]	*t*-value	0.037	−0.001	4.803	4.721
R-squared		0.334	0.292	0.564	0.603
Observation		35	34	33	32

Note[a]: ln (permission or completion) = c + ln (riceprice) or ln (landprice) + interest rate + policy dummy.
Note[b]: * significant in 10%, ** significant in 5%, *** significant in 1%.
Note[c]: Policy dummy variable is the dummy variable of CRPIP.

of the regression analysis show that in the case of the license model, rice price, land price, and interest rate have significant coefficients, but the interest rate shows a positive (+) value rather than a negative (−) one, which suggests that despite a high interest rate, many entities applied for permission to invest in reclamation projects in response to the increase in rice price or paddy land price and consequently, obtained licenses. On the other hand, in the case of the completion model, the regression coefficients of rice price and paddy land prices are not significant, and only interest rate and the policy dummy are statistically significant with the expected signs, that is, interest rate (−) and policy dummy (+). The trends in interest rates and the CRPIP affected the completion of reclamation projects that required fixed capital over at least seven to eight years. On the other hand, trends for rice price and paddy land price did not affect the completion of reclamation projects.

RECLAMATION PROJECTS BY ENTITY

Table 1.5 shows the license situation by ethnic group and business entity. First, the project cases promoted by ethnic Koreans numbered 800, which outnumbered the 590 cases promoted by ethnic Japanese. This indicates the ethnic Koreans' strong intentions to participate in reclamation projects. However, in terms of area, that of the Koreans' projects (only 47,332.5 *chobu*, or 23.5 percent of the total area) lagged behind that of the Japanese's projects (149,634.1 *chobu*, or 74.4 percent of the total area) because the average area per case for the Koreans (only 59.2 *chobu*) was less than that for the Japanese (253.6 *chobu*), representing a ratio of 1:4.3.

In terms of scale, the 590 cases promoted by the Japanese consisted of 259 cases (43.9 percent) of small- or medium-scale projects with an area of less than 50 *chobu* and 331 cases (56.1 percent) of large-scale projects with an area of more than 50 *chobu*, 210 cases (35.6 percent) of which were larger than 100 *chobu*. In contrast, the 800 cases promoted by the Koreans consisted of 608 cases (76 percent) of small- or medium-scale projects and 192 cases (24 percent) of large-scale projects, 83 cases (10.38 percent) of which were larger than 100 *chobu*. Compared to the 76 percent of small and medium reclamation projects by the Koreans, 56.1 percent of the projects by the Japanese had an area of more than 50 *chobu*, which shows the relatively small scale of the Korean projects. This aspect can also be confirmed in reclamation rights with an area of more than 500 *chobu*, including 12 for the Koreans and 76 for the Japanese. This phenomenon was caused by the gap in terms of capital and technology. Table 1.5 shows that the average participant in the reclamation projects was an individual, not a company. The average number of participants in a Korean project was 2.64 persons, higher than the average of

Table 1.5 Licensing and Completion Situation of Different Entities (Unit: Case, *Chobu*)

	License				Completion			
	Case	Area	Average Area	Average Participant	Case	Area	Average Area	Average Participant
Korean — Subtotal	800	47,332.50	59.2		242	12,009.30	49.6	
Korean — Individual	793	45,035.80	56.8	2.6	232	8,754.70	37.7	2.5
Korean — Company	7	2,296.60	328.1		10	3,254.60	325.5	
Japanese — Subtotal	590	149,634.10	253.6					
Japanese — Individual	544	123,345.90	226.7	2				1.4
Japanese — Company	46	26,289.00	571.5					
Korean and Japanese	15	2,395.90	159.7	5.2	2	18.8	9.4	2
Government	16	349	21.8		10	219.6	22	
Agro-Forestry Association and Groups, etc.	15	1,414.10	94.3		1	1,149.40	1,149.40	
Total — Subtotal	1,436	201,125.80	140		491	49,510.20	100.8	
Total — Individual	1,352	170,777.00	126.3	2.4	430	26,089.10	60.7	
Total — Company	53	28,585.50	539.4		50	22,052.00	441	2

2 persons per Japanese project. This outcome was because as ethnic Koreans were relatively inefficient in mobilizing the funds and technology needed to promote a project, they needed more participants to address the problem and avoid business failure.

The scale distribution of reclamation projects of individuals and companies shows that the latter were superior to the former in reclamation projects, because out of the 53 projects promoted by companies, there were no small-scale projects with an area of less than 10 *chobu*, and there were 12 medium-scale projects with an area of more than 10 *chobu* and less than 50 *chobu* and forty-one large-scale projects with an area of more than 50 *chobu*. It is not possible to directly compare cases or areas of reclamation projects between individuals and companies, but there was a big difference in average area per case between individuals (126.3 *chobu*) and companies (542.2 *chobu*). In other words, as in the case of Koreans and Japanese, a company, which was considered to have sufficient fund mobilization capability and technological capability in design, construction, and farming, was inevitably larger. In addition, a similar trend can be confirmed in the reclamation projects of agro-forestry associations and groups and other entities.

Transfers of reclamation rights, which followed almost the same trend as licenses over time, had 378 cases (51.7 percent) of small- or medium-scale projects with an area of less than 50 *chobu* and 353 cases (48.3 percent) of large-scale projects with an area of more than 50 *chobu*, 193 cases (26.4 percent) of which had an area of more than 100 *chobu*. Comparing the number of licenses, the transfer of reclamation rights occurred mostly in large-scale projects. There were 558 transfer cases within the same ethnic groups, and a majority of the transfer cases (651 cases) were between individuals. Transfer cases from Koreans and other ethnic groups to Japanese numbered 106, while those from Japanese and other ethnic groups to Koreans numbered 56. In addition, transfer cases from individuals to companies reached 59, more than 10 from companies to individuals. These results mean that the transfer of reclamation rights from Koreans and other ethnic groups to Japanese and companies, which had relatively plentiful capital and technology, was more noticeable than in the opposite direction.

On the other hand, according to the completion situation by ethnic group, 242 cases for ethnic Koreans had a total area of 12,009.3 *chobu*, while 236 cases for ethnic Japanese had a total area of 36,113.2 *chobu*. First, it can be pointed out that while the two ethnic groups had a similar number of cases, the project scale for the Korean cases was much smaller than that for the Japanese. This result can be confirmed by the average area per individual and company of each ethnic group. As in the case of licenses, the number of individuals participating in a project also indicates that Korean cases involved 1.07 persons more than Japanese cases to address capital limitations.

In addition, even though individual and company cases numbered 430 and 50, respectively, the total area for companies was 4,000 *chobu* more than that for individuals. This result shows how important the ability to mobilize capital was. Comparing the completions with the licenses in terms of each proportion by ethnic group and business entity, the proportion of the cases of Koreans became smaller, but that of the area slightly became larger. This outcome was because the proportion of the completed area of the Korean companies, which showed relatively better performance, complemented that of individual Koreans, which was relatively low.

The Japanese cases showed more dramatic differences. The proportion of the total number of cases of completed Japanese projects was 48.1 percent, slightly larger than that of the licensed Japanese projects (41.1 percent), while the proportion of the total area of completed Japanese projects was 72.9 percent, lower than that of the licensed Japanese projects (74.3 percent). Even though the cases for both Japanese individuals and companies became larger, the areas of the cases for Japanese individuals and companies show contrasting differences. The share of individuals became smaller from 61.3 percent to 35.0 percent, while that of companies became larger from 13.1 percent to 38.0 percent. Similar differences occurred in the cases for Koreans, albeit they were not as significant. As for the differences in the proportion for individuals and companies, individuals became smaller from 84.9 percent to 52.7 percent and companies became larger from 14.3 percent to 44.5 percent. These results indicate that the difference in average area per case between individuals and companies (especially, between Japanese individuals and companies) became larger at the time of project completion rather than at the time of gaining a license because of differences in capital, management, and construction supervision.

In terms of completion by ethnic group from the viewpoint of scale, the results show 186 cases for Koreans that had an area of less than 50 *chobu*, 56 cases with an area of more than 50 *chobu* and less than 100 *chobu*, and 18 cases with an area of more than 100 *chobu*; the cases for the Japanese numbered 124, 112, and 66, respectively. While the Koreans usually succeeded in small- and medium-scale reclamation projects, the Japanese usually succeeded in large-scale projects. Companies also had larger-scale projects than individuals. Compared with the number of licensed projects, small-scale reclamation projects were successful overall, with the number of completed projects relatively increasing while those of medium- and large-scale cases of completed projects decreasing across ethnic groups and business entities.

Nevertheless, with regard to the extinguishment, or failure of projects, there were 273 cases for Koreans, with a total area of 16,138.8 *chobu*, and there were 315 cases for the Japanese, with a total area of 92,904.3 *chobu*. The extinguished rates, which are calculated as the number of extinguished rights divided by the number of licenses, were 34 percent for the cases for

Koreans (34 percent for the cases for Korean individuals, 43 percent for the cases for Korean companies), and 53 percent for the cases for the Japanese (52 percent for the cases for Japanese individuals, and 67 percent for the cases for Japanese companies). These results, unexpectedly, show that the Korean cases had a lower extinguished rate than the Japanese cases, meaning that the cases for companies had a higher extinguishment rate than the cases for individuals. These results are in contrast with the results for completion. How could the contradiction between the project completed rate and extinguishment rate by ethnic group and business entity be like two sides of the same coin? The contradiction can be explained by transfers and recoveries. The transfers of reclamation rights from a Korean transferor to a Japanese transferee and from an individual transferor to a company transferee were stronger than those in the reverse directions. In terms of recoveries of reclamation rights, most of them were undertaken by Japanese, which indicates that the ethnic group that responded sensitively to the colonial reclamation projects was usually the Japanese, in particular, Japanese agricultural companies. Changes in reclamation rights, such as transfers, destruction, and recoveries, were remarkable in Japanese large-scale reclamation projects, which required long-term investment of fixed capital.

Table 1.6 shows the new land categories of reclamation projects. Under the permitted land category at the time of obtaining a license, there were 1,342 cases for paddies, with a total area of 191,760.3 *chobu*, which means that rice farming was the primary purpose of the reclamation projects. In addition, there were a few cases where the reclamation license was acquired for the purpose of farming, building housing, and building reservoirs. The final land categories at the time of project completion had a total area of 37,176.5 *chobu*, accounting for 75.0 percent of the overall total area, and the seawall, which was the core of the construction, had a total area of 10,347.78 *chobu*, accounting for 1.4 percent of the total area. Reclamation and irrigation facilities, such as seawall, drainage, and reservoir facilities, accounted for 20.9 percent of the total area with 10,347.78 *chobu*. It is important to note that these data do not include the reclamation projects licensed by provinces. According to the *Chosen Land Improvement Booklet* (1941), the completion area under the jurisdiction of provinces was 6,821 *chobu*, among the total area of 56,417.05 *chobu* until the end of 1941. This area is somewhat underestimated in that it does not include the completion area from 1942 to 1945. Nevertheless, these data show that reclamation projects were promoted actively during the colonial period because the total completion area of reclamation projects from 1946 to 1992 was 55,669.8 *chobu*, which is almost the same area as during Korea's colonial period. Even if this reclamation area was limited to the southern portion of the Korean Peninsula, it includes coastal industrial complexes, residential complexes, and harbor quay facilities, as well as agricultural areas.

Chaisung Lim

Table 1.6   Land Category of Reclamation Projects

	Permitted Land Category at the Time of License		Final Land Category at the Time of Completion	
	Case	Area	Case	Area
Paddy	1,247	162,968	478	37,188
Field	53	6,338	190	637
Field and Paddy	95	35,264		
Forest			21	101
Housing Site	2	14	164	204
Miscellaneous Land	6	914	172	1,123
Fishpond			1	7
Seawall			349	676
Drain			312	3,796
Reservoir			244	4,843
Estate	10	347	21	191
Tidal Pond			24	93
Road			191	361
River			17	387
Nonclassifiable	1	44		
Total	1,414	205,890	2,184	49,607

CONCLUSION

This study collects data from articles about reclamation projects from the *Official Gazette* of the Japanese Government-General of Korea and estimates long-term statistics to analyze the development of reclamation projects throughout the colonial period. The reclamation projects in colonial Korea reached a total area of more than 56,417.05 *chobu*, stabilized the food supply in the Japanese Empire, and promoted the formation of a colonial landlord-tenant system. In other words, it secured high-quality farmlands, expanded agricultural lands, and increased the food supply through relatively low-cost construction. The Korean Peninsula's natural environment features vast tidal flats on both the west and south coasts, which were favorable for reclamation projects. Unlike other land improvement projects, reclamation projects required considerable skill and long-term fixed capital. Even though the reclamation projects helped facilitate the food supply and stabilized the Japanese immigration business in the empire, its main goals were to increase business revenues when the opportunity cost of the reclamation project was taken into consideration.

The number of licenses for reclamation rights increased rapidly from the late 1910s to the early 1920s with increases in rice and farmland prices. On the other hand, the authorization of completion, which signified the success of a reclamation project, tended to increase significantly from the late 1920s to the early 1930s. Not only did the annual completion area increase, but so did the average scale of the projects, exceeding 100 *chobu*, because this period corresponded to the period of the CRPIP, which provided government subsidies of a maximum of 50 percent of major construction costs. In particular, the Great Depression brought about both cost savings and the negative effects of the collapse of rice prices. The progress of these reclamation projects also became impossible because of the shortage of materials and labor force in the 1940s.

Looking at the trends of the reclamation projects by ethnic group, there were almost the same number of subproject cases for Koreans as for the Japanese, but the project cases of Koreans had a much smaller scale than those of the Japanese. The Korean cases were inferior to the Japanese ones in terms of funding and technology, and to overcome these problems, Koreans increased the number of participants in each project. Nevertheless, the Koreans' reclamation subprojects had a significant average area of about 50 *chobu*. Reclamation projects of Koreans began to increase gradually from the beginning, reaching the level of the Japanese reclamation projects in the late 1930s. Moreover, in terms of business entity, that is individuals versus agricultural companies, the number of projects promoted by individuals was overwhelmingly more than that by companies, but the area of individuals' projects was only slightly more than that of companies' projects. This result shows that agricultural companies were superior to individuals in fund mobilization and civil engineering.

As was shown in the discussions in this chapter, reclamation projects in the colonial period were larger than reclamation projects in the Joseon Dynasty period, and civil engineering methods, which used modern design technology, such as bogies and rails, were introduced in the colonial period. In addition, administrative procedures by the Government-General and provincial governments were specified and the institutional arrangements for reclamation projects were improved by providing long-term and low-interest loans and subsidies according to the CRPIP. However, as can be seen from the scale of reclamation projects, this ethnic disparity could not be solved during the colonial rule, although many ethnic Korean entrepreneurs and companies participated. These reclaimed lands became the subject of agricultural land reform as the basis of food production after liberation.

NOTES

1. This chapter was previously published with the same title in *The Review of Korean Studies*, *21*(2), 7–35.

2. It can be pointed out that Taiwan's agricultural policy in 1920 was relatively high in *freedom*, while the agricultural policy in Korea was mainly focused on the increase of rice and its export to Japan (Yamamoto 1992, 137).

3. The CRPIP was an agricultural policy carried out from 1920 to 1934 to increase rice production in colonial Korea and rice export from Korea to Japan in order to address the food shortage and increase in rice prices in Japan.

4. As can be inferred from Matsumoto and Chung (2017) on the development and overflow of the Mangyeong River, the promotion of the reclamation projects may bring environmental changes to the terrain of the area. However, regarding this, another analysis is required because of length limitations.

5. Tidal flats refer to coastal sedimentary terrains where seawater enters during high tide and exits during low tide. In the academic sense, a tidal flat is the area between the highest tide, that is, the coastline, and the lowest tide (Geonseolbu 1979, 101).

6. Tidal flats can be categorized into sandy tideland, clayey tideland, and mixed tideland according to their main constituents, such as fine sand, silt, and clay (Park 1977, 11).

7. Refer to Article 4 of the National Uncultivated Land Utilization Law (July 1907, Law No. 4); Articles 9, 10, 11, and 12 of the enforcement regulation for the National Uncultivated Land Utilization Law (December 1911, Government of the Governor-General Ordinance No. 81); Article 2 of the Chosen Public Waters Reclamation Act (April 1921, Law No. 57); and Article 1 (2) of the enforcement regulation for the Chosen Public Waters Reclamation Act (June 1924, Government of the Governor- General Ordinance No. 36).

8. Refer to Article 3 of the National Uncultivated Land Utilization Law (July 1907, Law No. 4); Article 23 of the enforcement regulation for the National Uncultivated Land Utilization Law (December 1911, Government of the Governor-General Ordinance No. 81); Articles 22 and 24 of the Chosen Public Waters Reclamation Act (April 1921, Law No. 57); and Article 27 of the enforcement regulation for the Chosen Public Waters Reclamation Act (June 1924, Government of the Governor-General Ordinance No. 36).

9. For this, refer to Matsuyama 1918, 43.

10. In the case of a good harvest, it will be about 30 percent of that of a mature paddy (four to five *koku* of unhulled rice) in the first year, 60 percent in the second year, 80 percent in the third year, and 100 percent in the fourth year. In the case of a normal harvest that is not better than a good harvest, it will be 20 percent of that of a mature paddy (three to four *koku* of unhulled rice) in the first year, 40 percent in the second year, 60 percent in the third year, 80 percent in the fourth year, and 100 percent in the fifth year (Tochi kairyōbu 1928, 73).

11. This method of explanation seems to look at the situation optimistically. Because colonial Korea's position in the Japanese Empire had always been that of an agricultural country, even if colonial industrialization was promoted by the government of the governor-general, optimism about the reclamation projects should have been emphasized generally in the academic and journalistic fields.

12. A typical characteristic of a Korean tideland was a base shaped like a very soft wave-cut terrace (Park 1975, 7).

13. According to other data, the construction cost of a seawall in Korea was about one-tenth of that in Japan, because there were many cases where 30 yen per *tanbu*

to build a seawall was enough, while 300 yen was needed for the same in Japan (Syokusankyoku 1922, 30).

14. Around 75,000 *chobu* was planned for reclamation projects, of which 33,050 *chobu* was for marine reclamation, in the renewed Chosen Rice Production Increase Plan. The proportion of reclamation was only 21 percent of the total project area, but it accounts for 35 percent of the construction cost. In other words, a subsidy rate (30 percent, later 50 percent of construction cost) higher than other projects was applied to increase food production, because the construction cost of the reclamation projects was higher than that of irrigation projects and field changes (Chōsen sōtokufu 1928).

15. The rice price is the price of 180 liters of Seoul wholesale rice that can be observed over a long period of time (Hankuk eunhaeng 1968). The price of rice paddies is the national price estimated by reflecting the provincial area weights of 1918, 1922, 1932, and 1942 (Chōsen sōtokufu annual). The interest rate is the general loan rate of Chosen Agricultural Bank and Joseon Development Bank, which was closely linked to agricultural land improvement (Zaimukyoku annual; Joseon eunhaeng josabu 1948, 1949).

REFERENCES

Ayata, Y. (1922). Chōsen no Mikonchi Kaikon ni totte [Reclamation of uncultivated land in Korea]. *Chōsen [Korea],* October, p. 351.

Ban, Y. (1977). Incheon haean ui mud-flat jihyeong yeongu [A study on the mud-flat topography of Incheon coast]. *Gukto jirihak hoeji [Journal of Territory Geographical Society],* 3(1), 227–240.

Cha, M., & Hwang, J. (2015). 1910 nyeondae e ssal saengsan eun jeongche haetna? [The 1910s in Korea: Growth or stagnation decade?]. *Gyeongje sahak [Economic History],* 59, 77–104.

Chōsen sōtokufu [Government General of Korea]. (Ed.). (1928). *Chōsen no tochi kairyō jigyō [Chosen Land Improvement Project].* Seoul: Chōsen sōtokufu.

Chōsen sōtokufu [Government General of Korea]. (1941). *Chōsen tochi kairyō yōran [Chosen Land Improvement Booklet].* Seoul: Chōsen sōtokufu.

Chōsen sōtokufu [Government General of Korea]. (annual). *Chōsen sōtokufu tōkei nenpō [Statistics Annual Report of Government General of Korea].* Seoul: Chōsen sōtokufu.

Chōsen sōtokufu [Government General of Korea]. (daily). *Kwanbo [Official Gazette].* Seoul: Chōsen sōtokufu.

Daehan jeguk [Korean Empire]. (Ed.). (daily). *Kwanbo [Official Gazette].* Seoul: Chōsen sōtokufu.

Fujii, K. (1924). Chōsen ni okeru mikon-chi kaitaku to imin [Development of Uncultivated Area and Immigration in Korea]. *Chōsen nō kaihō [Korean Agricultural Association Report],* May, 19–20.

Geonseolbu [Ministry of Construction]. (1979). *Gancheok jawon yongdo jijeong gyehoek josa [Reclamation Resource Utilization Plan Survey].* Seoul: Geonseolbu.

Hankuk eunhaeng [Bank of Korea]. (Ed.) (1968). *Mulkka chongram [Prices Conspectus]*. Seoul: Hankuk eunhaeng.

Huh, S. (2011). *Ilje chogi Joseon ui nong-eop [Agriculture in the Early Colonial Period: Criticizing the Theory of Agricultural Development of Colonial Modernization]*. Seoul: Hangilsa.

Huh, S. (2014). Mangyeonggang mit Dongjingang yuyeok ui bangjoje wa hacheon ui jebang [Seawalls and embankments of the Mangyeong and Dongjin River Basin in 1910s]. *Gyeongje sahak [Economic History], 56*, 115–151.

Joseon eunhaeng josabu [Investigation Division, Joseon Bank]. (Ed.) (1948). *Joseon gyeongjeyeonbo [Chosun Economic Yearbook]*. Seoul: Joseon eunhaeng.

Joseon eunhaeng josabu [Investigation Division, Joseon Bank]. (1949). *Gyeongje yeon-gam [Economic Yearbook]*. Seoul: Joseon eunhaeng. Kang, Yeomuk. Joseon eunhaeng josabu [Investigation Division, Joseon Bank]. (1993). *Gancheok gonghak [Reclamation Engineering]*. Seoul: Hyangmunsa.

Kim, N. (Ed.) (2006). *Hanguk ui gyeongje seongjang: 1910-1945 [Economic Growth in Korea: 1910-1945]*. Seoul: Seoul National University Press.

Koh, C. (2009). Haebang ihu ui gancheok [Reclamation after liberation]. In C. Koh (Ed.), *Hanguk ui gaetbeol: hwan-gyeong, saengmul geurigo ingan [Korea's Tidal Flats: Environment, Biology, and Humanity]* (pp. 691–700). Seoul: Seoul National University Press.

Lim, C. (1995). Singminji Joseon e isseoseo ui gancheok sa-eop e gwanhan yeongu: Joseon-in ui neungdongjeok chamyeo wa seongjang [A study on the tideland reclamation project of colonial Korea]. Unpublished master's thesis, Seoul National University, Seoul, Korea.

Lim, Y., Lee, J., & Sin, D. (1988). *Gancheok gonghak [Reclamation Engineering]*. Seoul: Gyeongmunsa.

Matsumoto, T., & Chung, S. (2017). Water management projects and floods/droughts in colonial Korea: The case of the Man'gyŏng River in the Honam Plain. *Acta Koreana, 20*(1), 173–193.

Matsumoto, T. (1992). *Shinryaku to Kaihatsu: Nihon Shihon-shugi to Chūgoku Shokumin-chi ka [Aggression and Development: Japanese Capitalism and Chinese Colonization]*. Tokyo: Ochanomizu-shobō.

Matsumura, M. (1929). Kantaku kokuei to jisakunō sōsetsu [Nationalization of reclamation and establishment of independent farmer]. *Chōsen nō Kaihō, October*, p. 3.

Matsuyama, J. (1918). Higatachi kaikon jigyō ni tsuite [About reclamation project of tideland]. *Chōsen nō kaihō [Korean agricultural association report], September*, p. 43.

Misu, M. (1944). *Chōsen no Dojō to Hiryō [Korean Soil and Fertilizer]*. Seoul: Tōto shoseki.

Namgung, B. (1991). Hacheon jiyeok ildae ganseokji sang ui gancheok chwilak yuhyeong e gwanhan yeongu [A study on the type of reclamation settlement on the tidal flats in the river area]. *Jilihak nonchong [Journal of Korean Geographical Society], 12*, 1–198.

Nongeochon jinheung gongsa [Rural Development Corporation]. (Ed.) (1993). *Gancheok sa-eop ui damokjeok hyogwa [Multipurpose effects of reclamation projects]*. Suwon: Nongeochon jinheung gongsa.

Nongjigwalliguk, Nonglimbu [Bureau of Land Management, Ministry of Agriculture and Forestry] (Ed.) (1958). *Hanguk gancheok sa-eop ui jichim [Guidelines for Korean Reclamation Projects]*. Seoul: Nonglimbu.

Oh, S. (2009). Ilje sidae ui gancheok [Reclamation in the colonial period]. In C. Koh (d.), *Hanguk ui gaetbeol: hwan-gyeong, saengmul geurigo ingan [Korea's Tidal Flats: Environment, Biology, and Humanity]* (pp. 669–690). Seoul: Seoul National University Press.

Park, D. (1975). Urinara seohaean ui ganseokji yuhyeong [Morphology of the inter-tidal flat of the western coast of Korea in comparison with those of the Wadden Zee and the Bay of Fundy]. *Jirihak hoebo [Geographical Bulletin], 14*, 1–9.

Park, D. 1977. Won-gyeok tamsa bangbeop e uihan Cheonsuman ganseokji jihyeong yeongu [A study on the topography of Cheonsu Bay tidal flat by remote sensing method]. *Daehan jiri hakhoeji [Journal of the Korean Geographical Society], 15*, 1–15.

Park, S. (1989). *Mingan soyu daegyumo gancheok nongjang ui soyu mit iyong siltae e gwanhan josa yeongu [A Study on the Ownership and Utilization of Large Scale Reclaimed Farming Owned by the Private Sector]*. Seoul: Hanguk nongchon gyeongje yeonguwon [Korea Rural Economic Institute].

Park, S. (2015). Singminji Hanguk nong-eop tonggye sujeong jaeron [Review on the Korean agricultural statistics of the colonial period]. *Gyeongje sahak [Economic History], 59*, 149–171.

Park, Y., & Oh, S. (2004). *Joseon sidae gancheokji gaebal: gukto hwakjang gwajeong gwa iyong ui munje [Reclamation Development in the Joseon Dynasty: Territory Expansion Process and Utilization Problems]*. Seoul: Seoul National University Press.

Rhee, Y. (2012a). 17 segi huban—20 segi jeonban sudojak toji saengsanseong ui janggi chuse [The long trend of land productivity of the paddy farming from the late 17th century to the early 20th century]. *Gyeongje nonjip [Economic Journal], 51*(2), 411–460.

Rhee, Y. (2012b). Hollan gwa hwansang ui yeoksajeok sigonggan [The historical time-space in confusion and fantasy]. *Gyeongje sahak [Economic History], 53*, 143–181.

Shokusankyoku [Production Bureau], & Chōsen sōtokufu [Government General of Korea]. (Ed.) (1922). *Chōsen no kangai oyobi tochi kaikon jigyō [Korean Irrigation and Reclamation Project]*. Seoul: Chōsen sōtokufu.

Tochi kairyōbu [Reclamation Department], & Chōsen sōtokufu [Government General of Korea]. (Ed.) (1928). *Chōsen no tochi kairyō jigyō [Korean Land Improvement Project]*. Seoul: Chōsen sōtokufu.

Tochi kairyōbu. (1929). *Chōsen no kantaku jigyō [Korean reclamation projects]*. Seoul: Chōsen sōtokufu.

Woo, D. (2015). Iljeha migok saengsanseong ui chu-i e gwanhan jaegeomto [Growth and stagnation in agricultural productivity in colonial Korea: Causal effect or statistical artifact?] *Gyeongje sahak [Economic History], 58*, 53–93.

Yamaguchi, S. (1910). *Chōsen sangyō-shi (Chū) [Korean Industry Journal (middle volume)]*. Tokyo: Hōbukan.

Yamamoto, Y. (1992). *Nippon Shokumin-chi keizai-shi kenkyū [Japanese Colonial Economic History Research]*. Nagoya: Nagoya University Press.

Yamane, S. (1918). Higata kaikon wa yūri nari [Tideland reclamation is advantageous]. *Chōsen nō kaihō, February,* 14–15.

Yang, S. (Ed.) (2010). *Joseon hugi gancheok gwa suri [Reclamation and Irrigation in the Late Joseon Dynasty].* Seoul: Minsokwon.

Zaimukyoku [Finance Bureau], & Chōsen sōtokufu [Government General of Korea]. (Ed.) (annual). *Chōsen kin'yū jikō sankō-sho [Chosen Financial Matters Reference].* Seoul: Chōsen sōtokufu.

Chapter 2

The Narrative of Post-Childhood and Memories of Food

Study on the Symbolism of Food in Korean Postwar Formation Novels

Soh-yon Yi

This[1] study aims to investigate the formation novels written in the 1960s and 1970s after the Korean War, focusing on the symbolism of food that appears in varied forms. *Food* takes up the role of mediation where the so-called microscopic powers operate, and furthermore, becomes the motivation of desire that makes you participate in the energy cycle that operates in the whole ecosystem. Many researchers from different disciplines, such as philosophy, economics, and anthropology understand the act of cooking and eating as a highly diversified system of social and cultural symbolism. The social anthropologists, such as Claude Levy-Strauss and Mary Douglas, insist that "food" works as a code that transmits specific social messages including hierarchy, inclusion, exclusion, and interactions with other societies (Douglas 1999).

Therefore, many symbols related to food and the action of eating could be understood as a system of signs that carry various meanings.[2] In addition, because of the characteristics of food that is taken into the human body and assimilated, it is closely related with body discourse. The symbolism of food and the action of eating in a novel is expressed in combination of various aspects of parole in semiotics such as concrete situations, characters, and context.

In the post–Korean War novels, the problems that govern the situation and characters are the direct experiences of war and the pain of loss. It is not only writers such as Lee Dong-Ha and Lee Mun-Gu whom this chapter mainly studies, but also other writers, including Kim Won-Il and Oh Jeong-Hee, had more or less similar experiences during the Korean War. They all share in common in the expression of the fatal present caused by the painful memories of war or the absence of a father figure, with a sense of hunger that is particularly overwhelming among the physical senses. War traumas are in many cases formation epics that are self-realizing building blocks for the novel, growing out of childhood, especially in the novels of Lee Dong-Ha and Lee Mun-Gu, who often juxtapose incongruent episodes. To them, writing a novel was not to write about past experiences of loss, but to express a sense of hunger, an effort to reveal the existence of past pain still existing in the present.

The reason this study deals with Lee Mun-Gu and Lee Dong-Ha one after the other is that those two writers experienced the Korean War at about the same age and there are certain differences as well as similarities in the description of their memories. Whereas Lee Dong-Ha's main characters leave behind their hometowns to go to the cities and experience all the violence and poverty of modern society there, Lee Mun-Gu's characters are described more as having happy childhood memories spent in rural areas with rich images and rhetoric, amid the benevolence of elders and neighbors.

The Village *Gwan Chon* that is described in Lee Mun-Gu's novel is a place full of spiritual richness if not material wealth, an idealized space that exists in the memory of the narrator rather than in reality. Therefore, the work of recalling it from memory is related to the epic of sympathy that ironically reminds us of the huge loss that is the result of a terrible war disaster and the fetters of modernization.

On the other hand, the *toy-like* city described in Lee Dong-Ha's novel is a place that lacks adults who can educate and look after children, a fragile and degrading environment. There, whether adults or children, people look to survival, like animals, or to pursue their own personal gain or to fulfill their desire. There, in that absolute state of deficiency, children are described as being oppressed not only in their physical growth but also in their psychological maturity. In such cities, there cannot be anything like a long-lasting tradition or customs conveyed from a long history, nor the principle of living together based on human dignity. In those circumstances, the main characters try very hard to keep their self-esteem as human beings, but sadly end up in miserable failure. To Lee's main characters, the city is merely a frivolous place with as much value as a child's toy.

To the beings who live in the cities, there is only one option available to survive: the law of jungle, or violence in other words. The trauma from the dark point in history which cannot bear repetition is replaced by the sensation of hunger that is one of the worst pains remembered by the body, with only enough food to barely maintain life. Therefore, *Toy City*, the city that remains in the memory of the main character, is not an ideal place that inspires nostalgia, or a desire to return, but is something related to the epic of maturity and self-discovery, which triggers the separation of self through a strong negation of the present.

The traditional societies of the Orient where sharing is an important virtue, as well as western thinkers influenced by the Marxist anthropologists, such as Marcel Mauss (2007), have paid attention to the *gift economy* where traditional giving and distribution is an important model for solidarity of a community. According to them, in primitive societies where living together in a community was very important, people constructed a society model based on *values* that are mutually beneficial. In contrast, the market economy that pursues only the struggle for existence and materialistic value is expressed as modern violence.

This dark side of modern civilization is described in collective symptoms, such as lack of nutrition, feelings of hunger, voracity, and binge eating in many literary works. And furthermore, as such pathological situations surface as a consistent problem in the modern world, researchers, grounded in economics, cultural anthropology, and ethics, have examined an alternative to modernity, with post-modernism.

Therefore, the reason to re-examine the old-fashioned utopia, represented in the "Gwan Chon" village, in the context of today's post-modernism, is an effort to begin from a firm recognition of the sense of deficiency and reconstruct the memories of the past, and then to try to complete them in the form of condolences. The work of *signification of the past* completed by condolences provides a structured frame for the subjects to be able to treat their wounds and to relate to the future.

On the other hand, the novels of Lee Dong-Ha can be ascertained as a realization of a situation that lacks a community system. Thus, the analysis of his novel, *Toy City*, is focused on the process of the character's reconstruction of his inner world by replacing the negative experiences of the past with the experiences of an existential sense of loss.

THE EPIC OF LOST PARADISE AND CULINARY SEMIOTICS AS *GIFT*: *GWAN CHON ESSAY*

Agricultural Community: A System of Giving and Mutual Benefit

The first part of *Gwan Chon Essay* (Lee 1983) consists of eight chapters in total, centering on the story of recalling the past when the adult writer visits his hometown. His hometown before the Korean War where his grandfather was still living like the embodiment of the pre-modern order is described as an ideal world in his recollections with the sentiment of nostalgia. According to the narrator's recollections, *Gwan Chon* Village was a space very close to the Korean traditional community model where law and order are emphasized. Such a community is where the principle of giving and mutual benefit—what Marcel Mauss (2007) calls the *gift economy*—governs, unlike the principle of the market economy of the modern world. It was food items that were most required by the people of those days, especially when they were poor, and they were very important gifts most frequently given and received.

In the eyes of the young child, the cupboard where his grandfather stores bountiful snacks for himself is regarded as the symbol of limitless gifts, and also of the fertile Mother Nature where as much food as could be desired was stored. It was like a treasure trove, where surplus was abundant. The tradition of a community based on the riches of Mother Nature, endless surplus, and warm-heartedness is recollected as a mysterious power. It maintains the community so that its members do not die of hunger in the trauma of poverty for generation after generation, and also during the ordeal of the Korean War.

The narrator's family seems to be a distinguished one as descendants of *yangban* (Korean aristocrats), taking responsibility psychologically as well as economically in village life in a senior advisory role. The grandfather, who is symbolized as a king pine tree, not only makes it clear about the feudalistic order of *yangban* and *sangnom* (lower class) but is also the one who gives names to the village children, and the poor often come to his house to seek work or to be given old clothes.

In a Korean traditional community, the respectful class including *yangban* used the *gift* method, giving generously to obtain their fame and position. Such customs also induced a sense of duty to receive and also to return at the same time, which becomes a strong power to maintain a society and strengthen its solidarity. According to Marcel Mauss (2007), the principle of exchange-giving, that imposes a strong sense of duty just as much as spontaneity, was a system that most of the human race used before modernity.[3]

Therefore, in the background of the narrator being loved and protected in his childhood and being able to grow up playing in the whole *Gwan Chon* area as if it was his own garden lies the principle of mutual benefit that was what the traditional community was based on. In his home, it is Ongjeom who is the giving person in the kitchen, and outside of his house, it is Daebok who is the giver, representing nature and taking the role of giving food to the young narrator. And above them all, his grandfather positions himself as the source of all gifts including name giving. Food as the object of a gift becomes a homological sign to show most clearly the social relationship constituted by the order of giving. His grandfather who takes charge of the order of Gwan Chon was very strict about food-related ethics and palate discernment, and that shows us the importance of food in the whole social semantic network.

In contrast, the attitude of his father who possesses the modern way of thinking, unlike the grandfather, shows a different approach to everything including food. The narrator's father not only accepts the new culture of the West but is a revolutionary one with socialistic ideas, being also a successful businessman. Whereas the grandfather refuses any food that lacks proper formality, the father enjoys eating humble food together with the farmers.

The different attitude toward food the two characters represent can be explained as contrasts such as modern/pre-modern and upper class food/lower class food. However, the father character, reminding the narrator of a strict super-ego, actually appears as a beneficiary as far as food is concerned, being a recipient from the narrator in the story. The narrator's psychological distance from his father and the unconscious respect toward the modern ways of thinking and emotional ambivalence similar to Oedipus are symbolized in the act of bringing food to the father when he is put in prison.

In the meantime, there are scenes where relationships outside of his family, for example, with the neighbors, are part of the story and they are much more richly and affectionately described in quantity and content. They belong to characters who "liked me without any calculation but only by their good nature" (Lee 1983, 127) whom the narrator also likes. And the representative figure among them who gave food to him generously was the kitchen worker, Ongjeom. Especially moving is the scene where Ongjeom helps the narrator to keep his "independence" in his childhood through food. Ongjeom buys the young boy cheap snacks to prevent him from picking up the food items thrown away by the American soldiers who pass by the village during the Korean War. She pays for them with the money obtained by selling stolen foodstuffs from the kitchen.

The throwing of food gifts by the American soldiers from the train windows is not at all symbolized as a good-will or friendly gesture, but as a violent sign, despising and mocking, a typically "bad present." Often the food is half-eaten or covered with spit. Looking at the people who hurry to pick it up, Ongjeom laments: "What on earth do the soldiers think our people of Chosun are like, throwing their left-overs to us" (Lee 1983, 78).

While there are such bad gifts that show the ordeal of one period of history, there are also good gifts that show extreme generosity and warmth. When the family becomes broken up and put into a difficult situation having to worry about what to eat, the mother prepares a sixtieth birthday party feast for Mr. Youn and his family who are refugees of the war and have come to stay in the servants' room. The occasion becomes a decisive opportunity to show firm solidarity with the Youn family.

The traditional *yangban* custom where even if they go hungry themselves the guests who come to stay should be treated well is expressed clearly with the sixtieth birthday food, which is symbolized with bowls of cooked rice. After the generous gift, the Youn family works hard for the narrator's family while they stay with them and this event becomes an exemplary case that shows how the system of mutual benefit was established and united past rural communities. As the modern capitalist system based on market economics gradually reveals its shortcomings, we become more self-reflective about the loss of humanity and the phenomenon of marginalization, and the reflection on the principle of giving and sharing food of the past could become a reference point to suggest a new alternative.

The Pain of Lost Paradise and the Recalled *Body Memory*

The narrator's family that had been in a respected position in the agricultural community also becomes affected by the war and experiences a rapid crisis. The pillar of the family, the grandfather, passes away, leaving his son and the grandson behind. The narrator is only in the second year of primary school when that happens, and recognizes the war as "something extremely abstract that will be impossible to imagine even in dreams for a small boy like me" (Lee 1983, 109), but, on the other hand, writes also that "it was the most concrete and real among what I had experienced until then" (Lee 1983, 109).

To the narrator as a young boy, the war was not a historical event related to an international power struggle or ideology, but rather a family dissolution followed by hunger, a vivid reality experienced by his "body." The motivation for the writer who is now an adult to recall the hardship of those days without his father and grandfather came when he read in the newspaper about a sixteen-year-old boy killing a taxi driver and stealing his money because of hunger. He remembered his mother who used to give rice on a tray to a young beggar standing in front of their gate, or an old beggar under their angle rafter, and laments the passing of those past communities that believed in hearty food giving. In the seventies when society was regarded as more or less materialistically stable, the news of a boy killing an adult out of hunger reveals the combination of cold-heartedness and frivolity in modern civilization.

Experiencing poverty and violence due to the war, and being introduced to modern civilization armed with individualism and the monetary economy, modern society seems to have gradually lost the tradition of consideration for other people. Materialistically people may be more at ease now, but compared to the past with its sharing of food, modern people seem trivial. From a memory of enjoyment of belonging to a community, people's sense of loss has grown much bigger psychologically.

In the context of such absolute deficiency, the radish of *dongchimi* (radish water *kimchi*) that the narrator as a young boy could not yet eat, is contrasted with the white cooked rice, the coke, and grapes that the murderer and robber boy wanted so much. The food becomes symbols of something unreachably lost forever. As the narrator describes himself as a "displaced person" (Lee 1983, 11), *Gwan Chon* remains the lost paradise for him. The mutually benefiting community of the past has now collapsed and the young people who remained in the agricultural areas set their minds toward the modern capitalist society that presses for results. When the good traditional customs and the mutually benefiting regulations disappear, the results are shameless crimes and impulsive violence and the imposing of death sentences on people with the excuse of *unwritten law.*

In the process of growing up into an adult, the events of marginalization and separation experienced by the narrator are changed into a sense of lamentation toward the loss of hometown, with the recollections of food that his body still remembers one by one. To him, the lost hometown, gradually overtaken by modern violence and rapidly by the war, is recalled and reconstituted as an ideal community, an epic of the lost paradise.

THE EPIC OF SELF-DISCOVERY AND THE FEELING OF HUNGER AS A SYMPTOM: *TOY CITY*

Postwar City Space: *Placelessness* of Bare Life

In the novel *Toy City* (1995) by Lee Dong-Ha, the sense of loss in people who left their hometown, and the shallowness of city life are more vividly described. The narrator, "I," that is assumed as his young self, moves to the unfamiliar city hurriedly with his family because of something that is related to the ideology issue of one of his uncles. Then this novel describes the events that the narrator in the fourth year of a primary school experiences in Daegu City in three parts. According to the sequence of events, the losses experienced by the narrator and his family are revealed in three stages: (1) in the first series *Toy City*, he loses his father; (2) in the second series *Starved Soul*, he loses his mother; (3) and in the third series *Judah's Time*, he loses his sister and the sense of purity, and thus, his identity crisis arises.

The narrator who arrives in the city feels embarrassed facing the order of the city where you have to pay for everything, even for water that was abundantly provided for free in his hometown. He cannot digest the cold tea with orange color and vomits it up, as described in "one cupful amount, orange colored vomit" (Lee 1995, 22). In addition, the rice cooked with polluted water has a nasty smell and an orange color, and here it has to be noted that the color orange is not only an unfamiliar color in our traditional food which is based on five basic colors, but is also a color giving a visual image of the impression of city space filled with weak artificiality. To the narrator, the city causes the loss of people's purity, and it is a place where self-esteem cannot be maintained. The father, who had the position of head of the village, cannot support the family here and in the end even becomes a degraded criminal, useless as a head of the family. In the agricultural community where people have consideration for others and live together, the act of eating food was, before satisfying the instinctive physical desire, a form of meaningful behavior that strengthened the solidarity of the human body as well of the society.

However, the cities that do not have strong roots in nature change all relationships so that exchanging goods becomes an act of "de-humanization" that cannot help in maintaining the stability of life. According to Edward Relph (2005), a place is inherent in human existence, and offers the most original sense of identity. As a person and as a member of a community, Relph (2005) calls the characteristic of modern city space as *placelessness*. The meaning of *Toy City*—the title of the whole novel and subtitle of the first series—is connected with the *placelessness,* which refers to the state where the traditions and customs are lost and the space where the ethics of gift giving out of care are forgotten. This frivolous city, full of make-shift boxes and houses made roughly of wooden panels, is merely a *toy-like* space lacking the solidness of an existential base.

Such city space takes away the self-esteem of its residents and they degenerate into the state of animals or de-humanized beings struggling for survival. The narrator, in the poor environment where it is difficult to keep a minimum of self-respect not only in eating but also in excreting, experiences the feeling of self-loss with the sense of huge *hunger*. In the second series called *Starved Soul*, as the title tells us, it is the soul more than his body, the psychological deficiency which becomes a bigger problem for the narrator. The direct source of his psychological deficiency is the absence of a father, and the lethargic state of his mother who vegetates and then dies. With the sequence of such events, the narrator gradually loses his sense of identity and falls into the madness of violence. Such a state is described in *Judah's Time* as an intolerable sense of *thirst*.

The sufferings and anxieties experienced by the people who are expelled from their communities to be thrown into the devastated *toy-like* city where the strong govern the weak are common all over today's world. The novel of Lee Dong-Ha, in the extreme situation after the war, describes in a painstaking manner the process of a fall into violence, even for young children, after losing self-esteem through hunger and thirst, but never loses the critical tone of voice of an adult.

The Semiotics of Food as the Symbol of Trauma

For children in the growing period, if the supply of nutrition and love are insufficient, it may be said that they are in the state deprived of all the values necessary to grow properly, and the system of the whole society and family breaks down, with no-one managing their proper roles. Such a situation is clearly expressed in the scene of the family dinner at the beginning of the novel. Different from breakfast and lunch, which merely involved staving off hunger, *dinner* has greater meaning, including the order of food on the table, as well as the order of the participating people, showing their inter-relationships. It is an occasion to ascertain each individual sharing the group culture. And by cooking with the ingredients gathered from nature, they also participate in the cosmic order and energy cycle. In that sense, *dinner* functions as community semiosis as well as a social ceremony confirming the hierarchy and solidarity of the family members beyond the simple act of having a meal together.

The collapsed dinner scene of *Toy Story* is like an ironic blessing insinuating the approaching life in the city. "Considering that it was the first day of their new business after moving out into the city one month before, the dinner together that evening was a meaningful one" (Lee 1995). However, the left-over flour-based snack and cold tea replaces the proper food of the past, and thus the social system connected to the *symbol* of dinner is collapsed and dissipated. The laid out food on the table as well as the act of cooking and eating it all represent the value and ethics transferred through culture as a sign, therefore the act of having a meal together performs a function that gives a certain frame to the gathering. Ironically, the scene of dinner that evening hints at the augur that the family will end up being scattered and living separately.

In the meantime, the daily life of the narrator who struggles to fill the empty body and soul is described with the sequence of metonymic images of different food. The trivial food items that fill his hungry stomach in *Toy City* become the chain of signs that connect with past trauma. The father figure whom he believed would restore the destructed order when he returns home still shows a lethargic attitude when he does return, and the narrator feels an "enormous sense of betrayal and by degrees decides to leave the city space" (Lee 1995).

The ending of *Toy City* cannot be said to be gloomy as it ends with the scene where the main character, realizing his own deficiency, tries to be separated from his self. Rather, it has to be called an epic of self-discovery that describes the process of separating from his shameful past and at the same time denying the city space that degraded his and his family's life.

CONCLUSION

Lee Mun-Gu and Lee Dong-Ha share the same background in that they were born at about the same time and experienced the war and wrote actively in the chaotic time after war. The symbol of food in modern Korean novels has been marked as having a negative meaning. That could be explained in the colonial economy and exploitation under Japanese rule and full-scale destruction of the economic system due to the Korean War, but as we saw in *Gwan Chon Essay*, it is also due to the psychological and cultural deficiency following violent modernization.

In the 1960s and 1970s novels when the scars of the war were much healed, the capitalism and the violence of modernization deepened and appeared in many literary works in various forms. Especially for the food motif that was used in past literature works to represent absolute poverty and postwar poverty, it has to be noted that it now represents many more facets of life in the generation that has experienced more stability and wealth. As Korean society becomes highly industrialized, the ingredients to make food have become rapidly richer and people's concerns and interests in cuisine, diet, food hygiene, and so on have rapidly increased, and accordingly in literary works, the semantic network related to food has also become much more delicate.

Therefore, to reveal the various faces of Korean society with rapid changes, and the complicated semantic network of it, the effort to explore the various aspects of food should continue in the future.

NOTES

1. This chapter was previously published with the same title in *Literature and Environment*, *9*(2), 73–91.

2. Culinary semiotics is lately set as a subordinate category of semiotics. The history of food semiotics and Korean domestic research applying certain texts (especially, *pansori*) include "Culinary semiotics as a program of synchretische semiotik" by Park Yeo-Seong, "Study of semiotics (Vol. 14)," published by Korean Semiotics Academy (2003), "The theory and application of text linguistics: Ars culinae—Introduction to culinary semiotics," and "Text linguistics."

3. There is still such a system existent in limited scope mutually beneficial economy in some part of the society (Mauss 2007).

REFERENCES

Douglas, M. (1999). Deciphering a meal. In M. Douglas (Ed.), *Implicit Meaning: Selected Essays in Anthropology* (2nd ed., pp. 231–251). London: Routledge.

Lee, D. (1995). *Toy City (Compendium of Korean Novel Literature 54: Toy City and Others)*. Seoul: Dong-A Publishing Co.

Lee, M. (1983). *Gwan Chon Essay, Korean literature of 3rd generation*: *9*. Seoul: Samsung Publishing Co.

Mauss, M. *The logic of the gift*. (S. Lee, Trans.). Seoul: Hangil-sa.

Relph, E. (2005). *Place and Placelessness*. (D. Kim, H. Kim, & S. Shim, Trans.). Seoul: Non-Hyeong.

Chapter 3

Addressing the Agri-Food Crisis in Korea

Implications of Food Sovereignty and the UN Declaration on the Rights of Peasants

Byeong-Seon Yoon and Wonkyu Song

Recently,[1] a variety of discussions have been underway in the South Korea (hereafter Korea) on the revision of the constitution, last changed in 1987 as a result of the democratization movement of the 1980s. Among them, numerous organizations were calling for a revised constitution to include new provisions on the value of agriculture and food and the rights of peasants. Currently, the constitution contains only a land-to-the-tillers principle with respect to agricultural land (Article 121) and the obligation of the state to support and establish plans for agricultural development (Article 123). The Constitutional Amendment Movement Headquarters for the Realization of Peasants' Rights and the Fundamental Right to Food (hereafter, referred to as Headquarters), comprising 45 entities including agricultural organizations and civil society organizations, was inaugurated in August 2017, and the National Agricultural Cooperative Federation (NACF) has conducted a signature drive calling for agricultural values to be reflected in a new constitution.[2] Debates on what agricultural values should be included in the constitution and what is meant by sustainable agriculture based on such values are ongoing.

In Korea, discussions on the revision of the constitution have always included the rights of peasants. This is because there have been debates over adopting the United Nations Declaration on the Rights of Peasant and Other People Working in Rural Areas by the UN Human Rights Council and Open-Ended Intergovernmental Working Group (OEIWG) since 2012. The official recognition of the rights of peasants in the United Nations was first proposed by a transnational peasant movement, La Vía Campesina (LVC), and it was made into an official provision through cooperation with international human rights organizations such as FIAN International and Centre Europe-Tiers Monde (CETIM). The United Nations has moved to adopt a declaration on the rights of peasants in the international human rights system as peasants have been increasingly recognized as important players in the global agricultural production system since the world food crisis of 2007–2008. This has provided momentum to shed light on the importance of the agricultural sector and peasants who have sacrificed themselves for the sake of economic growth. Furthermore, the UN Declaration on the Rights of Peasants and a sustainable agriculture model has significant implications on the revision of the Korean constitution in relation to agriculture. In particular, an amendment of the constitution with regard to agriculture bears much significance in that it represents the first attempt to institutionalize food sovereignty since discussions of food sovereignty started within a grassroots movement in the mid-2000s.

This research will consider the significance of the UN Declaration on the Rights of Peasants for the Alternative Agri-food Movement in Korea and the ongoing discussions around a potential constitutional amendment. As scholars of global and local agri-food systems and food sovereignty, the authors have had continued discussions with activists within the Food Sovereignty Movement and Alternative Agri-food Movement in Korea, in particular, through participation in the Headquarters' research team. The direction and explanations of the Alternative Agri-food Movement found in this study were obtained through discussions with activists and collaborative research. This chapter is comprised as follows. First, it will track the development of Korea's agriculture and governmental agricultural policies under the postwar food regime. Second, it will review the process of the development of the Alternative Agri-food Movement that resisted both the postwar food regime and later neoliberalism and sought alternatives to them. Third, it will consider from Korean perspective food sovereignty and a declaration of the rights of peasants currently being discussed at an international level.

FOOD AID TO FREE TRADE: THE DEEPENING AGRI-FOOD CRISIS IN SOUTH KOREA

The eradication of hunger was one of the major national goals of almost all countries after World War II, and the Food and Agriculture Organization (FAO) of the United Nations was inaugurated in 1945 to promote international cooperation for this purpose (FAO 1985; Margulis 2013). In addition, the Universal Declaration of Human Rights included the right to food as a means to ensure an adequate level of life and social security.[3] After liberation from Japanese colonial rule in 1945, food consumption that had been suppressed by the colonial rule recovered, and Korea then faced a serious shortage of food along with population growth (Research Department of the Bank of Chosun 1948). The US Army Military Government in Korea that was formed after the liberation of 1945 implemented food aid through Government Appropriations for Relief in Occupied Areas (GARIOA) to relieve shortages, which helped to temporarily combat food shortages. The FAO advocated the right to food and thus pursued a balance between food aid, food trade, and the agricultural development of each nation after World War II (Pritchard et al. 2016, 6). However, the United States, which had a monopoly as the world's largest breadbasket, preferred to expand food aid and food trade rather than promote the agricultural development of each nation (Yoon 2006). The FAO appeared to support the balance between food aid and trade and the agricultural development of each nation on the surface, but food assistance provided in the name of realizing the right to food actually undermined the agricultural production of the beneficiary countries. In particular, Korea, which underwent US Military Government rule and the Korean War, became one of the key geopolitical focal points of US strategy during the Cold War period. The Korean Peninsula bordered communist nations and was also near Japan, an important stronghold in the United States' global strategy (McMichael 2009, 37–38; Yoon et al. 2013, 57). Hence, Korea became a representative of the international food assistance the United States implemented to achieve its dual political and economic aims of strengthening its superpower status and disposing of its surplus agricultural products.

After the Korean War (1950–1953), food aid was significantly increased under the US Farm Surplus Importation Agreement in 1955 based on the US' Agricultural Trade Development Assistance Law (Public Law 480), making a huge impact on Korean agriculture. The introduction of vast amounts of surplus foods without considering domestic production caused the fall of grain prices, which discouraged famers and destroyed the domestic agriculture base. Self-sufficiency in staple grains significantly decreased, not to mention the wheat and raw cotton that was also supplied from the United States (Yoon 1992, 140–145).

The conflict between the surplus agricultural products of the United States and the development of domestic agriculture is a leading example of the paradox of a postwar food regime that supported the necessity for both food aid and national agricultural development (Fairbairn 2010, 21). The United States chose food aid, which is effective in the short-term, instead of an increase in production through agricultural development, as the country needed to relieve hunger and grow the national economy to prevent the communization of a country—its geopolitical aim. During the years 1955–1971, the surplus agricultural products that were provided to Korea as per Public Law 480 (PL

480) amounted to $795 million, 47 percent of which was in the form of wheat (Korea Rural Economic Institute 1999, 1: 967). Such aid strongly contributed to solving the domestic surplus of the United States. For instance, PL 480 accounted for over 78 percent of total US wheat exports in 1964. From this perspective, US aid in the form of surplus agricultural products actually protected its own national agricultural sector (Myrdal 1971, 351). In Korea, more than 80 percent of the funds raised through this aid were used to bolster the South Korea's defense budget, contributing to its military capabilities during the Cold War. The US surplus agricultural products contributed to addressing the food shortage, but also resulted in a decrease in agricultural production and a farming crisis in Korea, essentially replacing the future right to food with immediate food aid.

With the 1970s world food crisis as momentum, the United States revised its mechanism to address surplus agriculture products by removing production limitations with the 1973 Farm Bill, and instead encouraging exports for commercial purposes, which drastically changed the relationship between US agriculture and the world economy (McMichael 2000, 131–132). However, this green power strategy has resulted in a steady decline in food prices by providing huge subsidies to exporters to promote commercial exports and by offering products that are exported at lower prices than production cost through dumping. This meant the end of food aid (McMichael 2005, 278).

The Korean government's main responses to this international market change were to pursue self-sufficiency of rice as a staple grain together with a low food price policy to achieve economic growth led by industrial sectors, the encouragement of the cultivation of cash crops to prepare for the agricultural crisis, and the rural community development of the *Saemaeul Undong* (New Community Movement). First, along with the decline in grain prices, the pursuit of self-sufficiency of staple grain is an industrial policy geared toward rapid economic growth led by industry as well as an agricultural policy to deal with the end of food aid. Increased production and self-sufficiency in staple grain was a deliberate policy to reduce living costs for workers, as peasants were hit severely by the massive influx of surplus crops such as wheat, raw cotton, and corn as food aid. The Rockefeller Foundation and the Ford Foundation established the International Rice Research Institute (IRRI) in the Philippines in 1962 and started to develop a high-yielding variety of rice that ultimately contributed to the development of the *Tongil* (Unification) rice variety in Korea (Kim 2017). Thanks to the green revolution of rice, Korea almost reached self-sufficiency in rice by the late 1970s. Production per 10 acres, which had been 287 kilograms in 1965, rose to 494 kilograms by 1977. The government forced peasants to cultivate this high yield variety of rice, implement a policy of monoculture, and conduct specialized farming, as farm households were in financial difficulties due to farming costs and the government's low grain pricing policy. As a result, farm households focused on the cultivation of a few select cash crops such as red pepper, garlic, and onions. As the share of these cash crops in agricultural income significantly increased, demand for external agricultural input such as seeds, fertilizers, and pesticide sharply rose. Furthermore, government policy to encourage the livestock industry, without consideration of the domestic production of feedstuffs, replaced animal husbandry as a supplement to farm households' income with industrialized factory-style livestock. This resulted in a rapid decline in grain self-sufficiency and an unstable food supply, significantly threatening the livelihood of peasants (see figure 3.1).

As the Doha Development Agenda (DDA) did not make much headway after the inauguration of the World Trade Organization (WTO), multilateral trade negotiations faced a crisis. The Korean government responded by opening agricultural markets fully, signing multiple free trade agreements (FTAs) at the same time.[4] After the launch of the WTO and the signing of FTAs, imports of foreign agricultural products and livestock rose sharply, reaching US$12 billion by 1996, temporarily declining during the foreign currency crisis of 1997, and then rising again significantly to over US$20 billion by 2010 and US$34.8 billion in 2015. The government advocated for the enhancement of international competitiveness in domestic agriculture and products amid the complete opening of the agricultural market. The government restructuring policy encouraging the expansion of farming scale and monocultures has accelerated the exit of peasants, leading to a sharp decline in the grain

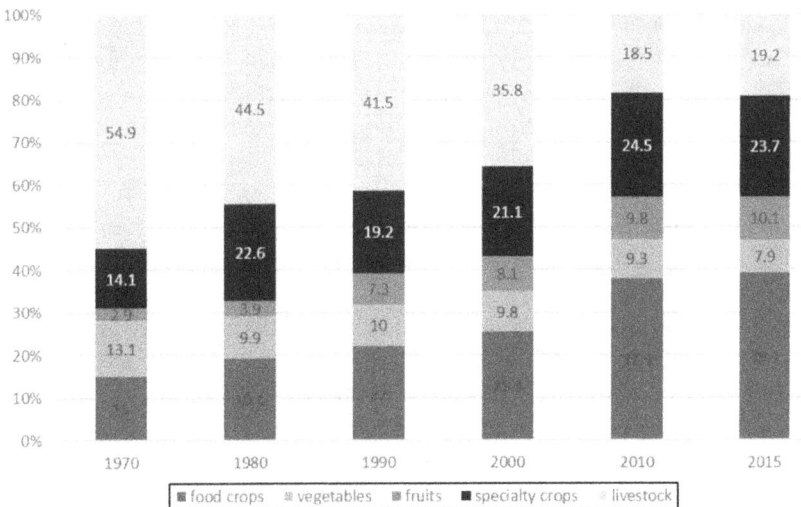

Figure 3.1 Changes in the Value of Korean Agricultural Production, 1970-2015.
Source: Statistics Korea.

**Table 3.1   Income Disparity between Farm Households and Urban Laborer House-
holds in South Korea, 1970–2015ᵃ**

Year	Farm household (A)	Urban laborer household (B)	A/B (%)
1980	2,693	2,809	95.9
1985	5,736	5,085	112.8
1990	11,026	11,319	97.4
1995	21,803	22,933	95.1
2000	23,072	28,643	80.6
2005	30,503	39,025	78.2
2010	32,121	48,092	66.8
2015	37,215	57,800	64.4

Source: Adapted from "Farm Household Economy Survey and Household Income and Expenditure Survey,"
   by Statistics Korea.
*Note*ᵃ: Unit: ₩1,000, %.

self-sufficiency rate and the exodus of the rural population.[5] Subsequently, the income gap between urban and farm households has widened (see table 3.1).

The complete opening of the agricultural market by the government and food security dependent on the world market led to a number of adverse outcomes. First, the policy resulted in a crisis of peasants and small-holders, which are the main pillars of Korean agriculture. Hit by full-scale trade liberalization, peasants and small-holders, which comprise the absolute majority in terms of total farm households, faced serious polarization. Still worse, as regulations on farmland were relaxed, actually dismantling the land-to-the-tillers principle guaranteed by the constitution, they faced difficulties in even securing farmland, the basic tool of production.

Second, the basic rationale of the agricultural and food policy—a stable food supply and food security guarantee—weakened considerably. Due to significant price fluctuations of agricultural products, underproduction and overproduction, price spiraling and collapse occurred repeatedly with the import of foreign agricultural products. In addition, distrust of citizens deepened as a result of food safety incidents such as the conflict over full resumption of the US beef imports in 2008, the Fipronil eggs contamination in 2017, and the ongoing genetically modified organism (GMO) issue.

Third, the right to food for socially vulnerable groups in both cities and rural villages worsened due to social polarization. This came at the same time as the Korean government failed to fulfill its obligation as a state to guarantee food as a basic human right, although it indirectly recognizes the right to food as per Article 6 (1) of the constitution, which states, "Treaties duly concluded and promulgated under the constitution and the generally recognized rules of international law shall have the same effect as the domestic laws of the Republic of Korea."[6]

Fourth, the segregation of agricultural policy from food policy was an issue. During the period of economic development in the 1960s–1980s, agricultural policy focused on production expansion, which was a food policy. However, when self-sufficiency in rice was achieved in the late 1970s and quantity shortages were resolved thanks to the sharp rise of agricultural imports, production policy began to split off from consumption policy. Production policy concentrated on increasing competitiveness through scale expansion and quality improvement, while consumption policies left to the market function except for some food welfare programs. The local market that used to closely connect production to consumption disappeared.

CONVERGENCE OF THE ALTERNATIVE AGRI-FOOD MOVEMENT AND FOOD SOVEREIGNTY MOVEMENT

Korea's agriculture and food crises have deepened as the nation has faced challenges such as food aid, the spread of the green revolution, and the full opening of agricultural markets to imports. Various resistance and alternative movements have emerged to address such crises. The development of these resistance and alternative movements has had two main directions in terms of the players and core values pursued.

First, the alternative agri-food movement initiated by some farmers who adopted organic agriculture as an alternative to industrial agriculture later evolved into a producer-consumer linkage movement. In the 1970s, the Corean Catholic Famers' Movement (CCFM), a member of the International Federation of Adult Catholic Farmers' Movements (FIMARC) and Right Farming Association, through exchanges with Japanese farmers, established an organic farming movement amid growing awareness of the hazards of chemical farming. Direct trade of agricultural products cultivated by organic farming has increased since small-scale direct trade started between farmers and citizens in the 1980s and later direct trade through Consumers' Cooperatives in the 1990s. As a result, the organic farming movement evolved into an alternative agri-food movement linking producers and consumers. In particular, with the enactment of the Environment-friendly Agriculture Promotion Act in 1997 and Consumer Cooperatives Act in 1999, the production and consumption of eco-friendly agricultural products increased sharply in the 2000s.[7] In 2009, when the production of eco-friendly agricultural products peaked, 16.6 percent of farms carried out eco-friendly farming and eco-friendly products accounted for 13.3 percent of the total agricultural production in Korea.

Second, the peasant movement emerged to protect the rights and interests of peasants and later to resist the agricultural market opening and neoliberalism. In the late 1960s, the gap between agriculture and manufacturing widened as a result of the government's policy to foster a manufacturing industry-led growth. In the early 1970s, peasant movement organizations were formed, demanding a guarantee for farmers' incomes and agricultural products pricing. However, the dissemination of the peasant movement was highly restricted under the military regime in Korea. The peasant movement grew up in the mid-1980s with the democratization movement and supported farmers through the Korean Women Farmer Association founded in 1989 and the Korean Farmers League founded in 1990. It established a unified political stance of opposition to the market opening of agricultural imports.[8] In 1994, it gained popular support by waging a struggle to oppose market opening to imports under the Uruguay Round. Ultimately it suspended imports of rice, a staple grain of Korea, and established an institutional basis to introduce a direct payment system through the enactment of the Special Act on the Implementation of the Agreement Establishing the WTO.

In the 2000s, these two movements encountered new issues. First, as the peasant movement largely focused on economic issues such as opposition to market opening, the guarantee of agricultural products prices, and government purchases of agricultural products, critics said that the peasant movement may have lost its fundamental value as an alternative. Second, although the organic farming movement had evolved into an alternative agri-food movement linking producers and consumers, some suspected that the movement was being *conventionalized* as it relied on the government for eco-friendly farming facilities, materials, and certification system. These movements were faced with a fundamental question: By whom and how food is produced? In addition, local food, slow food, and fair trade movements newly emerged to fight problems associated with food globalization such as inequity, safety, and disruption between production and consumption. Divergence between existing movements and various alternative movements prompted discussions to answer a fundamental question of *by whom and how food is produced*, and brought about a need to explore practical ways in which individual movements could collaborate.

These issues were resolved through the following two innovations in Korea. First, in the mid-2000s, through the peasant movement's linkage with transnational peasants' movements, the concept of food sovereignty was introduced and civic societies promoted discussion of it. In 2001, the KWPA and KPL came into contact with LVC in the World Social Forum and participated in the South East and East Asia regional meeting of LVC as observer organizations. Following an incident in Cancun, Mexico during a WTO Meeting in 2003 in which farmer Lee Kyung Hae committed suicide, they became official members of LVC in 2004. The KWPA launched a food sovereignty movement through linkage with transnational peasants' movements and reinforced solidarity with various civic organizations through the Native Seeds Movement and Sisters' Kitchen Garden Subscription Box

Project. In 2012, the KWPA was awarded a Food Sovereignty Prize from LVC (Yoon et al. 2013). The KWPA is striving to define food sovereignty suitable to Korea and to reach social consensus by working together with various social organizations. Second, after 2010, the peasant movement, alternative agri-food movement, and local food movement joined forces to create an eco-friendly free school meal movement. The school meal movement, which began as an effort to create a local ordinance for school meals in the 1990s, achieved the change from the commissioned school meal system to a direct management system in the 2000s and an expansion of eco-friendly free school meals after 2010.

Especially in Korea, school meals and local food movements overcame the interruption between production and consumption, which had worsened under the agri-food system led by transnational corporations. They contributed to restoring public confidence in food as a medium as well as promoting the public policy of agri-food. School meals that started with foreign food aid in 1953 are one of the oldest public policies regarding food and developed into the most popular alternative food movement of Korea since the mid-2000s. After the enactment of the School Meals Act in 1981, the proportion of schools offering school meals increased. Since the late 1990s, against neoliberal policies, school meals that had been mostly supplied by commissioned contractors were converted into a service directly operated by the school itself after massive food poisoning incidents in 2003 and 2006—against the international trend. As eco-friendly free school meals emerged as one of the social issues in the nationwide local elections in 2010, free school meals were expanded nationwide, despite the so-called age of austerity after the 2008 Global Financial Crisis. In 2009, 16.2 percent of elementary, middle, and high schools nationwide offered free school meals, but by 2016, 74.3 percent adopted this policy, including 95.6 percent of elementary schools (Kim 2016, March 15). The distribution of eco-friendly agricultural products for school meals rose sharply. A 2014 survey showed that 16.2 percent of eco-friendly agricultural products were consumed at schools, but increased to 31.5 percent in 2015 (Ministry of Agriculture, Food and Rural Affairs of Korea 2016, July 15).

COLLABORATING UNDER THE NEW AGENDA: FOOD SOVEREIGNTY AND RIGHTS OF PEASANTS

For the past ten years, the Korean free school meal movement has aimed to replace the contract school meal service by companies to one in which this service was directly operated by schools themselves. Local governments enacted ordinances to support free school meal costs and the procurement of eco-friendly food materials. Despite progress made by the school meal movement, however, food material procurement for school meals, like other existing food regimes, relied on farms with a certain scale of production, showing a lack of consideration for small family farms and peasants who can foster an eco-friendly, sustainable food regime. As a result, some local governments began to devise ways to ensure the participation of small-scale farms and peasants in the school meal procurement system. Recognition of the role of small-scale farms as an important contributor to the food regime transition coincided with two major international events. The first was the world food crisis of 2007–2008, and the other was the designation of the year 2014 as the International Year of Family Farming (IYFF) by the United Nations. In the wake of the world food crisis, the World Summit on Food Security, held in Rome in 2009, declared that solutions to a food crisis must include the need to reinvest in local agriculture and the right to food (Golay 2010). Furthermore, Olivier De Shutter, the UN Special Rapporteur on the Right to Food, emphasized that what matters in human rights terms is determining who will produce food, and for the benefit of whom (De Shutter 2008). In this way, peasants, the most vulnerable and important entity in terms of the right to food, began to gain attention. An initiative was launched by the World Rural Forum in collaboration with more than 350 civil society and farmers' organizations to declare an IYFF. In 2011, the government of the Philippines proposed IYFF in the 37th FAO Congress, and the 66th UN General Assembly officially declared the year 2014 as IYFF (IFAD 2014). During this process, the right to food regained traction and consideration and the rights of peasants presented by LVC, a transnational indigenous peasants' movement, began to be discussed in the United Nations.

At the same time as such attention was given to peasants and small-holders as indispensable actors in sustainable agriculture after the global food crisis of 2007-2008, rights to the food movement were prevalent throughout the world. LVC criticized the privatization of food security and the food system led by businesses and proposed a new food sovereignty concept as an alternative to food security or a real food security. Food sovereignty is broadly defined as "the right of peoples to healthy and culturally appropriate food produced through ecologically sound and sustainable methods, and their right to define their own food and agriculture systems" (Forum for Food Sovereignty 2007). The concept of food sovereignty includes a human rights perspective of the right to food and emphasizes people's right to decide their own food system from seed to table. Recently, food sovereignty movements have gradually expanded multilevel practices by encouraging peasants to take action under local, national, and regional circumstances while providing the universal tool of food democracy and rights-based approaches. Each nation began to include the obligations of the state to realize food sovereignty through the amendment of national constitutions and enactment of basic laws. Discussions on officially establishing such rights within the international human rights framework through the UN Declaration on the Rights of Peasants are underway (Golay 2015).

The declaration of the rights of peasants requested by LVC was drafted in collaboration with international human rights organizations and was included on the official agenda of the UN Human Rights Council. It has taken nearly ten years, and working-level debates to draft a declaration have been underway for five years. Although the declaration has not yet been adopted within the UN General Assembly, the discussions of the past fifteen years have significant implications for the international community and nations including Korea. The term *rights of peasants* was coined by the Indonesian Peasants Union (SPI), a member organization of LVC. Later, the first declaration draft was written at the Southeast/East Asia Regional Conference of LVC in 2002 and the declaration was completed at the 6th International Conference in 2008. It was approved by its International Coordination Committee (ICC) at a meeting that was held in Seoul in March 2009 (Golay 2015, 10n10; La Vía Campesina 2009). LVC demanded that the rights of peasants should be established as a convention of the UN in its final declaration of the International Conference on Peasant's Rights in 2008 and pushed to make the declaration institutionalized at its international body (La Vía Campesina 2008, June 24). International human rights organizations such as FIAN and CETIM have worked together with LVC regarding peasants' issues with regard to the International Covenant on Economic, Social and Cultural Rights (ICESCR) and drafted a declaration on the rights of peasants, ensuring that this draft was discussed within the framework of the United Nations (Clayes 2015, 56–58). As the rights of peasants and family farming began to be recognized in the wake of the 2007–2008 food crisis, in 2009, the UN Human Rights Council and the General Assembly, respectively, invited LVC and listened to its opinion on a declaration of the rights of peasants. An advisory committee of the UN Human Rights Council was inaugurated in 2008 to give more attention to the right to food issue and proposed needs for the UN Human Rights Council to study food crises, the right to food, agricultural subsidy, and the rights of peasants. The UN Human Rights Council instructed the Advisory Committee to launch a study on policies and strategy to eliminate discrimination toward rural communities in terms of the right to food. Research on the advancement of the rights of peasants and other people working in rural areas was conducted from 2010 to 2012 (Golay 2015, 11–14). Through this process, LVC and international human rights organizations successfully made the rights of peasants an official agenda item of the United Nations through a decision (see UN Human Rights Council 2012) regarding the establishment of an open-ended intergovernmental working group (OEIWG) to draft a declaration at the UN Human Rights Committee in 2012. A procedure for making a declaration is underway. Recently, in the fifth session of OEIWG held on April 5, 2018, a draft declaration was discussed, and in the 39th Regular Session of the Human Rights Council, the declaration was adopted. This declaration is to be confirmed by the 73rd UN General Assembly in November 2018 (table 3.2).

As a member of Human Rights Council, South Korea voted four times. South Korea voted against resolution A/HRC/RES/26/26 and abstained from voting on resolution A/HRC/RES/30/13, A/HRC/RES/36/22, and A/HRC/RES/39/12. The Korean government's shift from opposition to abstention may be a meaningful change, but despite a strong opposition from peasants' organizations, the government continued to abstain until the end.

Recently in Korea, with the movement to revise the constitution, various alternative agri-food movements (peasants' movement, school meals movement, consumer cooperatives movement, etc.) are collaborating under a new agenda of the rights of peasants. These groups once formed a nationwide coalition at a candlelight vigil to voice their opposition to the import of US beef in 2008 and jointly conducted an eco-friendly free school meals movement in the 2010 local elections. During this process, they agreed on the need to shift to a sustainable agri-food system that as the common objective of all alternative agri-food movements, and translate the value of sustainability into a system. As a result, the Headquarters, comprising major agricultural organizations, organic farming organizations, consumer cooperatives, and school meal organizations, was launched in October 2017 to push for the revision of the constitution in the agriculture sector.

A democratic government was inaugurated and the constitution was revised in 1987 as a result of the democratization movement. However, at that time, clear evidence of damage from neoliberalism and globalization had yet to appear, and sustainable agriculture was not sufficiently understood. Therefore, a separate provision regarding agriculture and food was not considered in discussions regarding the revision of the constitution. With the full opening of the agricultural product market that placed peasants and smallholders as the main pillar of Korea's agriculture production into crisis, discussions on food security resumed after the world food crisis and the insertion of a provision on the guarantee of sustainable agriculture in the constitution became an important social issue. As discussions of food sovereignty spread within the alternative agri-food movement, efforts were made to reflect the agricultural production model envisioned by a declaration of the rights of peasants in the constitution, thereby ensuring that small-scale farmers and peasants are incorporated as important producers in school meal, public meal, and local food strategies. In this process, tensions and conflicts related to the content of the revised constitution have emerged among the alternative

Table 3.2 Adopted Resolutions and Major Decisions on the Promotion and Protection of the Human Rights of Peasants and Other People Working in Rural Areas

HRC Session	Year	Resolution (Result of the Vote)	Major Decisions
21st	2012	A/HRC/RES/21/19 (YES 23/ ABST 15/ NO 9)	To establish an open-ended intergovernmental working group with the mandate of negotiating, finalizing, and submitting to the Human Rights Council a draft United Nations declaration on the Rights of Peasants and Other People Working in Rural Areas, on the basis of the draft submitted by the Advisory Committee, and without prejudging relevant past, present and future views and proposals
			That the working group shall hold its first session for five working days in 2013, before the 23rd session of the Human Rights Council
26th	2014	A/HRC/RES/26/26 (YES 29/ ABST 13/ NO 5)	That the working group with the mandate of negotiating, finalizing and submitting to the Human Rights Council a draft United Nations Declaration on the Rights of Peasants and Other People Working in Rural Areas shall hold its second session for five working days before the 29th session of the Council
			That the Chairperson-Rapporteur of the working group should be asked to prepare a new text on the basis of the discussions held during the first session of the working group, including on the draft declaration presented by the Advisory Committee, and for informal consultations to be held, and to present these to the working group at its second session for consideration and further discussion
30th	2015	A/HRC/RES/30/13 (YES 31/ ABST 15/ NO 1)	That the working group with the mandate to negotiate, finalize and submit to the Human Rights Council a draft United Nations Declaration on the Rights of Peasants and Other People Working in Rural Areas shall hold its next two annual sessions for five working days each before the 36th session of the Council
33rd	2016	A/HRC/33/59 (Report of the Chair-Rapporteur, No Vote)	That the Chair-Rapporteur should prepare a revised text on the basis of the discussions held during the first, second, and third sessions of the working group

(Continued)

Table 3.2 Adopted Resolutions and Major Decisions on the Promotion and Protection of the Human Rights of Peasants and Other People Working in Rural Areas (*Continued*)

HRC Session	Year	Resolution (Result of the Vote)	Major Decisions
36th	2017	A/HRC/ RES/36/22 (YES 34/ABST 11/ NO 2)	That the open-ended intergovernmental working group on a United Nations Declaration on the Rights of Peasants and Other People Working in Rural Areas shall hold its fifth annual session for five working days before the 38th session of the Human Rights Council, in accordance with its mandate, to negotiate, finalize, and submit to the Council a draft United Nations declaration on the rights of peasants and other people working in rural areas; That the updated version of the draft declaration that will be presented by the Chair-Rapporteur of the working group at its fifth session, taking into consideration the report of the Chair-Rapporteur on the fourth session, and the version of the draft declaration resulting from the fifth session will be translated into all official languages of the United Nations
39th	2018	A/HRC/ RES/39/12 (YES 33/ABST 11/ NO 3)	Adoption of United Nations Declaration on the Rights of Peasants and Other People Working in Rural Areas, as contained in the annex to the resolution

Source: Adapted from United Nations Human Rights Council Resolutions. Retrieved from https://www.ohchr.org/EN/Issues/IDPersons/Pages/Resolutions.aspx.

agri-food movement, mainstream food regime entities and policy makers, and even within alternative agri-food movement participants.

CONCLUSION: EVOLUTION OF THE FOOD
SOVEREIGNTY MOVEMENT AND ITS CHALLENGES

The United Nations Declaration on the Rights of Peasants is very significant in that it could create critical momentum to evolve the outcome of the food sovereignty movement into an international system. Historically, social movements have facilitated institutionalization and this institutionalization has invigorated the same social movements, creating a virtuous cycle. Evidence of this can be found within Korea's alternative agri-food movement.

The organic farming movement, which started to resist green revolution agriculture in the 1970s, has evolved into a popular alternative agri-food movement through eco-friendly product certification and institutionalization through Consumers' Cooperatives. In the 1990s, the peasant movement, which gained popular support through its opposition to opening to imports and neoliberalism, has become an important civic movement and political force. Nevertheless, these movements have revealed a preference for conventionalization and focused on economic issues while exhibiting weakness as a societal movement seeking alternatives to various social issues. In the late 2000s, as discussions on food sovereignty gained support from civic society and the school meal movement formed solidarity with other social movements, the alternative agri-food movement revived in Korea. Recently, as several agendas pursued by the alternative agri-food movement achieved institutionalization, it has been revitalized. First, the alternative agri-food movement successfully pushed for the establishment and policy implementation for a *public plate* and *local food strategy* to be included as one of the campaign pledges of candidate Moon Jae-in, who was elected president in 2017. Second, the Alternative Agri-food Movement encouraged some local governments to adopt and implement public plate and local food strategies. The Seoul Metropolitan Government drew from a consensus on rights to food and food sovereignty among civic organizations and adopted the public plate as one of its local food projects.

Expanding eco-friendly free school meals such as public plates and promoting local food strategy in local governments are attempts to institutionalize the Alternative Agri-food Movement on a subnational level. Efforts to include the principle of food sovereignty in the national constitution through an amendment would mean an institutionalization of food sovereignty on a national level. In this respect, the declaration of the rights of peasants has two important implications for the revision of agriculture-related provisions of the constitution. First, it strongly supports the argument of the Alternative Agri-food Movement that the principle of food sovereignty should be included in discussions of the constitutional amendment. Mainstream food regime entities assert that the nation's agricultural sector, dominated by small family farming and small-scale producers, is inefficient and lacks a vision for the future. Against such arguments, an international recognition of the food sovereignty model through a declaration of the rights of peasants would act as a powerful support, in addition to the alternative agri-food models being built on a subnational level. Second, it is creating tension due to differing views on food sovereignty inside the Alternative Agri-food Movement and also providing an opportunity to review the movement itself. The varieties of views on food sovereignty, sustainable peasant, and family farm agriculture, which have not been exhibited in the process of fighting the government's neoliberal agricultural policy, are being revealed. The dynamics of the movement are observed on various occasions. Differences were clearly exhibited over the minimum wage hike among organizations that participated in the constitutional amendment campaign. The Korean Advanced Farmers' Federation (KAFF) criticized the minimum wage hike as it does not consider the difficulties of farmers. The KAFF said that the increased minimum wage raises the cost of immigrant workers as well as local workers in the agricultural sector, thus adding pressure to the overall agricultural economy. That provided an opportunity to look at the agricultural immigrant workers issue, which previously had not drawn attention from the Alternative Agri-food Movement. On the other hand, as the peasant movement continues to focus on economic issues, it gives the impression that it avoids presenting a clear stance on the future agenda of agriculture, which seeks an answer to a question of *by whom and how food will be produced?* as is contained in the food sovereignty movement and the UN Declaration on the Rights of Peasants.

This paper derived implications of the UN Declaration on the Rights of Peasants with regard to the food sovereignty movement and institutionalization, by reviewing historical changes and crises of agriculture in Korea and by looking into the development and limitations of the Alternative Agri-food Movement. As a solid consensus has not been reached on the implications of a declaration of the rights of peasants in Korea, this research could not make a detailed analysis. Further research is needed to analyze diverse views about food sovereignty, and the declaration of the rights of peasants as well as the dynamics inside the movement such as the tension and conflict of interests among farmers. Additionally, more research is required to pursue and analyze the underlying reasons why social movements repeat a cycle of evolution and conventionalization and how such a dialectic evolution of social movements is related to a change in agriculture and farms. This may enable us to identify factors enabling Alternative Agri-food Movement to have a virtuous cycle of institutionalization and evolution, instead of a vicious cycle of institutionalization and conventionalization.

NOTES

1. This chapter was previously published with the same title in *Korea Journal*, *58*(4), 143–166. The original work was supported by Konkuk University in 2015.

2. Over ten million people (about 20 percent of the total population) participated in the signature campaign organized by the NACF.

3. See Article 25-1 of the "Universal Declaration of Human Rights," by United Nations (1948).

4. With the market opening of agricultural products since the late 1970s, Korea's import liberalization rate, which was 64.3 percent in 1984, rose to 92.1 percent in 1994. In 2015, the liberalization of the market was completed by removing tariffs on the rice market altogether.

5. The self-sufficiency rate of grains dropped sharply to 23.8 percent in 2015 from 56.0 percent in 1980, and the proportion of farm households to total population dropped dramatically from 28.4 percent in 1980 to 5.0 percent in 2015.

6. Article 6 (paragraph 1) of the Constitution of Republic of Korea. Retrieved from http://www.moleg.go.kr/english/korLawEng;jsessionid=2L4ba0F4AzkTY 81iUIfsQofxLT17RXSiMKwoeyRugEXhU4xLrO0os54bmpUcYXrb?pstSeq=54769 &pageIndex=6

7. The Environment-friendly Agriculture Promotion Act includes *no-pesticide certification* in which organo-synthetic agricultural chemicals are not used and less than one-third of the recommended amount of chemical fertilizers are used, as well as *low-pesticide certification* in which less than half of the permitted amount of pesticide, and less than half of the recommended level of chemical fertilizers are used. Low-pesticide certification was suspended in 2009 and abolished in 2016 (National Agricultural Products Quality Management Service n.d.).

8. As it became an official member of the LVC, the farmers' movement was renamed as the peasants' movement. Instead of the term *farmer* that represents multiple classes in Korea, organizations used the term *peasant* in order to emphasize that they represented a specific class. In 2004, after official approval as a member organization at the LVC's International Conference both organizations changed *farmer* to *peasant* in their name. Their names are now the Korean Women Peasant Association (KWPA) and Korean Peasant's League (KPL).

REFERENCES

Claeys, P. (2015). *Human Rights and the Food Sovereignty Movement: Reclaiming Control*. London: Routledge.

De Schutter, O. (2008). Building resilience: A human rights framework for world food and nutrition security. A/HRC/9/23. UN Human Rights Council. Retrieved from https://www.refworld.org/docid/48cf71dd2.html.

Fairbairn, M. (2010). Framing resistance: International food regimes and the roots of food sovereignty. In H. Wittman, A. Desmarais, & N. Wiebe (Eds.), *Food Sovereignty: Reconnecting Food, Nature and Community* (pp. 15–32). Oakland: Food First Books.

FAO (Food and Agriculture Organization of the United Nations). (1985). *FAO: The First 40 Years (1945–1985).* Rome: Food and Agriculture Organization of the United Nations.

Forum for Food Sovereignty. (2007). Declaration of Nyéléni. Retrieved from https://nyeleni.org/IMG/pdf/DeclNyeleni-en.pdf.

Golay, C. (2010). The food crisis and food security: Towards a new world food order? *International Development Policy Series, 1,* 215–232.

Golay, C. (2015). *Academy in-brief No.5: Negotiation of a United Nations Declaration on the Rights of Peasants and Other People Working in Rural Areas.* Geneva: Geneva Academy of International Humanitarian Law and Human Rights.

IFAD (International Fund for Agricultural Development). (2014). The international year of family farming: IFAD's commitment and call for action. Retrieved from https://www.ifad.org/documents/10180/5fe2f0d8-4b43-4598-8b7b-429ee24b6635.

Kim, C. (2016, March 15). Jeonbuk musang geupsik silsi hakgyo biyul 91.7% [Implementation of free school meals in Jeonbuk province is 91.7%]. Retrieved from https://blog.naver.com/PostView.nhn?blogId=kimcj334&logNo=2206553 38806.

Kim, T. (2017). *Geunhyeondae hanguk ssal-ui sahoesa [Social History of Rice in Modern Korea].* Paju: Dulnyouk.

Korea Rural Economic Institute. (1999). *Hanguk nongjeong 50 nyeonsa [50 years of Korean Agricultural Policy].* Vol. 1. Seoul: Ministry of Agriculture and Forestry of Korea.

La Vía Campesina. (2008, June 24). Final declaration of International Conference on Peasants' Rights. Retrieved from https://viacampesina.org/en/final-declaration-of-international-conference-onpeasants-rights.

La Vía Campesina. (2009). Declaration of the rights of peasants: Women and men. Retrieved from http://viacampesina.net/downloads/PDF/EN-3.pdf.

Margulis, M. (2013). The regime complex for food security: Implications for the global hunger challenge. *Global Governance: A Review of Multilateralism and International Organizations, 19*(1), 53–67.

McMichael, P. (2000). Global food politics. In F. Buttel, F. Magdoff, & J. Foster (Eds.), *Hungry for Profit: The Agribusiness Threat to Farmers, Food and the Environment* (pp. 125–143). New York: Monthly Review Press.

McMichael, P. (2005). Global development and the corporate food regime. In F. Buttel & P. McMmichael (Eds.), *New Directions in the Sociology of Global Development* (pp. 265–299). Bingley: Emerald Group Publishing Limited.

McMichael, P. (2009). The world food crisis in historical perspective. *Monthly Review, 61*(3), 32–47.

Ministry of Agriculture, Food and Rural Affairs of Korea. (2016, July 15). Chinhwangyeong nongsanmul sobi, hakgyogeupsik-gwa jikgeolae-ga daese [School meal and direct sales are most important in consumption of eco-friendly agricultural products]. Retrieved from http://www.mafra.go.kr/list.jsp?newsid=1 55448282&section_id=b_sec_1&listcnt=5&pageNo=1&year=&group_id=3&m enu_id=1125&link_menu_id=&division=B&board_kind=C&board_skin_id=C3 &parent_code=3&link_url=&depth=1.

Myrdal, G. (1971). *The Challenge of World Poverty: A World Anti-poverty Program in Outline.* New York: Vintage Books.

National Agricultural Products Quality Management Service. (n.d.). *Environment-friendly Agricultural Products Certification.* Retrieved from http://www.enviagro.go.kr/portal/content/en/html/sub/system.jsp.

Pritchard, B., Dixon, J., Hull, E., & Choithani, C. (2016). 'Stepping back and moving in': The role of the state in the contemporary food regime. *Journal of Peasant Studies, 43*(3), 693–710.

Research Department of the Bank of Chosun. (1948). Joseon gyeongje yeonbo [Annual Economic Review of Korea].

UN Human Rights Council. (2012). Promotion and protection of the human rights of peasants and other people working in rural areas. A/HRC/RES/21/19. Retrieved from https://ap.ohchr.org/documents/alldocs.aspx?doc_id=20840.

UN Human Rights Council. (2016). Report of the open-ended intergovernmental working group on a draft United Nations declaration on the rights of peasants and other people working in rural areas. A/HRC/33/59. Retrieved from https://ap.ohch r.org/documents/dpage_e.aspx?si=A/HRC/33/59.

UN Human Rights Council. (2017). Draft declaration on the rights of peasants and other people working in rural areas presented by the Chair-Rapporteur of the working group. *A/HRC/WG.15/4/2.* Retrieved from https://ap.ohchr.org/documents/ dpage_e.aspx?si=A/HRC/WG.15/4/2.

United Nations. (1948). Universal declaration of human rights. Retrieved from https ://www.un.org/en/universal-declaration-human-rights/.

Yoon, B. (1992). The modification of agricultural crisis and the role of state monopolistic capital in the post-war (Doctoral Dissertation). Konkuk University, Seoul.

Yoon, B. (2006). Who is threatening our dinner table? The power of transnational agribusiness. *Monthly Review, 58*(6), 56–64.

Yoon, B., Song, W., & Lee, H. (2013). The struggle for food sovereignty in South Korea. *Monthly Review, 65*(1), 56–62.

Part II

NATIONAL CUISINE IN THE ERA OF GLOBALIZATION

Chapter 4

Food and Nationalism
Kimchi *and Korean National Identity*
Hong Sik Cho

INTRODUCTION: FOOD AND NATIONALISM

For[1] Ernest Gellner (1983), "nationalism is primarily a political principle, which holds that the political and the national unit should be congruent" (1). From this simple definition follows that of the nationalist sentiment, which is described as "the feeling of anger aroused by the violation of the principle, or the feeling of satisfaction aroused by its fulfillment" (Gellner 1983, 1). This politics-centered definition, in spite of its operational value as a research and analysis tool, reveals to be problematic when dealing with the subjective dimension and micro-level nationalism. It can be appropriately argued that nationalist movement has originated from, for example, the feeling of anger against colonial situation, a flagrant case of the violation of the nationalist principle. But this macro-level explanation does not account for why specific individuals engage in nationalist movement and why people feel anger or satisfaction depending on the violation or fulfillment of a principle. Furthermore, nationalism needs to be explained not only from the functionalist perspective a la Gellner as a prerequisite and concomitant of modernization, but also in its subjective dimension of affection, attachment, or hatred.

Micro-level or subjective interpretative analysis has largely contributed to our understanding of nationalism. Benedict Anderson (1991) duly underlines the cultural roots of nationalism in building *imagined communities*, stating that a new way of apprehending time and space rendered possible the imagination of *horizontal-secular, transverse-time*, while print-capitalism allowed the emergence of national consciousness by broadly diffusing *national print-languages*. Historians point to *the invention of tradition* as a process or mechanism permitting the use of history as legitimator of action and cement of group cohesion (Hobsbawm and Ranger 1983).[2] These invented traditions,

69

defined as "a set of practices . . . with a ritual or symbolic nature, which seek to inculcate certain values and norms of behavior by repetition, which automatically implies continuity with the past" (Hobsbawm and Ranger 1983, 1), often serve as an efficient instrument of nationalism. Michael Billig (1995) explores a new perspective in his book *Banal Nationalism.* According to him, the national consciousness does not always manifest in its political and extreme form but also in more unconscious and less visible way in everyday life through routine symbols and habits of language. All these studies pay particular attention to how individuals come to think, imagine, manipulate, or are manipulated by the national phenomenon in their everyday life. In this perspective, nationalist sentiment is not only, neither principally, a sentiment of anger or satisfaction depending on the congruence of political and national units. Rather, the national identity of individuals "comprises both a cultural and political identity and is located in a political community as well as a cultural one" (Smith 1991, 99).

For Anthony Smith (1991), the fundamental features of national identity are: (1) an historic territory, or homeland, (2) common myths and historical memories, (3) a common, mass public culture, (4) common legal rights and duties for all members, and (5) a common economy with territorial mobility for members (14). Food and eating can be considered as one of the most important nexus of national identity: every human being has to eat several times a day, every day, as long as (s)he lives, and every human society has its own food preferences and way of eating. Furthermore, food is potentially related to all the principal features of national identity: it is often produced on the soil of homeland; culinary tradition is full of myths and memories; eating is an important part of mass public culture; food for survival forms an implicit element of modern citizenship; and food production and consumption constitutes the basis of national economy. Therefore, recent literature on nationalism and national identity takes seriously the issue of culinary habits (Bell and Valentine 1997; Mennel 1985; Scholliers 2001; Watson 1997; Watson and Caldwell 2005).

Individuals decide what, when, and how to eat, or at least have preferences.[3] Mouth is considered the "gateway to the body" (Rozing and Fallon 1981, 45) and "the act of consuming food may represent the basic locus of identity, conformity and resistance" (Smith 2006, 480). Of particular interest for national identity is the fact that food can have two contrasting functions: "it can serve to indicate and construct social relations characterized by equality, intimacy, or solidarity; or, it can serve to sustain relations characterized by rank, distance, or segregation" (Appadurai 1981, 496). National food serves of course the former function of reinforcing equal, intimate, and solidarity-based relations among members of national community. For Palmer

(1998), it is of utmost importance to understand "how individuals became consciously aware of cultural community" and "how a sense of nationality is constructed that links individuals to a particular cultural tradition" (180). She considers food, along with the body and the landscape, as the three flags of identity. Thus, Nir Avieli (2005) sees the study of national iconic dishes as bridging the gap between theory and praxis of nationalism by concretization of the imagined community.

In the current study, the case of *kimchi*, a hot and spicy Korean side dish, is analyzed in light of the aforementioned theoretical perspective. *Kimchi* is considered as the Korean culinary symbol not only by the Koreans themselves but also by many foreigners. According to a poll by Gallup Korea in 2006, *kimchi* was cited as the "symbol of national culture representing Korea" by 22.1 percent, second only to the national flag *taegeuggi* with 34.9 percent. These were followed by *hangeul* (the Korean writing system) (17.2 percent), *mugunghwa* (the national emblem-flower) (13.9 percent), and *dogdo* (small islets over which Korea and Japan both claim sovereignty) (13.2 percent).[4] At first sight, it is surprising that a mere side dish appears as a national cultural symbol along with the trinity of national identity symbols like the national flag, anthem, and emblem (Firth 1973),[5] as well as with the *noble* writing system and *sacred* territory. Outside Korea, *kimchi* is perceived as the characteristic Korean dish as reflected in the title of books such as *The Kimchi Cookbook: Fiery Flavors and Cultural History of Korea's National Dish* (Kim, Lee, and Lee 1999), *The Kimchi Matters: Global Business and Local Politics in a Crisis-Driven World* (Zonis, Lefkovitz, and Wilkin 2005), or in the naming of a club of Korean-French international couples, *Kimchi-Fromage.*

Therefore, it appears to be of particular interest to investigate this symbol of national identity in order to deepen our understanding of the relationship between food and nationalism in general, and of Korean national identity in particular. My approach is to analyze historically three different phases of the emerging process of *kimchi* as national symbol: (1) declaration of independence in taste, (2) promotion of the national food, and (3) international conflicts around *kimchi* as national food. These three phases are chronologically ordered in case of *kimchi* without necessarily being exactly sequenced. This case study is an attempt to answer to several theoretically oriented questions: What are the determinants of the selection process of national symbols, and put simply, why *kimchi*? Who are the principal promoters of this particular food as the national symbol, and what are their main motives? What are the consequences for *kimchi* to become the national cultural symbol, especially in light of internationalization and globalization of national cuisines and economies?

"DECLARATION OF INDEPENDENCE IN TASTE"

Kimchi[6] has been for a long time an important part of Korean cuisine, more precisely an essential side dish accompanying rice, the main staple, and other dishes. It belongs to the family of pickled vegetables whose consumption can be documented and traced back to antiquity. It has undergone many profound transformations concerning its raw materials, the spices utilized, and the preparation method. In order to understand the sudden ascension of *kimchi* as national food in the 1980s, I discuss the value of *kimchi* as a national symbol and the historic context of its emergence.

Value as Symbol

The value of *kimchi* as national symbol comes from its generalized daily consumption among ethnic Koreans. Most Koreans eat *kimchi* every day, even at every meal. Rice is the main staple, but can be occasionally replaced by noodles: whatever the main staple is, *kimchi* is the *sine qua non* of Korean meal. As for many national myths and symbols, the pseudo-scientific studies trace their origins back in history abound, but serious historical studies about their actual evolution are rare or absent. We do not have the history of *kimchi* consumption, but some literary episodes or historical facts show the generalized daily consumption of *kimchi* among Koreans at least in the twentieth century: The South Korean troops sent to Vietnam in the 1960s and 1970s, and Korean construction workers in the Middle East in the 1970s were the first clients of massive *kimchi* exports. International migration of Koreans was followed by their indispensable side dish.

The equation reproduces itself in the United States among Korean migrants. Exposed to a foreign environment, *kimchi* rapidly became the symbol of Koreanness: "Just as the smell of *gimchi*[7] signifies for me my mother's love and my homeland culture, for her it signifies a daughter who remains proudly Korean despite the dominant white culture in which I was raised" (Heijin 2004, 384). It seems that well before the advent of *kimchi* as national food in Korea herself, it had already acquired the heart of Koreans in foreign countries as a popular psychological and physiological connection tool with the Homeland.

Kimchi presents several intrinsic characteristics which perhaps explain the degree to which Koreans are so much attached to the consumption of that side dish, and the extent to which Koreans adhere to it as a national symbol. (1) *Kimchi* is a very hot and spicy dish with abundant use of salt and red pepper. There are many pickled vegetables in China and Japan, but they usually do not taste so hot and spicy. (2) Korean *kimchi* is a fermented vegetable rich in minerals and vitamins. But it also means that *kimchi*'s odor is very strong and unsupportable but for meal time, even for everyday consumers. Naturally, in a multi-ethnic environment, *kimchi* with its odor and particular taste becomes the ethnic identity marker of Koreans. (3) *Kimchi* presents a great variety with more than 200 sorts according to the *Kimchi* Museum.[8] This richness and variety are supposed to represent those of Korean culture, just like hundreds sorts of wine or cheese in Western countries.

But so far as *kimchi* was considered "smells awful BUT indispensable," it could not be raised as a national symbol: "Up until the early sixties, *kimchi* was an embarrassment in the intercultural settings. Koreans admitted that *kimchi* smells awful. Although Koreans could not stop eating *kimchi*, they dared not publicly urge foreigners to learn to enjoy *kimchi*" (Han 2000, 229). But in the 1970s, some nutritionists began to praise *kimchi* as health food full of vitamins, minerals, and lactic ferments, making it "smells awful BUT good for health." In the 1980s, *kimchi* became "tasty AS WELL AS good for health and environmentally correct," acceding to the status of national symbol.

Historic Context of Emergence

It is always difficult to date the emergence of national symbols unless they are officially adopted by state act or some conscious declaration. For Han (2000), the 1988 Seoul Olympics was the occasion for the "declaration of independence in taste" by proclaiming *kimchi*, the national food. Actually, at this time, *kimchi* was no more a stinking dish to eat by hiding from foreigners, but a healthy traditional food to be presented and promoted among foreigners. The venue of this world event surely represented an opportunity for Korean people to exhibit their proud of economic success and, at the same time, to be recognized by foreigners as a nation possessing a cultural heritage worth the world respect. This thirst for international recognition is very representative of social processes involving identity, and it is in this sense that the Olympic Games can be symbolically considered the turning point of the status of *kimchi*. The coronation of *kimchi* as national symbol in the 1980s reflected several historical streams of the time. First, it was the culminating point of economic development since the 1960s which transformed the country from an agriculture-based poor nation to a dynamic industrial power. Korean people were proud of the economic miracle they had achieved and expected for international recognition of the value and superiority—or at least equality—of their cultural tradition. Second, the student and associative movements of the 1980s underlined the importance of three *min*: *minju* (democracy), *minjog* (nation), and *minjung* (people). These were reactions against the military dictatorship during more than two decades and against a society ruled by cosmopolitan elites. From this perspective too, *kimchi* was an ideal symbol because it was not only typically Korean in its taste and character, but more importantly representative of popular culture because it constituted daily diets of peasants, workers, and poor people opposed to cosmopolitan elites enjoying varied and refined foreign food. Third, the 1980s was also the decade of the emergence of food industry, especially interested in traditional foods like *kimchi*. Industrialization, urbanization, the generalization of nuclear family, the increased participation of women in labor market, and these socio-economic changes promoted the large-scale food industry. *Kimchi*, the popular Korean side dish, represented an enormous potential market, even though the traditional way of thinking considering that *kimchi*'s taste comes from the housewife's attention, care, and devotion, formed a high cultural barrier to its industrialization.

The first Kimchi Museum opened its door in 1986 established by a small food manufacturer *Myeongga*. The next year, it is another food manufacturer *Pulmuone* who bought the Museum and still owns and manages it in 2006. In 1988, the year of the Olympic Games, the Museum was transferred from Seoul's ancient center to the newly built international exhibition center COEX and enlarged to present the culinary *national treasure* to foreign visitors. The opening of this private museum is another event helping us to date the coronation of *kimchi* and also another fact showing the interrelation between cultural nationalism and economic interests. This museum contributed greatly to elevate the status of *kimchi* by providing an institutional base camp for its promotion and prestige. In 1992, a Kimchi Museum University was organized and officially registered as a Museum at the Ministry of Culture and Tourism in 1993 achieving the process of institutionalization.

One can hardly doubt *kimchi*'s status as an indispensable side dish in everyday life for most of Koreans. Its particular, taste and strong odor made it a very suitable candidate as a symbol of Koreanness. With scientific inquiry establishing the nutritional value and the variety of *kimchi*, it ascended rapidly to the status of national symbol in the 1980s during the preparation of the 1988 Seoul Olympics. The establishment of the Kimchi Museum in 1986 by the food industry is another step in its institutionalization as the national dish.

PROMOTION OF THE NATIONAL FOOD

Once the Korean declaration of independence in taste proclaimed in the name of *kimchi*, a surprising national mobilization took off in different spheres of society for the promotion of the national food. The period beginning with the organization of the Olympic Games to the 1990s is characterized by several trends: continuous economic development that reinforced the thirst for international recognition; increased economic internationalization and the corresponding reaction with frequent appeal to national identity; burgeoning civil society in the era of political liberalization and democratic consolidation; industrialization of the food industry in general, and of the *kimchi* industry in particular. These trends form the historic context of the consolidation of *kimchi* as a symbol of national identity.

Symbol of Korean Strength: Sports and Health

The affinity of *kimchi* with the Olympic Games has reiterated and even reinforced since 1988. For every Olympic Games since 1988, *kimchi* entered the official menu for athletes and Korean food manufacturers supplied it. This internationalization of the national food is considered and presented as a triumph of Korean culture by the media. Each time, the demand for *kimchi* supply by the Organizing Committee was news for Korean media, reflecting the psychological need for international recognition. The titles of newspapers coverage are eloquent: "*Jonggajib kimchi* of Doosan Foods, selected in the official menu of the [Barcelona] Olympic,"[9] "*Kimchi*, on the Atlanta Olympics menu,"[10] "Korean *kimchi* on the Sydney Olympics table,"[11] and "Athens Olympics D-6, 1.5 tons of *kimchi* and side dish air-transported."[12] We can expect for similar media coverage for the 2008 Beijing Olympics.

It is interesting to observe that, recently, the attention of Korean media turned not only to the selection of *kimchi* in official menu but also to its popularity among foreign athletes: under the title "Chinese athletes rush on *kimchi*," *Financial News* deplores that because *kimchi* is so popular among foreign athletes, Korean athletes cannot eat it if they arrive late in restaurant.[13] *Segye Ilbo* insists on the popularity of *kimchi* not only among Asians like Chinese and Japanese, but also among "European athletes who know that [it] is good for body."[14]

The logical extension is to explain the performances of Korean athletes by their consumption of *kimchi*: the TV station Korean Broadcasting System did not hesitate to title a report, "*Kimchi* is our strength."[15] The Korean national dish, which also entered in the official menu of 1998 Soccer World Cup in France, was presented as an explanation for the excellent performance of Korean team in 2002 Korea-Japan World Cup: "Korean soccer is the force of *kimchi*, said the Asahi TV,"[16] "According to some foreign media, the good performance of Korean team attaining the semi-final in this World Cup, using strong pressing and tenuous attack, is related to the strength of physical conditions which seems to originate from ginseng and *kimchi*."[17]Once again, the analysis is not presented as singing one's own praises. Rather, by quoting the analysis or the perception of foreign media, Korean media seek the appearances of objectivity. *Kimchi* has also been praised for its beneficial effects on health. Several research teams underlined the positive impact of *kimchi* in preventing cancer, constipation, high blood pressure, and diabetes.[18] Along with these traditional diseases, *kimchi*'s positive effect was cited every time a new disease appeared: "Financial Times, Absence of SARS case in Korea due to garlic in *kimchi*,"[19] "*Kimchi*' s lactic ferments subjugate avian flu."[20] As the title of the first article indicates, foreign media are considered as more efficient in elevating the objectivity of the claim. But it can be also pernicious because the *Financial Times*' article just quoted a Korean researcher claiming the preventive effect of *kimchi*. Thus, the citation forms a circle with Korean media quoting foreign media, quoting Korean researcher.

This large, frequent, and repetitive media coverage on the beneficial effects of *kimchi* contributes to its consolidation as a national symbol: it not only is recognized by international society but also receives the affection of foreigners. *Kimchi* is not only tasty, but also good for health and prevents traditional as well as new diseases like *deus ex machina* medicine. Koreans should be proud of this culinary heritage coming from *ancestors' wisdom*.[21]

Scientific Legitimacy

The promotion of the national symbol can be reinforced by elevating the scientific legitimacy of the claims on *kimchi*'s beneficial effects, as well as on its long history. The pseudo-scientific discourses often trace the origin of *kimchi* back to the Three Kingdoms period (fourth to seventh century A.D): "The safety of *kimchi* is proved by historical experience because our ancestors have been eating it everyday since the Three Kingdoms period."[22] But more serious historical studies show that the most popular and generalized form of *kimchi*—hot and spicy, with a lot of red pepper and prepared with Chinese cabbage—is a rather recent invention. The red pepper was introduced to Korea by Japanese during the Korea-Japan War of 1592–1598, but its utilization was generalized only around 1800. Furthermore, the Chinese cabbage was introduced only at the end of the nineteenth century (Han 2000, 222–223). From this perspective, *kimchi* can also be considered a representative fusion food generalized in modern Korea rather than an invariable form of food representing Korean long-term tradition and wisdom. But as scholars of nationalism know, time is an important legitimating power elevating the status of national symbols. The mobilization of the scientific community was much stronger in natural sciences. The study of *kimchi* has known continuous development since the 1950s as follows (table 4.1).

After a period of sporadic studies during 1955–1978, the 1980s are the era of more consistent and continuous investigation of *kimchi*. The period 1989–1991 is characterized by a sudden upsurge in the number of studies reflecting perhaps the heightened status of *kimchi* as national symbol.

With a growing number of scientists studying *kimchi*, the institutional basis for research was created in 1994 by the establishment of the Kimchi

Table 4.1 Number of kimchi studies from 1955 to 1996

55	56	57	58	59	60	61	62	63	64	65	66	67	68	69	70	71	72	73	74	75
2	1	1	3	3	6	2	3	1	1	2	5	6	4	2	5	2	1	2	7	5
76	77	78	79	80	81	82	83	84	85	86	87	88	89	90	91	92	93	94	95	96
4	8	4	11	4	4	16	20	19	15	12	17	17	30	34	38	15	12	27	40	8

Source: Adapted from "1955nyeon-eseo 1996nyeon ggaji-ui gimchiyeongu munheon moglog [The list of literature on kimchi from 1955 to 1996]" in *Sigpumsan-eobg-wayeongyang [Food Industry and Nutrition]*, by Sinyang Choe (1996, 88–101).

Research Institute in Pusan National University.[23] A Department of *Kimchi* Food Science was launched in 2000 at Chungju National College of Science and Technology for the formation and training of *kimchi* specialists.[24] The Department aims at "studying the specialized knowledge and technology for the industrial development of *kimchi*, which is the representative Korean traditional food, and training specialized technicians of food industry."

For a part of scientific community, especially that of food and nutrition science, the emergence of *kimchi* as national symbol was an excellent opportunity to develop a subfield of study. Research on *kimchi* could be considered an act of patriotism as well as a professional activity. At the same time, the need for industrialization of *kimchi* production reflected a more profound change in Korean society with a growing number of people eating outside or consuming manufactured food even at home. In the 1990s, the national food was on the industrial track.

Industrialization of *Kimchi*

The 1990s is the period of industrialization of *kimchi*: the number of manufacturers increased from 160 in 1992 to 400 in 2000, and industrially manufactured *kimchi* production was 450,000 tons in 2000. Large conglomerates such as *Lotte*, *Doosan*, and *Cheiljedang* were among the *kimchi* producers as well as companies specialized in the food industry such as *Dongwon* and *Pulmuone*, the latter being the owner of the Kimchi Museum.[25] *Kimchi* produced by relatively large industrial corporations with high level of quality control was destined to be sold to and consumed by households, while a large number of small- and medium-sized companies produced low-quality and competitive-price *kimchi* to be sold to collective meals providers or restaurants.

In 1993, a big *kimchi*-related industrial market was created with the launch of *kimchi* refrigerator: traditionally, a large quantity of *kimchi* was made in autumn for winter consumption, and it was conserved in jars buried in soil. With urbanization, a majority of Koreans lived in apartment and did not possess the soil where to bury and conserve their *kimchi*. Refrigerator was a good functional substitute but presented some problems: it was too small to conserve large quantity of *kimchi*, and the strong odor of *kimchi* was imbibed into other cohabitants. *Samsung* and *Golstar* (later *LG*), two leaders in Korean electronics industries, quasi-simultaneously launched their *kimchi* refrigerator in 1993. Two years later, *Winia Manda* launched a very popular model of *kimchi* refrigerator called *Dimchae*, which is the ancient name for *kimchi*: this model became the leader of the market with its cumulated production reaching 100,000 in 1998, 1 million in 2000, and 2 million in 2002.[26] In 1994, only 0.03 percent of households possessed a *kimchi* refrigerator, but the rate was 57 percent in 2004, reflecting the importance of *kimchi* in Korean families' food habits.[27]

It was thus proved that *kimchi* and its derivative products had an enormous industrial and commercial potential. The scientific and technological approach of *kimchi* was emphasized with proliferation of *kimchi* research centers and teams: *Hanyang Yutong*, a chain of supermarkets, opened a research center in 1995 in Seoul;[28] *LG* founded the Kimchi Research Center in their home electronics industrial complex of Changwon in 2002; the same year, *Samsung, kimchi* refrigerator manufacturer, made alliance with *kimchi* producer *Pulmuone*, which had already organized its own *kimchi* research team since 1985; *Winia Manda* created its research team in 1993, and experimented different *kimchi*-making and -conserving technology with one million Chinese cabbages in ten years.[29]

Finally, the Korean Kimchi Association was established on August 24, 2005, for "the globalization of *kimchi* by enhancement of quality, increase of exports and diffusion of *kimchi* culinary culture, to elevate the status as the original *kimchi* country, and to contribute to the improvement of revenue for farmers and the development of domestic *kimchi* industry."[30] This association is located in the Kimchi Research Institute in Pusan National University and represents an effort to mobilize both scientific and industrial actors of *kimchi* and derivatives. So far, the promotion of *kimchi* has been exclusively the fact of civil society: journalists bragging the mysterious strength of Korean traditional food, food scientists creating the subfield of *kimchi* studies, and industrials catching the opportunity of Korean societal change to create a market for industrially processed *kimchi* as well as for *kimchi* special refrigerator.

State Support

Contrasting with the extent to which the various sectors of civil society were mobilized in the emergence and promotion of *kimchi* as a symbol of national identity, Korean state's participation is relatively late. The role of the state began with the symbolic manipulation: in 1996, the Ministry of Culture and Sports proclaimed the best five Korean cultural symbols. *Kimchi* and *bulgogi*[31] couple was among the five along with *hanbog* (traditional dress), *hangeul* (Korean alphabet), *Bulgug* Buddhist Temple and *Seoggul-am*, and *taekwondo* (national martial arts).[32] Ironically, these symbols were called the Corporate Identity of Korean Culture reflecting the mixed-influence of mercantilism (exports rather than imports even in cultural matters) and neoliberalism (commodification of everything, including culture).

Ten years later in 2006, the Ministry of Culture and Tourism (2006) publicized the ambitious list of One Hundred Symbols of National Culture, with, of course, *kimchi*. One of the proclaimed objectives of this list is to "find out the cultural DNA of our nation." The official reason of selection for *kimchi*: it is "the best vegetables fermented food created by Koreans." *Kimchi* figures among eleven symbols related to eating and drinking: others are *ddug* (rice cake), *jeonju bibimbab* (Jeonju style rice with assorted mixtures), *gochujang* (red pepper paste), *doenjang* (bean paste), *samgyetang* (chicken broth), *onggi* (Korean pottery), *bulgogi, soju* and *maggeolli* (traditional alcohol), *naengmyeon* (cold noodles), and *jjajangmyeon* (Chinese-style noodles).[33] The criteria for selection were symbolic value, possibility for commercial and industrial development, globalization meaning exports possibilities, commonness in both South and North Korea, and affirmation of Koreanness for disputed territories like *Dogdo*. In a sense, *kimchi* fulfills all these criteria, even the last one because of the disputes on *kimchi* standardization with Japan, as will be considered later.

This state policy of symbolic manipulation is symptomatic of the government efforts to generalize the trajectory of *kimchi* as a successful cultural item. *Kimchi*, from stinking but indispensable everyday foodstuff, has become a proudly proclaimed Korean national treasure, good for health and environment, and simultaneously very profitable business in both domestic and international markets. The example of *kimchi*, whose development was entirely autonomous, was to be emulated in other cultural domains.

In 2004, the Planning and Promotion Unit for Kimchi Industry was created with government funding in Gwangju Technopark. Financed by the Ministry of Industry, it is a consortium including central government, local governments of Gwangju and Jeonnam, a research center, and six universities. It seems to be the first case of government funding for a concrete industrial promotion project of *kimchi* reflecting the policy interest for *cultural mercantilism*.

The 1990s can thus be characterized as the period of *kimchi*'s consolidation as an important national symbol, with repetitive journalistic promotion and generalized scientific legitimation. As we have examined, all these developments are related to the surprising ascension of the *kimchi* industry, igniting research and development activities, improving *kimchi*'s qualities as everyday health food, and enlarging the consumption basis of *kimchi* with nationalist appeal in domestic market.

INTERNATIONAL DIMENSION

Because *kimchi* is not a trivial food, but one of the most popular cultural symbols of Korean national identity, it possesses a particularly high sensitivity when it is put on the international stage. I underlined earlier how much the

praise of *kimchi*'s qualities by foreign voices was quoted, utilized, and sometimes over-exploited by Korean media. In this part, I examine three cases of
international issues concerning *kimchi*: the Korea- Japan conflict about the
international standardization of *kimchi*, the Korea-China conflict upon *kimchi*
trade and hygiene, and the internationally buried potential controversy over
kimchi's effect on health.

Korea-Japan *War* for International Recognition

The utilization of martial terminology like *war* by media is symptomatic
of *kimchi*'s status as national cultural symbol involving identity and sovereignty. The first *Kimchi* war was between Korea and Japan over the international recognition and standardization. The media reported the "Victory of
Olympic '*Kimchi* War'" and "Official Provider of Atlanta Olympics, Beating
Japan";[34] and the Korean Agricultural Cooperative, *Nonghyeob*, signed a
supply contract of *kimchi* with the Organizing Committee of the Atlanta
Olympics. Because Japanese *kimchi* manufacturer was also candidate for this
contract, it was for *Nonghyeob* a matter of national sovereignty; its representatives insisted that Korea was the "sovereign house of *kimchi*" and deployed
efforts "to block the Japanese supply of *kimchi*."[35]

The basic problem between Korea and Japan on *kimchi* is that Japan has
developed its own kind of *kimchi*, called *kimuchi*—simply the Japanese
pronunciation of *kimchi*, which is less hot and spicy, and not necessarily
fermented like the Korean version, thus with less strong odor. This was a perfectly normal consequence of local adaptation, but unacceptable for Koreans,
because (1) Japan was the formal colonial power of Korea, (2) Japanese
kimuchi recipe was a clear violation of the Korean authentic *kimchi* fabrication method, and (3) Japanese *kimuchi* market had an enormous potential for
enlargement and Japanese manufacturers were potential competitors in the
global *kimchi-kimuchi* market.

The most feverish phase of Korea-Japan *Kimchi* War was the period 1995–
2001 during which the international Committee Alimentarius Codex (CAC)
discussed, examined, and finally fixed an international standard for *kimchi*.
In this process, the Korean Ministry of Agriculture and Forestry played a
leading role by first submitting a draft proposition in 1995. The Korea Food
Research Institute under the Ministry, created in 1987–1988, was the concrete actor and negotiator of this internationalization of *kimchi*. Following
the symbolic manipulation by the Ministry of Culture, the main motive of
state intervention was *cultural mercantilism* in order to export merchandises
of Korean culture.

The war was in fact a series of negotiations between Korea and Japan
over what to call *kimchi-kimucbi*: Korea favored the traditional method of

natural fermentation, while Japan opposed such a restrictive definition.[36] Ogawa Toshio, from the Japanese National *Tsukemono* Cooperatives Union, is against calling *kimchi* only Korean style *kimchi*, because every food should adapt to the local market and one cannot ignore the demand of Japanese consumers. Kim Yeongyeol, president of the Korean Food Consortium of Japan, argued that "if Korean *kimchi* and Japanese *kimchi* were called by the same name, it would be a second Japanization of name."[37] On July 2001, the *kimchi* standard was officially registered at the CAC as a consequence of Korean-Japanese compromise; the Korean version of food name, *kimchi*, was internationally recognized, while a large definition of fabrication method was adopted, opening the way for Japanese manufacturers to legitimately call their products *kimchi*.

The international standardization policy reflected the state's commercial interest in expanding the *kimchi* international market and in stimulating Korean *kimchi* exports. But, confronted with Japanese commercial interests, Korean government was forced to accept a broader definition of its national dish. Once *kimchi* was internationally standardized, another war was awaiting, this time concerning the cost of production and international competitiveness.

Korea-China *Kimchi* Trade War

The registration of *kimchi* in 2001 on the internationally recognized CAC was undoubtedly a victory of the Korean national symbol on world stage. Once the rules of the game were defined, it was up to the main actors, Korean and Japanese manufacturers to compete in growing markets. But it was counting without a terrible new actor, China.

At the turn of the century, the prospective for the Korean *kimchi* industry seemed brilliant: in 2000, the Korean annual production of *kimchi* was estimated 1.5 million tons with 450,000 tons for manufactured *kimchi*, the majority being still prepared in households. But the industrial part of the market was steadily growing. The Japanese market of *kimchi-kimuchi* was estimated at 180,147 tons in 1998, and Korean exports of *kimchi* to Japan were also increasing, from 12,080 tons in 1997 to 24,561 tons in 1999, the Japanese market representing the quasi-totality of Korean exports (97 percent). It was perfectly natural to expect for continuous development of the Korean *kimchi* industry on both domestic and foreign markets: the sovereign house of *kimchi* was to reign on world market.

At the dawn of the new century, China began to export *kimchi* to Korea in small amounts. In 2002, it was only 1,041 tons, which means less than 1 percent of the manufactured *kimchi* market. But the low production cost of China and the consequent international division of labor provoked a rapid delocalization of the *kimchi* industry from the sovereign house to foreign lands. Chinese *kimchi* exports to Korea traced a dramatic ascension curb to 28,701t in 2003, to reach about 100,000 tons in 2005 (Kim 2005, 37). The latter number means that the average annual individual consumption of Chinese *kimchi* by Koreans is 2 kg!

On this strange and explosive context of Koreans importing their national dish from China, the War was ignited by an opposition politician Ko Kyeonghwa, member of National Assembly. As the chief of Food Security Task Force for the opposition Grand National Party, and based upon results from the Research Institute of Public Health and Environment of the City of Seoul, she declared that imported *kimchi* from China contained a dangerous level of lead.[38] But the Korea Food and Drug Administration (KFDA) replied that the amount of lead contained in imported *kimchi* was not dangerous for human body according to WHO criteria.[39] The central government administration proceeded to analyzing imported and domestic *kimchi*, and found that some contained lead, but the level was far lower than declared by the opposition politician.[40] On October 21, 2005, the KFDA announced that further investigations showed that some imported Chinese *kimchi* contained parasitic insect eggs, thus deepening the social scandal over and concern with food security. The import of Chinese *kimchi* fell dramatically and was practically blocked by Korean customs for hygiene inspection. On October 31, China retaliated by announcing that Korean *kimchi* and food products contained parasitic insect eggs, and prohibited their imports.[41] The *kimchi* war was declared, but rapidly found the way to the cease-fire around November 10, with an arrangement and promise of closer cooperation for hygiene and customs inspection. It was reported that the Chinese government was particularly dissatisfied with the media coverage of the news inclining to China-bashing.[42]

The Korea-China *kimchi* war of 2005 revealed that (1) the low-end market of the national dish was "occupied" by foreign production, and (2) because of this international division of labor, the domestic political confrontation on food security provoked an international trade war. But more concrete analysis indicates that most of the manufacturers producing *kimchi* in China and exporting to Korea are Korean entrepreneurs, so that (3) the Chinese government's firm reaction must be understood as an identity-based dissatisfaction rather than a commercially motivated move. It seems that this constitutes an interesting case of spillover from a domestic political debate to the international conflict.

Kimchi's Effect on Health

Kimchi's beneficial effects on health have been abundantly studied, publicized, and promoted not only by food scientists and nutritionists but also by Korean media and Korean people in general, especially in the context of international encounters. In a sense, the national treasury could have but beneficial effects on health. When an American periodical, *Health*, chose Korean *kimchi* among international health food in its March delivery of 2006, major important Korean newspapers reported the news with flashing titles: "American Magazine Health Chose *Kimchi* among Five Healthiest Food in the World with Abundant Vitamins and Repressing Effect on Cancer,"[43] "Wonderful *Kimchi*, among World Five Best Health Food,"[44] or "Seduced by *Kimchi*, American Monthly Magazine's Selection as the World's Five Healthiest Foods."[45] The Spanish olive oil, the Japanese soy, the Greek yogurt, and the Indian lentils were the other world health foods. After the declaration of independence in taste, Korea has finally reached the highest level of international recognition not of mere independence but of its superior quality.

What is much less known and publicized is the fact that Korean and Japanese generalized daily consumption of pickled food—*tsukemono* in Japan and *kimchi* in Korea—is considered a risk factor of frequent gastric cancer. Medical studies have established that salted food as well as high salt diet were main risk factors for this type of cancer along with smoked food and barbecued meat or fish (Ahn and Shin 1995). These studies also underline that vitamins and yellow-green vegetables are protective factors of gastric cancer so that the effects of *kimchi* on health cannot be unilaterally and uniformly said to be good or bad. But because *kimchi* is the cultural symbol of Korean national identity, it is surrounded by an aura of sanctity, which is difficult to attack.

Recently in 2006, Korean newspapers reported an article by *Los Angeles Times* criticizing Korean *kimchi patriotism*, which hinder possible risks induced by over-consumption of national food.[46] It is too early to say if these reports will be the beginning of a more objective public discussion on the effects of *kimchi* on health.

So far, Korea fought two *kimchi* wars, one against Japan about the very definition of *kimchi*, and one against China about food security in *kimchi* trade. These international conflicts are the logical consequences of *kimchi*'s internationalization in consumption as well as in production. As in most wars, *kimchi* wars were also fought by state soldiers, the Ministry of Agriculture (Korea Food Research Institute) in the first one, and the Ministry of Foreign Affairs (Korean Embassy in Beijing) and the Ministry of Agriculture (Korean Food and Drug Administration) in the second one. This contrasts with the declaration of independence and national promotion phases largely dominated by civil society actors. Perhaps a third war on the objective and universal value of *kimchi* as health food is being generated. The internationalization of *kimchi* has ineluctably brought about these conflicts and pushed the state to the line of confrontation.

CONCLUSION: THE POLITICS OF *KIMCHI*

In a sense, the emergence of *kimchi* as national food followed a trajectory similar to that of Korean nation: (1) the liberation from symbolic domination of imported foreign food and declaration of independence in taste by raising the popular domestic food; (2) the large social mobilization and promotion of the national food to praise its superior qualities, and consequently the scientific institutionalization and industrialization; and (3) the international promotion of *kimchi* encountering some conflicts, either on the standardization or international trade.

During this process of emergence and institutionalization of about two decades, several characteristics can be underlined. First, eating and drinking are one of the most private acts of human life so that their cultural and political manipulation as national symbol seems to have a very deep and strong appealing power on individuals. Even compared to several national culinary symbols of other nations, *kimchi* possesses particularities such as its generalized everyday consumption, contrary to some noble, elegant, but high-class or extraordinary festive foods, or its reinforced ethnic marker function due to its strong odor, like some French *fromage* in Western environment. In a word, *kimchi* has some intrinsic qualities as a national symbol.

Second, the timing of *kimchi*'s emergence as national symbol indicates that this kind of cultural nationalism must be intimately related to the general ascension of national status in international society. The 1988 Seoul Olympics constitutes not only the symbol of Korean economic miracle but also the culinary declaration of independence. It seems that the shifting involvements between public action and private interest *à la* Hirschmann can metaphorically be applied to the shifting preferences between foreign imitation and national affirmation.

Third, the case of *kimchi* is of particular interest because its emergence was purely societal. In many cases, the third world countries' nationalisms are stimulated and directed by postcolonial state in its efforts to forge a strong country. In these Asian developmental states like Korea, society has been continuously mobilized in order to reinforce the state power and plenty. But in the case of *kimchi*, it emerged autonomously among societal actors including media, scientific communities, and industries, as a national symbol. The invention of the culinary tradition was also the fact of several universities and industrials. This article indicates that the congruence of industrial interest and psychological need for international recognition was determinant in the emergence of *kimchi* in such a speed and extent.

Fourth, the state followed the societal emergence by officially legitimating the national symbol and participating in the international promotion of the national treasure. But such a strong nationalistic involvement in this side dish provoked international conflicts because, even for national dish, the law of international division of labor applies especially if the production is industrialized. Now, the biggest manufacturer of *Korean kimchi* is China, reflecting the globalization process.

In this study, I did not treat *kimchi*'s status as national symbol in North Korea. The generalized daily consumption of *kimchi* is the common feature in South and North, and it must be of particular interest to follow and observe the *kimchi* trajectory as national symbol or merely a basic food in communist North. Furthermore, this research should be completed by other studies of Korean national symbols, and by comparative study of different representative national food.

NOTES

1. This chapter was previously published with the same title in *The Korean Journal of International Studies*, *46*(5), 207–229. The original work was supported by the Soongsil University Research Fund.

2. "Because so much of what subjectively makes up the modern 'nation' consists of such constructs and is associated with appropriate and, in general, fairly recent symbols or suitably tailored discourse (such as 'national history'), the national phenomenon cannot be adequately investigated without careful attention to the 'invention of tradition'" (Hobsbawm and Ranger 1983, 14).

3. Food preference is defined as "the way in which people choose from among available comestibles on the basis of biological or economic perceptions including taste, value, purity, ease or difficulty of preparation, and the availability of fuel and other preparation tools" (Smith 2006, 480).

4. This opinion poll was ordered by the Ministry of Culture and Tourism in the selection process of "One Hundred National Cultural Symbols," presented as "the cultural DNA of Korean people." *Hankyoreh*, July 27, 2006.

5. "The National Flag, the National Anthem and the National Emblem are the three symbols through which an independent country proclaims its identity and sovereignty, and as such they command instantaneous respect and loyalty. In themselves, they reflect the entire background, thought and culture of a nation" (Firth 1973, 341).

6. The title of this section is an expression borrowed from Han's (2000) work, "Some foods are good to think: *Kimchi* and the epitomization of national character," published in *Korean Social Science Journal*, *27*(1).

7. *Gimchi* is the new spelling of *kimchi*, following the new system of romanization of Korean language. Nevertheless, I maintained the ancient one because it had already become a word of English language recognized by dictionaries.

8. *Hankyoreh,* September 4, 2001.

9. *Chosun Ilbo,* May 1, 1991.

10. *Kookmin Ilbo,* April 13, 1996.

11. *Hankook Ilbo,* August 23, 2000.

12. *Segye Ilbo,* August 7, 2004.

13. *Financial News,* August 12, 2004.

14. *Segye Ilbo,* August 10, 2004.

15. *Korea Broadcasting System,* August 20, 2004.

16. *Kyunghyang Sinmun,* June 20, 2002.

17. *Kookmin Ilbo,* June 28, 2002.

18. *Chosun Ilbo,* September 2, 1993; *Hankyoreh,* November 5, 1994.

19. *Dong-a Ilbo,* April 15, 2003.

20. *Chosun Ilbo,* March 7, 2005.

21. *Seoul Sinmun,* June 9, 1993.

22. This quote is from Eungsu Han, a professor of food science at the Agricultural Cooperative University, published in *Munhwa Ilbo,* October 28, 2005.

23. Kimchi Research Institute (http://www.kimchiresearch.com/index.html)

24. *Chosun Ilbo,* November 9, 1999; Department of Pickled Food Science, Chungju National College of Science and Technology (http://www.kimchiresearch .com/index.html)

25. *Munhwa Ilbo,* March 6, 2001.

26. *Dong-a Ilbo,* November 6, 2002.

27. *Hankyoreh,* October 12, 2004.

28. *Kookmin Ilbo,* May 10, 1995.

29. *Chosun Ilbo,* July 9, 2002.

30. Ministry of Agriculture and Forestry, *Public notice 2005-W.*

31. Usually translated Korean barbecue, *bulgogi* is beef meat marinated in bean sauce and barbecued. Very popular till the 1980s, it fell out of favor in the 1990s and somehow became a Korean food for foreigners. *Galbi,* which is prepared in the same manner but utilizing more expensive beef ribs, is more popular today.

32. *Chosun Ilbo,* December 1, 1996.

33. The Ministry explains that "even though it comes from China, it was localized in a different manner in our country. It is a representative eating out menu for most Koreans with a possibility for globalization." But, some foods coming from Japan, even localized, could not be included among the symbols of national culture, reflecting the particular sensitivity of Korea-Japan relations.

34. *Dong-a Ilbo,* April 13, 1996.

35. *Dong-a Ilbo,* January 11, 1996.

36. See the debate in *Dong-a Ilbo,* September 15, 1999.

37. In 1939, Japan adopted a policy of cultural assimilation in her Korean colony and forced people to take Japanese family and given names in place of Korean ones.

38. *Kookmin Ilbo,* September 26, 2005.

39. *Chosun Ilbo,* September 29, 2005.

40. *Hankyoreh,* October 11, 2005.

41. *Munhwa Ilbo,* November 1, 2005.

42. *Kyunghyang Sinmun,* November 11, 2005

43. *Chosun Ilbo,* March 27, 2006.

44. *Dong-a Ilbo,* March 27, 2006.
45. *Kyunghyang Simnun,* March 27, 2006.
46. *Kyunghyang Sinmun,* May 23, 2006.

REFERENCES

Ahn, Y., & Shin, M. (1995). Epidemiology of gastric cancer in Korea. *Korean Journal of Epidemiology, 17*(1).
Anderson, B. (1991). *Imagined Communities: Reflections on the Origin and Spread of Nationalism.* London: Verso.
Appadurai, A. (1981). Gastro-politics in Hindu South Asia. *American Anthropologist, 8*(3), 494–511.
Avieli, N. (2005). Vietnamese new year rice cakes: Iconic festive dishes and contested nationalidentity. *Ethnology, 44*(2), 167–187.
Bell, D., & Valentine, G. (1997). *Consuming Geographies: We are Where We Eat.* London: Routledge.
Billig, M. (1995). *Banal Nationalism.* London: Sage.
Braudel, F. (1986). *L'identite de la France.* Paris: Arthaud-Flammarion.
Firth, R. (1973). *Symbols: Public and Private.* Ithaca: Cornell University Press.
Gellner, E. (1983). *Nations and Nationalism.* Ithaca: Cornell University Press.
Han, K. (2000). Some foods are good to think: *Kimchi* and the epitomization of national character. *Korean Social Science Journal, 27*(1), 221–235.
Hobsbawm, E., & Ranger, T. (1983). *The Invention of Tradition.* Cambridge: Cambridge University Press.
Kim, J. (2005). Junggugsan gimchi-e beomuryeojin hangugsan jeongchigyeongjehag [Korean political economy seasoned by Chinese *kimchi*]. *Mal,* November, 32–39.
Kim, M., Lee, K., & Lee, O. (1999). *The kimchi cookbook: Fiery flavors and cultural history of Korea's national dish.* North Clarendon: Periplus Editions.
Lee, C., & An, B. (1995). Gimchi-e gwanhan munheonjeog gochal [A literature review on *kimchi*]. *Hangug Sigsaenhwal Munhwa Haghoeji, 10*(4), 311-319.
Lee, S. (2004). The story of *gimchi chigae. The Massachusetts Review, 45*(3), 381–385.
Mennel, S. (1985). *All Manners of Food: Eating and Taste in England and France from the Middle Ages to the Present.* London: Basil Blackwell.
Ministry of Agriculture and Forestry. (2005). *Public Notice 2005-111.* Seoul: MAF.
Ministry of Culture and Tourism (2006). *One Hundred Symbols of National Culture.* Seoul: MCT.
Palmer, C. (1998). From theory to practice: Experiencing the nation in everyday life. *Journal of Material Culture, 3*(2), 175–199.
Rozin, P., & Fallon, A. (1981). The acquisition of likes and dislikes for foods. In J. Solms & R. Hall (Eds.), *Criteria of Food Acceptance: How Man Chooses What He Eats.* Zurich: Forster Verl.
Scholliers, P. (Ed.). (2001). *Food, Drink and Identity: Cooking, Eating and Drinking in Europe since the Middle Ages.* Oxford: Berg.
Smith, A. (1991). *National Identity.* Reno: University of Nevada Press.

Smith, M. (2006). The archeology of food preference. *American* Anthropologist, *109*(3), 480–493.

Watson, J. (1997). *Golden Arches East: McDonald's in East Asia.* Stanford: Stanford University Press.

Watson, J., & Caldwell, M. (2005). Introduction. In J. Watson & M. Caldwell (Eds.), *The Cultural Politics of Food and Eating* (pp. 1–10). Malden: Blackwell.

Zonis, M., Lefkovitz, D., & Wilkin, S. (2005). *The Kimchi Matters: Global Business and Local Politics in a Crisis-driven World.* Evanston: Agate.

Chapter 5

Buddhist Temple Food in South Korea

Interests and Agency in the Reinvention of Tradition in the Age of Globalization

Seungsook Moon

Food[1] is a source of nourishment and quotidian pleasure. It is also a significant aspect of individual and collective identities, as indicated by religious regulations of diet and regional variations in dietary customs (Khare 1992; Reinders 2004; Ulrich 2007). As a social fact, food signifies rank and hierarchy, intimacy and solidarity, and exclusion and distance between social groups (Appadurai 1981; Chang 1977; Goody 1982; Sterckx 2004). In the current era of globalization, food is not only a major target of transnational agribusiness, the fast food industry, and the leisure and entertainment industries, it is also an important focal point where localized responses to globalization are articulated. To illuminate local responses that reveal the complicated process of globalization as a lived experience, the current study examines the cultural politics of reinventing *jeontong sachal eumsik* or *jeol eumsik* (traditional Buddhist temple food) in South Korea.[2] Since the mid-1990s, there has been growing mass media attention to Buddhist temple food. Especially in the 2000s, cookbooks on this subject have been steadily published and Internet sites on it have multiplied. Major dailies have increasingly reported on Buddhist cuisine by focusing on these cookbook authors and Buddhist cooking classes in urban areas; within these articles, newspapers have commonly introduced handy recipes of Buddhist cuisine and restaurants specializing in temple food.[3] National television networks have broadcast documentaries on temple food particularly around the Buddha's birthday (April 8 in the lunar calendar) and cable television channels have featured regular cooking shows on temple food.

The apparent revival of Buddhist temple food as Korean tradition is a curious phenomenon and raises the following questions: Why is it happening at this moment after the long public oblivion of temple food? What sorts of interests are at work to generate this phenomenon? What does it mean to revive tradition in this age of globalization, characterized by the transnational flows of capital, labor, images, ideas, and technology? What does the redis-covery of the tradition reveal or illuminate about the complicated process of globalization as a lived experience? While diverse versions of Buddhist temple food have existed since Buddhism was introduced to the Korean Peninsula in the late fourth century, it has been considered (by contemporary Koreans) to be food for monks and nuns living in remote temples to pursue enlightenment. In the past decade or so, however, the mass media have repre-sented this rather esoteric category of food as an alternative diet to fast food, processed food saturated with artificial additives, and the *westernization* of dietary habits leading to serious disease. Urban middle-class women have taken Buddhist cooking classes to improve their family diet, personal health, and appearance. As this interest in healthy food has affected restaurant busi-nesses, men and women with entrepreneurial inclinations have also taken such cooking classes to open specialty restaurants or incorporate temple food into their existing menus. This array of health concerns and economic interest among the public partly account for the surge in popularity of temple food among segments of the population.

Another recurring theme in mass media discourse on temple food is the significance of Buddhist cuisine as a source of national identity in the age of globalization; it is important to know Korean culture and maintain its unique identity not only for its own sake, but also for its economic potential. The Korean government is interested in utilizing temple food for this potential, as well as for the political purpose of affirming the unique Korean identity. Because of its economic potential, the government has supported the tourism industry and the Buddhist establishment in order to promote temple food as a cultural resource to be branded and sold as a value-added product. Aspiring to be influential in the larger society, Buddhist orders have begun to pay some belated attention to temple food. In a nutshell, the reinvention of traditional Buddhist temple food in contemporary Korea allows us to examine the inter-play between popular concerns for health and economic security, and the interests of the state, business, and the Buddhist establishment in reinventing tradition and mobilizing cultural differences, to further larger national and transnational politics. It also enables us to reflect on the postcolonial view of agency tied to consumption and pleasure, rather than intentional and orga-nized action.

THE POLITICS OF *INVENTED TRADITION* AND LOCAL CULTURE IN THE AGE OF TRANSNATIONAL GLOBALIZATION

As Joseph Gusfield (1967) argues, the idea of tradition is the product of rapid social change, accompanied by a pervasive sense of loss and temporal distance from what has passed. It connotes a self-conscious relation to the past, and an attempt to identify it with continuity in the midst of disruptive change. Contemporary globalization has accelerated social change, as exemplified by the spread of the market economy and transnational flows, and it has generated a growing public interest in localized traditions. In his theory of cultural globalization, which underscores the constitutive role of imagination mediated by the combined effect of the mass media and migration in shaping the modern subjectivity, Arjun Appadurai (1996) argues that "space and time are themselves socialized and localized through complex and deliberate practices of performance, representation, and action" (180). Hence, locality needs to be understood as *a structure of feeling* (to use Raymond Williams' words), rather than a geographical space, that emerges from the practices of local subjects in the forms of "resistance, irony, selectivity and in general, agency" (1996, 7). Similarly, Richard Wilk (2006) observes that globalization seems to "produce local culture and promote the constant formation of new focus of local identity, dress, cuisine, music, dance and language" (10).

In his seminal work on invented traditions in the context of modern Europe, Eric Hobsbawm and Terence Ranger (1983) observes that such traditions are intended to establish social cohesion among members of a group, legitimize existing institutions and authorities, and inculcate conventional values and behavior in individuals (11). In this constructionist view of tradition, they highlight the dominant role that the state and organized political and social movements played, between 1870 and 1914, in inventing such traditions as political ceremonials, national myths, and national sports (Hobsbawm and Ranger 1983, 283). While Hobsbawm and Ranger recognize unofficial social groups and businesses as significant actors in this invention, the prominence of official political actors in their work reflects the era marked by the spread and consolidation of the nation-state (and colonial empire) as the political unit. In their historical study, the salience of political interests over economic and popular ones also reflects their focus on European metropolises without analyzing the economic exploitation of their colonies and the difficulty in accessing the unrecorded lives of ordinary people in the past.[4]

As I discuss further, in the case of Buddhist temple food in contemporary Korea, however, popular and economic interests (rather than political interests in social cohesion) play a conspicuous role in the cultural politics of reinventing tradition in the current era of globalization. Popular concerns for health and economic security are not merely the object of manipulation by the state, business, and religion but also a formative element in shaping the actions of these major institutions. Responding to the economic potential of temple food that became trendy among middle-class urbanites, the state began to promote temple food as tradition. I argue that the reinvention of this tradition not only serves to reaffirm national identity and ease a collective anxiety about rapid social change but also promotes national competitiveness in the global market. In the face of deterritorializing globalization, tradition appeals as a source of territorializing the collective identity of Korea, and a crucial means to differentiate one's commodity from others' in the global market. This analysis of the cultural politics of reinventing temple food as tradition does not deny the continuing political function of tradition as the source of authority and legitimacy of a nation-state. Rather, it highlights the fact that such political function hinges on the effective appropriation of popular interests in health and economic security to enhance the state's economic performance.

Analysis of cultural politics also allows us to examine the post-enlightenment view of agency that is not rooted in the rationality of political intention, which has been promoted by a dominant brand of postcolonial studies in American academia.[5] In line with the postcolonial concept of agency, Appadurai (1996) explores the agency of people who encounter the forces of globalization in their consumption of mass-mediated popular culture, rather than organized and intentional movements. While he recognizes that the consumers of mass-mediated commercial culture are not free agents and that consumption is frequently embedded in repetitious regulations of individual behavior, he highlights the pleasure involved in the consumption that generates agency. Appadurai (1996) further contends that the transnational flow of mass-mediated images, ideas, and sensations engenders a "diasporic public sphere" that undermines the nation-state bounded by a given territory (19). From the angle of the cultural politics of reinventing tradition, however, it is too premature to announce the near end of the epoch with the emergence of the diasporic public sphere in urban areas in the world. Because such a fluid public sphere is open to ongoing interplay among converging and diverging popular and institutional interests, the consumerist agency rooted in pleasure is often appropriated by better organized political and economic interests. Moreover, as analyzed further in the cultural politics of reinventing temple food, popular agency in this case is not so much rooted in the pleasure of consumption as in concerns for health and economic security. These concerns are also expediently appropriated by the government, business, and the Buddhist establishment. While this article does not focus on the historical development of Korean Buddhist temple food, a brief discussion of its history is needed to contextualize the contemporary cultural politics of reinventing it as tradition.

A BRIEF HISTORY OF BUDDHIST CUISINE IN KOREA AND ITS CONTEMPORARY CHARACTERISTICS

Mahāyāna Buddhism was introduced to the Korean Peninsula during the Three Kingdoms period (fourth to seventh centuries). *Goguryeo*, one of the three kingdoms, first adopted Buddhism as its court religion in 372. The other kingdoms of *Baekje* and *Silla* accepted Buddhism in 384 and 528, respectively. Under the patronage of these royal courts, numerous Buddhist temples were built and the commandment against eating meat was disseminated. During the Unified *Silla* period (668–935), the prohibition against meat-eating was modified but Buddhist temples spread tea-drinking as a central component of Buddhist rituals. During the *Goryeo* Dynasty (919–1392), which adopted Buddhism as the state religion, the prohibition against meat-eating became strict and temples invented various culinary techniques to prepare vegetarian dishes and preserve them (General Affairs Office 2006, 22). Marinated and fermented vegetables, the predecessors of *gimchi*, were developed along with *guk* (vegetable soup), *ssam* (lettuce wraps), and *namul muchim* (salad). Wang Geon, the founder of the *Goryeo* Dynasty, instituted two annual Buddhist festivals, *yeondeunghoe* (gathering for the lighting of lotus lamps) and *palgwanhoe* (gathering to observe the eight prohibitions).[6] These national festivals and other ceremonies catering to wealthy aristocratic patrons facilitated the development of elaborate vegetarian cuisine and the spread of tea-drinking (KBCEG 2006, 7).

The aristocratic Buddhist cuisine underwent a transformation during the Joseon Dynasty (1392–1910), which established neo-Confucianism as the state ideology and suppressed Buddhism. The Confucian dynasty imposed a series of legal restrictions on monks and temples. It restricted the number of monks and forbade them from entering the capital. It closed hundreds of temples and banned the construction of new ones. It also confiscated such properties as land and slaves from temples. Consequently, Buddhism became confined to the countryside, where its followers were illiterate and poor peasants and women (Buswell 1992a, 23). Impoverished and marginalized in the process of this sociopolitical change, Buddhism since this period has concentrated on other-worldly activities of *seon* (meditation) and studies of scriptures.[7] As Buddhism lost its wealthy and powerful patronage by royal court and nobility, opulent Buddhist ceremonies accompanied by luxurious temple food disappeared. Tea drinking declined and temple food was reduced to the mainstay of vegetarian culinary dishes, which would resemble rural peasants' diets (Kim 1995, 10).

Rustic vegetarian cuisine continued to characterize Buddhist cuisine in Korea, outliving tumultuous sociopolitical change during Japanese colonial rule. The colonial power, with its strong Buddhist tradition, tried to support Buddhism in Korea; at the turn of the nineteenth century, Japan pressed the declining Joseon court to eliminate restrictions on Buddhist activities in the capital and allow monks to enter cities for the first time after a roughly three-century hiatus (Buswell 1992a, 24). During its colonial rule of Korea (1910–1945), Japan introduced the practice of marriage into the Buddhist priesthood in Korea, where monks and nuns had observed strict celibacy for centuries, sowing the seed of internecine conflict within Buddhism after Independence. This internal strife over marriage not only led to the division of Buddhism into the Jogye Order (which has upheld celibate priesthood and dominated contemporary Korean Buddhism) and the Taego Order (which has accepted married priesthood) in 1962 but also aborted the potential to revive Buddhism in contemporary Korea for a few decades.

Against the backdrop of this checkered political and social history, Buddhist cuisine in Korea developed into a distinct form of vegetarian diet that has been prepared and consumed by monks and nuns. At the same time, as will be discussed ahead in this chapter, there are some significant differences between Buddhist temple food and a generic category of vegetarian food in terms of Buddhist injunctions against the use of "stimulating vegetables" and artificial or chemical ingredients. Two factors were significant to the emergence of temple food as an integral part of the monastic culture. First, unlike Buddhist temples in South Asia that were built in residential neighborhoods, temples in Korea were mostly located in mountains away from populous residential areas due to the history of the persecution of Buddhism. Hence, while monks in South Asia obtained their daily food through alms collections from local villagers, monks and nuns in Korea cultivated or collected their own food. Second, as mentioned earlier, Korean Buddhism stressed meditation as the vehicle to achieve enlightenment, and monks and nuns devoted their lives to *suhaeng* (meditative training) (KBCEG 2006, 4). Hence, food is conceived as a means to achieve enlightenment. While food is recognized as being essential to the human body, it is not viewed as a source of bodily indulgence and pleasure. Rather, it is a source of nourishment and even medicine to gain and sustain physical health and composure, and thereby cultivate human capacity to obtain enlightenment. This metaphysical and instrumental view of food is also reflected in how food eaten by monks and nuns is characterized: *sangsik* (regular food), *juksik* (porridge), and *byeonginsik* (medicinal food). Buddhist Sutras recommend that the porridge is eaten for breakfast, the regular food for lunch, and fruit juice (which is included in the regular food) for dinner. The medicinal food includes such categories of food as fish, meat, and alcohol that are banned for a healthy person. The Sutras admonished monks and laity against gluttony and eating within two hours before sleep, and considered these practices to be toxic (KBCEG 2006, 14–16).

The significance of food as an instrument of enlightenment underlies specific guidelines of Buddhist cuisine. First, a carnivorous diet is prohibited (with dairy products allowed), because it requires killing living life forms that are caught in the cycle of birth, death, and rebirth. The *yeolbangyeong* (*Nirvana Sutra*), a major sutra of Mahāyāna Buddhism, teaches that eating meat destroys the seed of compassion toward living beings (KBCEG 2006, 11). Second, *osinchae* (five pungent or stimulating vegetables) are forbidden because they are believed to intensify sexual desire when they are eaten cooked, and are believed to make people aggressive and impetuous when eaten raw. Those vegetables include *buchu* (chive), *maneul* (garlic), *pa* (scallion), wild *dalle* (rocambole),[8] and *honggeo* (Persian dropwort).[9] Ginger and peppers are not included in the category of these five stimulating vegetables because the criterion is not a spicy taste but a lingering smell and stimulation after eating them. Third, alcohol is also forbidden because it intoxicates people, destroys their wisdom, and disrupts their training.

Three basic principles underlie general culinary techniques in Buddhist cuisine in contemporary Korea: (1) how to make fibrous grains and vegetables *yuyeon* (soft and palatable), (2) how to prepare *cheongjeong* food (cleans, not contaminated), and (3) how to comply with Buddhist teachings and *yeobeop* (the law of nature) (KBCEG 2006, 17). Due to the prohibition against meat-eating and the emphasis on harmony with nature, Buddhist cuisine uses seasonal and local vegetables, fruits, grains, legumes, and seaweeds. The concern with clean food forbids the use of chemical additives and other synthetic ingredients and has promoted the development of natural flavor enhancers like mushroom broth, seaweed broth, and wild sesame. The emphasis on harmony with nature has enabled the development of various culinary methods designed to preserve natural ingredients' own flavors and textures, even minimizing the use of (natural) condiments.[10]

THE REINVENTION OF TRADITIONAL TEMPLE FOOD IN CONTEMPORARY KOREA: CONVERGING AND DIVERGING INTERESTS AND POPULAR AGENCY APPROPRIATED

While popular interest in Buddhist cuisine has grown rapidly in larger society, its practice in actual temples has been in gradual decline, along with the stagnant shortage of new recruits for the priesthood in recent decades.[11] As a result, there are many temples without abbots and some temples do not even have a monk; such temples are taken care of by local laities.[12] This broad problem is reflected in the dietary practices in many Buddhist temples in Korea. According to a national survey of thirty-one major temples (seventeen monasteries and fourteen nunneries) conducted by the Korean Buddhist Culture Enterprise Group of the Jogye Order in early 2006, the characteristics of contemporary Buddhist cuisine discussed earlier have been undermined in the process of industrialization and urbanization. First, while monks and nuns continue to cultivate vegetables and beans for their own use, a majority of those surveyed combine this practice with the purchase of food ingredients from traditional markets (81.8 percent), big supermarkets (9.1 percent), and local grocers (4.5 percent). There is also a significant gender difference in food consumption. In the case of monasteries, 26.7 percent of them purchase all food ingredients, whereas none of the nunneries purchase all food ingredients. The reasons for the use of commercial food ingredients include difficulties involved in cultivation (45.5 percent), absence of labor (32.7 percent), lack of land (12.7 percent), and lack of time (9.1 percent) (KBCEG 2006, 94–95). The growing practice of purchasing commercial food ingredients undermines the principle of *cheongjeong*. Second, while none of the nunneries use the *osinchae* in nun's meals, 26.2 percent of the monasteries occasionally use them and 6.6 percent of the monasteries use them frequently to enhance flavor and health. A parallel trend is observed in the use of artificial flavor enhancers. While a majority of the temples do not use any synthetic flavor enhancers in their cooking, 28.9 percent use them occasionally. These growing practices violate the principles of *cheongjeong* and *yeobeop* (KBCEG 2006, 98, 100). Against the backdrop of the decline of Buddhist cuisine in contemporary temples, culinary experts, consumers, the state, business, and the Buddhist establishment are involved in reinventing temple food in the name of its rediscovery and preservation.

The Emergence of Individual Buddhist Culinary Experts

Just as national cookbooks in contemporary India can be categorized as the literature of exile and nostalgia that is usually written by authors who reside outside India (Appadurai 1988, 18), the reinvention of Buddhist temple food as indigenous tradition in contemporary Korea implies its codification by nuns, monks, and lay experts who commonly reside outside the conventional monastic context (in remote mountains). Prior to the publication of Buddhist cookbooks in the 2000s,[13] popular texts focusing on the subject were rare. One exception was Kim Yeon-sik, a former Buddhist monk, who has written on Buddhist cuisine since 1971 when he first published temple food recipes in the *Busan Ilbo* (April 16, 1971).[14] This absence of texts reflects the legacy of monastic life in Korean Buddhism, as mentioned earlier, which has elevated the importance of meditation and scriptural studies and neglected ritual performance. In this ascetic monastic culture, cooking has not been considered a prestigious activity, and therefore has been relegated to novice monks and *bosal* (lay women) at the bottom of the temple hierarchy (Buswell 1992a, 117, 118). Dietary knowledge in general and recipes in particular have been orally transmitted from one generation to the next mostly through informal learning and practices (General Affairs Office 2006, 7; Kim 1995, 11). As late as the early 1990s, the Bohyeonhoe, an association of Buddhist nuns, was one of a few venues for preserving temple food.[15] Another rare venue in the 1990s was a dozen vegetarian restaurants inspired by Buddhist cuisine.[16]

It was not until the 1990s that a few monks and nuns of a younger generation, who cross the boundary between monasteries and the larger society, began to draw increasing mass media attention to their research on temple food, due to its appeal to the popular concern for health and economic security. In late 1992, monk Jeogmun, a sophomore at Seungga Daehak (a Buddhist Seminary) at the time, founded the first Traditional Buddhist Temple Food Culture Studies Center, composed of his fellow students at the seminary.[17] Since then, as the director of the center, he has promoted the preservation of temple food and its "scientific studies" through publications, lectures, exhibitions, and regular cooking classes.[18] He became the abbot of the Sudosa temple in Pyeongtaek, Gyeonggi-do province in 2003 and made this temple a major site of annual temple food festivals.[19] In 1993, nun Seonjae, a student of the Buddhist Seminary at the time, wrote her thesis on Buddhist temple food culture, and began in 1995 a two-year long Buddhist cooking show on the Buddhist Television Network. She has a unique family background, with her maternal grandmother being a court lady of the royal kitchen in the Joseon Dynasty. In 2001, she established the Seonjae Temple Food Studies Academy in the Buddhist Nuns' Center (Biguni Hoegwan) in Seoul, and has taught regular cooking classes there and given lectures outside the Center. She has also been an adjunct professor at the Home Economics Department at Dongguk University, to train experts on Buddhist cuisine.[20] In 1995, Kim Yeon-sik wrote a paper exploring the potential of temple food for advancing the restaurant business at the Graduate School of Industrial Education at Chung-Ang University in Seoul, and presented it at a seminar organized at the university the following year.[21] Nun Daean, an abbot of Geumseoam temple in Gyeongsangnam-do province, founded the Geumdang Temple Food Studies Center to research and teach about temple food in the provincial area and beyond. She became interested in temple food in order to cure her own illnesses, and studied traditional medicine in China for six years.[22] Nun Hongseung, a former officer of the Academy of Dissemination of Buddhism in the Jogye Order, opened her temple food studies center in Seoul in late 2005.[23] She has taught cooking classes and given lectures in Seoul and provincial areas, and in 2008, she moved to Busan to continue her activities at the newly opened Asia Seon Culture Center.[24] As these experts have gained media attention and offered regular cooking classes, other lay practitioners have emerged to publish books on Buddhist temple food and run specialty restaurants.

The current revival of Buddhist temple food by priests and lay practitioners indicates its reinvention in the following senses. First, Buddhist temple food is gaining popular attention outside the monastic settings where it had previously been ignored. According to the national survey mentioned earlier, most of the thirty-one temples surveyed do not pay attention to the transmission of temple food to the younger generation of nuns and monks. A majority of these temples neither offer Buddhist cuisine classes (83.3 percent) nor intend to establish such classes in the future (70.4 percent) (KBCEG 2006, 110). This institutional indifference has been the main cause of the decline in temple food in a rapidly industrializing Korea. The national survey also documents that monks and nuns are not directly involved in cooking in a majority of the thirty-one temples, and *bosal* are entirely or primarily responsible for cooking. While there is a significant gender difference between the monasteries and the nunneries,[25] the combination of institutional negligence and lack of culinary practices among monks and nuns themselves, contribute to the marginalization of temple food.

Second, those five leading experts discussed above do not concur as to what constitutes the body of temple food. My individual interviews with three of them reveal that they harbor different views concerning how much innovation is acceptable while still maintaining the integrity of temple food and how Buddhist teaching guides the preparation and consumption of temple food (beyond mere vegetarianism).[26] Despite institutional attempts to standardize and codify temple food recipes (HED 2006; KBCEG 2006), some experts insist on the traditional recipes collected exclusively from old monks and nuns, whereas others are willing to incorporate fusion dishes. For example, Kim Yeon-sik maintains the orthodox view of what constitutes Buddhist temple food and is critical of other practitioners who incorporate contemporary innovations or fusion dishes into it. Nun Seonjae is somewhat more open to innovation but insists on the strict observance of the injunction against the use of *osinchae* and chemical or artificial ingredients. She also emphasizes the importance of attitudes and state of mind in preparing and consuming temple food; hence it is not desirable to cook and sell temple food for profit; nor is it desirable to consume it while occupied with vicious or destructive ideas. Nun Hong-seung is more active (than the other two experts) about integrating fusion dishes and new ingredients (like colorful peppers and broccoli) into temple food.[27] She also offers a special class designed for chefs and restaurateurs who approach temple food as a business idea. These heterogeneous views are reflected in the content of the recent compilation of the standard recipes for temple food mentioned earlier. It contains not only traditional dishes using old Buddhist food ingredients such as lotus roots and leaves, mushrooms, and soybean products, but also such popular non-Buddhist dishes as *gimbap* (seaweed rice rolls) with tofu in place of meat, or *tangsuyuk* (sweet and sour pork) with mushrooms instead of pork (HED 2006, 49–52).

The differences among the leading experts coexist with their shared interests in preserving and disseminating temple food as a valuable element of Korean culture, and its relevance for contemporary Koreans. Hence, they hope to promote systematic studies to excavate buried knowledge and preserve disappearing knowledge about temple food, and reach out to the wider public through diverse forms of mass media, ranging from newspapers to the internet. At the same time, while they have joined government-sponsored projects to promote temple food, they are cautious about the negative implications of such projects, including the loss of Buddhist teaching and spirit through excessive commercialization and popularization.

Third, as amply illustrated by current publications, temple food tends to be colorful and sophisticated in its visual presentation, using natural plant colors and decorative displays of dishes. This visual emphasis is present even in simple dishes using traditional Buddhist ingredients. The range of innovations in the reinvention of temple food demonstrates that culinary practitioners are actively accommodating urban middle-class tastes and practical needs. In the era of globalization, the willingness of leading culinary experts to innovate and learn from non-Buddhist culinary practices has made the tradition of temple food a fluid category, rather than an exclusionary nativist one.

Popular Interest in Health and Economic Security

Widespread public concerns about unhealthy processed food and fast food lie at the heart of the growing popularity of Buddhist temple food as an alternative health food or even as preventive medicine. According to a report published by the Ministry of Health and Welfare (1997, 2002),[28] there has been a significant dietary shift among Koreans, indicated by the decreasing consumption of grains and the increasing consumption of fat and meat. Between 1969 and 1994, calories from carbohydrates diminished from 80 percent to 65 percent, whereas those from fat more than doubled from 7 percent to 19 percent. The average per capita annual consumption of rice, the staple food, decreased from 120 kilograms in 1990 to 77 kilograms in 2007.[29] According to statistics compiled by the Korean Meat Processing Industry Association, the consumption of meat steadily increased by an annual average of 7 percent between 1987 and 2006, with the exceptions of 1998 and 2004, reflecting the scare of mad cow disease.[30] As a result, average daily per capita meat consumption more than doubled from 47 grams in 1986 to 107 grams in 2002.[31]

With these drastic shifts in dietary practices, Koreans have encountered escalating problems of diet-related illness and obesity since the 1990s. The most common illnesses among Koreans now include cancer, heart disease, and diabetes related to the over-consumption of fat, refined sugar, and salt, and the under-consumption of complex carbohydrates.[32] In the 2000s, breast cancer has ranked first among female cancer patients, and rectal cancer has ranked second among all cancer patients. Overall, breast cancer, prostate cancer, and rectal cancer, which are associated with high incomes and the aforementioned dietary change, have increased far more rapidly than stomach cancer, liver cancer and uterine cancer, which are linked to low incomes and poor hygiene.[33] In line with this epidemiological shift, obesity among Koreans has drastically increased. In 2005, the Health Insurance Public Corporation reported that about 31 percent of the adult population over 40 years old were obese (as defined by a body mass index of 25 and higher), as a result of a rapid increase in obesity over the past three years,[34] and 43 percent of the entire population is either overweight or obese.[35]

The global outbreak of mad cow disease and avian flu and the local outbreak of contaminated food have sensitized the Korean public to food safety.[36] The local spread of atopic allergies has also contributed to public concern about food safety. There are a growing number of children suffering from atopic symptoms, which are associated with processed food in particular and environmental pollution in general. A national survey conducted by the Korean Association for Child Allergy and Respiratory Disease Studies reported that 25 percent of elementary school respondents and 13 percent of junior high school respondents were diagnosed for atopic dermatitis.[37] As a result, according to a national survey conducted by Research Plus, a professional polling institute, almost 62 percent of 1,000 adult respondents replied that they believed the food they consumed daily was "unsafe," and only 11 percent replied that it was "safe."[38]

The array of negative health consequences, coupled with shifting dietary habits and the problem of food safety discussed above, has stirred numerous Koreans to reflect on the safety and quality of the food they consume daily, and has sensitized them to pay attention to alternatives to mass-produced processed food. In particular, mothers who are still primarily responsible for the care of their families look for dietary remedies for ailments suffered by their children and other family members. A growing number of middle-class mothers are frequent food cooperatives specializing in organic and healthy food, which have been spreading in urban areas.[39] Capitalizing on this popular concern, urban supermarkets in Korea now commonly carry organic vegetables, fruits, and grains or Korean agricultural products that have been promoted as being tastier and healthier than foreign imports requiring long-distance transportation.

Appropriating the widespread public concern about food safety and health, the mass media have disseminated useful (and not so useful) information about food and health problems to attract viewers and readers. Large food manufacturers also take advantage of this pervasive concern and promote various food commodities in the name of health and well-being. The popular interest in health converges with the leading culinary experts' shared view on the relevance of temple food for contemporary Koreans. Yet the mass media have been more than a passive broker between consumers and Buddhist culinary experts. In collaboration with the food industry and related retail businesses, the mass media have represented temple food as the indigenous example of "slow food" that relies on natural condiments and flavor enhancers, seasonal fruits and vegetables, and fermented and preserved food ingredients beneficial for health.[40]

This aggressive marketing reflects local appropriation of the global spread of the "slow food movement," which began in Bra, Italy, in the late 1980s (Petrini 2001) and was introduced to Korea between 2002 and 2003. The introduction of the slow food movement developed into active promotion of the "well-being lifestyle" or "slow living" by business interests and the mass media. By 2003, the "well-being lifestyle" had become very trendy.[41] Hotels have featured food festivals and seasonal and weekend events to introduce Buddhist temple food to middle-class consumers searching for well-being and a higher quality of life. Major department stores have created special corners for temple food, in addition to organic food, carrying various products ranging from fermented bean paste to preserved pickles and snacks. Big food companies have competed to attract consumers with trendy temple food events and cooking classes.[42]

Urban middle-class mothers take courses on Buddhist cuisine not only in Buddhist organizations[43] but also in non-sectarian public and private cultural centers located downtown and in their neighborhoods.[44] These classes teach diverse recipes along with varying degrees of emphasis on Buddhist ideas about food, eating, health, and life; they are offered at various levels, depending on the level of culinary skills necessary for recipes. While these classes observe the basic tenets of vegetarianism and avoidance of the *osinchae*, those who take the classes are free to innovate and selectively practice what they learn. This flexibility is fairly common because a majority of students in the classes are not Buddhists. It is noteworthy that temple food is appealing to the general public as a healthy alternative, regardless of religious orientations. According to some Buddhist culinary experts, roughly 60 percent of

students in their cooking classes are Protestant, and approximately 15 percent are Catholics.[45] During my own fieldwork in nun Hongseung's Temple
Food Studies Center, I found that a majority of students were non-Buddhist,
whereas Buddhist believers made up about 40 percent of students in cooking
classes.[46]

While married women make up the largest group among students of
Buddhist cooking classes, young or middle-aged men with entrepreneurial
interests constitute a significant minority. Unlike urban middle-class mothers,
they study Buddhist cooking to become a specialist chef, open a specialty
restaurant or incorporate Buddhist dishes into already-existing menus in
their restaurants. To accommodate this specific business concern, some of
the temple food study centers mentioned earlier offer special or intensive
courses for this entrepreneurial group. In light of the current well-being trend
and the ever-growing practice of dining out in urban Korea, such considerations appear to be practical, if they can capture their customers' capricious
palates.[47] The economic potential of temple food is particularly appealing
to Koreans because of the employment structure in the country; among
industrialized countries, Korea has one of the lowest percentages of people
employed by large corporations, and one of the highest percentages of self-
employed workers.[48] This self-employed group has increased in the aftermath
of the Asian economic crisis (1997–1998), which aggravated employment
insecurity in the name of flexible labor markets in this era of globalization.
This means a large number of Koreans are faced with unstable and insecure
employment, and therefore, small business remains one of the few viable
employment options.

The Government's Interest in the Economic Potential of Temple Food and Development of the "Han Brand"

The popular interests in health and economic security that have contributed
to the popularity of temple food converge with the government's interest
in keeping the body of its population healthy and productive. Sharing the
culinary experts' interest in preserving and disseminating temple food,
the government is also interested in its promotion as a valuable element
of Korean culture to reaffirm Korean identity in the era of globalization.
For example, it has sponsored "temple stay programs" to educate young
Koreans, who are perceived to be *westernized*. This political interest in
Korean identity resonates with a populace searching for stability and
meaning in the midst of globalization marked by unstable employment and
westernization. NGOs also use temple visits to educate foreigners about
Korean culture.[49]

The governmental interest in temple food, however, is primarily economic (unlike its political interest in group cohesion and ensuring loyalty) in this era of "global cultural economy" (Appadurai 1996, 27). The central government has been keen on the economic potential of temple food as a cultural commodity tied to tourism, identifying it as the new strategic industry that would lead economic growth in the twenty-first century.[50] Since the late 1990s, the Korean Tourism Public Corporation (KTPC) has paid attention to Buddhist rituals and practices in general, and temple food in particular, as a cultural resource to be marketed for the promotion of international and domestic tourism. It has encouraged Buddhist orders to develop Buddhist cultural products. In 1998, the KTPC collaborated with Bongwonsa temple to perform *yeongsanjae*, a forgotten ritual that symbolically enacts the Buddha's address to the laity, which was designated as an Intangible Cultural Treasure and an experiential commodity presented to foreign tourists. This revived performance was accompanied by the display and tasting of temple food.[51] For tourist consumption, the ritual was expediently reduced to a thirty-five-minute performance from its original three-day version. In 1999, expanding on the idea of cultural products marketed to tourists, the KTPC attempted to turn Buddhist rituals in major temples in the Seoul area into tourist commodities.[52] During the 2002 World Cup Soccer event, it asked twenty-five major Buddhist temples nationwide to host temple stay programs that included the tasting of temple food as an integral part of consuming the experiential commodity.[53] In addition to international sports events, international political conferences such as the ASEM were used as occasions for introducing temple food to a wider array of domestic and foreign visitors by bringing together the Buddhist establishment, businesses, and leading culinary experts. Between 2004 and 2006, the government subsidized the Jogye Order's project to build a *"Jeontong Bulgyo Munhwa Saneop Jiwon Ssenteo* (Traditional Buddhist Culture Industry Support Center)," equipped with a meditation center, performance center, and research facilities, in order to develop cultural products to be marketed. The government funded approximately half of the 25 billion Korean won invested in the construction of the support center.[54]

Behind the series of government efforts to develop Buddhist cultural commodities, there are two significant sociopolitical developments that allow for the rise of Buddhist culture in general, and temple food in particular, as a tourist commodity: (1) the increase of leisure time in the 2000s among the employed, with the recent adoption of a five-day work week; and (2) administrative decentralization pursued through the strengthening of *jibang jachi* (local government autonomy) since the 1990s. The growth of leisure time has led to the expansion of leisure and entertainment industries, including tourism. To stressed urbanites, Buddhist temples, usually located in mountains, are appealing sites for restful vacations. The revival of local rule in

1991 with the election of local assembly members[55] has also facilitated the growth of diverse interests in local culture, primarily because of the potential for producing tourist commodities. Local governments invented regional food festivals such as the Grand Gangwon Province Potato Festival, Grand Southern Province Food Festival, Busan Jagalchi Cultural Tourism Festival, Hanbat Food Festival, and Halla Cultural Festival. Since 1994, the KTPC has sponsored these folk food festivals as a regular feature of local culture festivals, held every October. In particular, the Grand Southern Province Food Festival, organized near famous old Buddhist temples like Songgwangsa temple and Seonamsa temple, has featured a display of temple food. In 2002, the local government sponsored a symposium to develop the southern food as a brand.[56] Since 2004, Gyeonggi-do province has developed "slow food villages" to market local specialty food as an integral part of its "well-being tourism" industry. Ten villages were chosen for their specialty food items, including Sudosa temple mentioned earlier, which has become a center of the temple food festival. These slow villages have been popular among Seoulites as a weekend retreat course; the number of visitors to these villages grew from 46,000 in 2004, to 240,000 in 2005, and the province expected over 1 million visitors in 2006.[57]

The (central) government's interest in temple food as a unique *munhwa sangpum* (cultural commodity) evolved into the project to develop the "Han brand." *Han* refers to Koreanness and the brand is a vehicle to sell Korean cultural products in the global market. This project is inspired by the unexpected economic success of Korean popular culture—television dramas, popular music, and film—in the late 1990s and early 2000s, which began in China, Taiwan, and Japan, and has spread to Vietnam and other Southeast and West Asian countries (Bak 2005). This phenomenon, commonly called the "Korean Wave" or *hallyu*, is crucial to the thinking behind the Han-brand project.[58] In the global market, where ideas and images circulate transnationally along with people, money, and other tangible material goods, a unique cultural identity and tradition can be a source of value-added products. Under the project, the Han brand encompasses a range of unique cultural items, including *hansik* (Korean food), *hanbok* (Korean clothes), *hangeul* (the Korean alphabet), *hanok* (Korean architecture), *hanguk eumak* (Korean music), and *hanji* (Korean paper). Like any other branded commodities, the list of the Han brand can expand and shift altogether because brand capitalism is about the accumulation of profit through selling abstract ideas about, and images of, success, glamour, happiness, and sophistication, rather than selling specific and fixed material products (Klein 1999). In 2006, the Korean government began to explore ways to brand temple food and encourage the Jogye Order and scholarly community to develop value-added cultural products (KBCEG 2006). In response, the Jogye Order established the Traditional

Buddhist Temple Food Culture Preservation Society to exhibit temple food at the Han Brand Expo, held in September, 2006.[59]

The government's economic interest in temple food led to collaboration between the KTPC and the Buddhist establishment around high-profile international or local events through which temple food is publicized and the governmental support for instituting some elements of the infrastructure of the Buddhist culture industry. Although it is rather ambiguous at the current stage of the Han brand project who will be the main beneficiary of the economic effort to capitalize on temple food, there is potential for economic conflict between the Buddhist establishment and the tourism industry that are brought together by the government for the project. The bigger the economic success of the temple food marketing and sales, the sharper the competition between these two actors is likely to be. It is also likely that these two actors will compete for control over the content of temple food as a raw material for producing value-added products. If this competition indeed develops, the heterogeneous views of the body of temple food held by the leading Buddhist culinary experts can turn into an intellectual tool to wage a fight in the economic (culture) war. As discussed ahead, the Buddhist establishment has begun to assert its position as a major player in capitalizing on temple food as Korean tradition.

The Buddhist Establishment's Interest in Strengthening Its Influence

Belatedly responding to the mass media and the government's attention to temple food, the Buddhist Order of Jogye joined the reinvention of temple food to strengthen Buddhism's influence in the larger society. It established the Academy of Dissemination of Buddhism and has collaborated with *Hanguk Bulgyo Jeontong Munhwa Cheheom Saeopdan* (the Group for Korean Buddhist Traditional Culture Experience).[60] The academy has developed various types of temple retreat programs to attract urban families, looking for affordable leisure activities. Building on the experience of accommodating foreign tourists during international events, temples have hosted weekend camps and vacation camps, which include meditation practices and the eating of temple food. The academy also developed temple stay programs for school children during their summer and winter vacations.[61] Major temples have begun to provide both the Buddhist and non-Buddhist public with ingenious programs that combine temple retreats or visits with film festivals, rock music concerts, and therapy sessions beyond the established practices of meditation and sampling of temple food.[62] In response to the popularity of these programs, Haeinsa temple, a major temple renowned for its strong tradition of meditation, held a big entertainment festival that featured a fashion show, music concert, dance performance, and poetry reading, along with Buddhist temple food and meditation.[63] Similarly, Woljeongsa temple and Sangwonsa temple in Gangwon-do province hosted large-scale Buddhist cultural festivals that drew over 100,000 visitors.[64] This type of cultural festival emerged as a common feature of Buddhist temple events held in autumn.[65]

Under the auspices of the government, the Jogye Order and its culinary experts participated in such business events as the World Cultures Exposition and Food Expositions.[66] The Buddhist Broadcasting System worked with Jay Convention Inc. to organize the 2006 Korean Buddhism Expo to promote Buddhist culture and develop cultural products to be marketed.[67] In August 2006, the Jogye Order organized a seminar on the popularization of temple food and announced its plan to open temple food specialty restaurants in order to develop temple food as a tourist commodity.[68] It also brought individual culinary experts together to form the aforementioned Traditional Buddhist Temple Food Culture Preservation Society to facilitate the standardization of temple food textbooks and educate temple food experts. The society also planned to construct a temple food culture center to disseminate information among the wider public.[69]

CONCLUSION

The reinvention of Buddhist temple food as tradition in contemporary Korea reveals the complex interplay between popular concerns for health and economic security and the interests of the government, business, and the Buddhist establishment, in the service of larger national and transnational politics. These concerns and interests converge, and at times diverge. The popular concerns converge with the interests of the Buddhist establishment to promote its culture and expand its influence. These political interests of the establishment are inevitably entangled with its economic interest in capitalizing on temple food. On the economic front, the establishment can be drawn into a conflict with the tourism industry, with whom it has collaborated in the initial development of the Buddhist culture industry. At the same time, Buddhist political and economic interests dovetail with the government's interest in developing Buddhist cultural commodities that can be competitively sold in a global market. This governmental interest converges with the interests of the tourism industry to reap profits domestically and internationally from leisure and entertainment activities. Yet the salient economic interests of the state, as well as the institutional interests of the Buddhist establishment, tend to be at odds with the culinary experts' interest in preserving the integrity of temple food.

The cultural politics of reinventing temple food generates different meanings of tradition for the various parties involved. To grassroots Koreans, traditional temple food means a valuable alternative to unhealthy processed food and the *westernization* of dietary habits, and a useful business idea for a specialty restaurant in an era of increasing employment insecurity. For the government, which has a strong legacy of directing economic development, this tradition means primarily a strategic cultural asset to be capitalized on as the national economy has shifted from labor-intensive manufacturing to capital-intensive manufacturing, in addition to information and culture industries. Secondly, it signifies a source of Korean identity to be reaffirmed in the age of globalization, particularly for the younger generation who grew up in industrialized Korea. For the Buddhist establishment, temple food represents a valuable legacy, which can strengthen Buddhism's influence in the larger society.

The close collaboration between the government and the Buddhist establishment in the cultural politics of reinventing temple food has its historical precedents. Over a millennium ago, Buddhism as the state ideology enjoyed immense material and political support from royal courts in exchange for its promotion of the state's welfare. The most visible aspects of Buddhist culture in contemporary Korea are usually products of the symbiotic relationship between Buddhism and the state, including the idea and practices of *hoguk bulgyo* (state-protecting Buddhism). In contemporary Korea, Buddhist monks not only perform mandatory military service, but the Jogye Order has also maintained *hoguk seungdan* (the Monks' Militia for National Defense), which all monks are required to join (Buswell 1992b, 2). In the era of globalization, Korean Buddhism aspires to regain a position of sociopolitical influence by serving the governmental interest in developing distinct cultural commodities. Indeed, the Jogye Order has tried to revive its popular influence during the past decade or so. For example, it repackaged its *yeondeung chukje* (lotus lanterns festival) as a national festival reaching out to the general public beyond Buddhist believers.[70] In 2007, the number of participants in this festival reached 300,000. The Jogye Order aspires to transform this festival into a distinct Korean festival open to all peoples in the world.[71]

In the midst of converging and diverging interests involved in reinventing temple food, the agency of the grassroots population lies in the concerns for health and economic security. Although the production and consumption of temple food would involve culinary and dietary pleasure, what has popularized temple food is not so much pleasure as concerns for health and economic security. These urgent and serious concerns triggered the mass media, food industry, and related businesses to capitalize on them. Responding to the growing popular appeal of temple food and building on the economic success of the Korean Wave, the government has appropriated temple food to reinvigorate its economic program in the age of globalization, making local cultural differences a profitable resource.

NOTES

1. This chapter was previously published with the same title in *Korea Journal*, *48*(4), 147–180. The original work was supported by the Jane Rosenthal Heimerdinger Fund, the Carolyn Grant '36 Endowment, and a Mellon Faculty Research Award at Vassar College.

2. This approach is different from historical accounts of the development of Korean Buddhist temple food and therefore this article is not concerned with the comparison of Korean temple food with temple food in other Asian societies.

3. According to my survey of major newspapers' articles on Buddhist cuisine between January 1990 and January 2008, the number of substantial articles on the subject multiplied in the 2000s. Around 98 percent of the total 722 articles from the major national newspapers surveyed were published in the 2000s.

4. Yet, Hobsbawm and Ranger (1983) consider the importance of popular sentiments regarding the effectiveness of invented traditions when they write that "it also seems clear that the most successful examples of manipulation are those which exploit practices which clearly meet a felt—not necessarily a clearly understood—need among particular bodies of people" (307).

5. For the discussion of postcolonial agency, see Homi Bhabha's "Of Mimicry and Man" and "Interrogating Identity: Franz Fanon and the Postcolonial Prerogative" in Bhabha (1994).

6. The first festival was organized to commemorate Buddha on a full-moon night of the first lunar month of the lunar calendar, and the second one was held to wish prosperity for the royal court under the auspices of indigenous Korean spirits in the eleventh lunar month of the calendar (Buswell 2005, 9).

7. This meditative tradition *seon* was introduced to Korea by a *Silla* monk in the late seventh century, but it remained subordinate to the earlier tradition of scholasticism and did not become dominant until the thirteenth century. By the beginning of the sixteenth century, however, the meditative tradition overshadowed all other branches of Korean Buddhism (Buswell 1992a, 21–22, 1992b, 9).

8. This is "a name used erratically for more than one plant in the onion family." It occasionally refers to a form of garlic that has chive-like leaves with a milder flavor than garlic, and tiny bulbs forming from the flower head. It grows wild throughout Europe, often in dry or rugged places. See Davidson (2006, 667).

9. Persian dropwort grows in Iran and Afghanistan and was called *augwa* in medieval Persian. It is similar to a Korean vegetable, *minari*, which has a strong scent and flavor and therefore is commonly used in fish soup or stew.

10. The commonly used condiments are roasted sesame oil, salt, soy sauce, sugar, red pepper paste and powder, sesame salt, fermented soybean paste, black sesame seeds, and barley glucose syrup (KBCEG 2006, 74).

11. As of 2004, the Jogye Order, the largest order representing over 90 percent of the Buddhist population in Korea, had approximately 12,000 monks and nuns (*Kyunghyang Daily News*, July 2, 2004). According to a Jogye Order census, in 1986, it controlled 1,628 temples and had ordained some 7,708 monks and 4,153 nuns (Buswell 1992a, 34).

12. This information is based on my conversation with the nun Hongseung in June of 2007. During that month, I took an intensive cooking course with her and conducted fieldwork at her temple food research center in Yangjae-dong, Seoul.

13. For example, see Jeokmun (2000), Jeong (2000), Seonjae (2000), Kim Yeon-sik (2002), Yi (2002), Daean (2003; 2008), and Hongseung (2003).

14. This information is based on my conversation with Kim Yeon-sik in July 2008 and *Kyunghyang Daily News*, March 8, 2002.

15. *Hankyoreh*, November 25, 1992

16. *Munhwa Ilbo*, April 23, 1996. The original model for this category of restaurant was a specialty restaurant that Kim Yeon-sik opened in 1980 and has run ever since. When he opened this restaurant, he was criticized by the Jogye Order and individual monks who viewed his unusual activity as "unfit" for a Buddhist monk. Finally, he left the order and later joined the Taego Order and has also been pursuing his career as a painter. Currently, he is the Chair of the Department of Temple Food Culture Studies at Tongsan Buddhist College. This information is based on my conversation with him in July 2008.

17. *Hankyoreh*, November 25, 1992.

18. *Hankyoreh*, May 16, 1996; *Kyunghyang Daily News*, May 16, 2002.

19. *Kyunghyang Daily News*, November 7, 2003.

20. This information about her activities is based on my interview with her in July 2008. See also *Kyunghyang Daily News*, May 16, 2002 and *Hankyoreh*, March 29, 2006.

21. This information is based on my conversation with him in July 2008. See also *Munhwa Ilbo*, April 23, 1996.

22. *Seoul Shinmun*, May 21, 2004.

23. *Munhwa Ilbo*, May 23, 2007.

24. This information is based on my interview with her in June 2007 and our phone conversation in July 2008.

25. Cooking is done by monks only in 1.6 percent of the monasteries; in 28.6 percent of the monasteries monks collaborate with bosals for cooking. In contrast, nuns cook their own meals in 42.9 percent of the nunneries, and in 28.6 percent of the nunneries they collaborate with bosals (KBCEG 2006, 90).

26. Newspaper articles on these five experts also corroborate my findings. Because of different ideas and views, they have not maintained a regular professional network to develop collaboration except for a 2006 seminar sponsored by the Ministry of Culture and Tourism and the Culture and Tourism Committee of the National Assembly. For this seminar, see General Affairs Office (2006).

27. Similarly, monk Jeokmun stressed the importance of using natural ingredients to make healthful food regardless of their origins (*Hankook Ilbo*, December 20, 2002).

28. Quoted in KBCEG (2006, 28).

29. *Chungbuk Media*, June 8, 2008; *Finance and Economy News*, January 18, 2008.

30. *Seoul Economic Daily*, May 28, 2008.

31. *Maeil Business Newspaper*, February 3, 2004.

32. KBCEG 2006, 29; *Oh My News*, October 22, 2005.

33. *Kukmin Daily*, January 7, 2008; *Seoul Shinmun*, October 22, 2007; *Kangwon Ilbo*, September 6, 2007; *Dong-A Ilbo*, June 20, 2007.

34. *Kyunghyang Daily News*, September 20, 2005.

35. *Munhwa Ilbo*, January 23, 2006.

36. *Korea Economic Daily*, June 11, 2004; *Dong-A Ilbo*, December 25, 2003; *Hankyoreh*, September 28, 2001.

37. *Money Today*, March 28, 2007.

38. *Hankyoreh*, June 15, 2004.

39. The number of food cooperatives that directly link urban consumers to rural producers multiplied in the 2000s and their membership surpassed 100,000 in 2003. The production of environment-friendly agricultural products increased tenfold between 2000 and 2003 (*Hankyoreh*, June 15, 2004).

40. *Kyunghyang Daily News*, April 2, 2001; *Hankook Ilbo*, December 20, 2002; *Seoul Shinmun*, September 3, 2003; *Kyunghyang Daily News*, October 31, 2003; *Kyunghyang Daily News*, November 28, 2003; *Munhwa Ilbo*, April 16, 2004.

41. *Hankook Ilbo*, January 16, 2004; *Seoul Shinmun*, May 21, 2004; *Korea Economic Daily*, February 27, 2004. The "well-being lifestyle" emerged as a trend in 2003 and has been a slogan for a wide range of commercials.

42. *Segye Times*, September 30, 2005; *Seoul Economic Daily*, August 15, 2006.

43. For example, the major Buddhist organizations include the National Buddhist Nuns' Center in Seoul, Heungbeop Temple in Busan, and several temple food studies centers established by the aforementioned Buddhist culinary experts.

44. *Maeil Business Newspaper*, February 25, 2000. By 2007, temple food cooking classes were no longer an exclusively urban phenomenon. An Agricultural Technology Center began to offer such classes for local residents (*Incheon Times*, April 16, 2007).

45. *Kyunghyang Daily News*, May 16, 2002.

46. This information is based on my interviews with the nun and her assistants for cooking classes in June 2007.

47. *Korea Economic Daily*, August 28, 2006.

48. KEF and *Chosun Ilbo* (2007).

49. For instance, the Taegu chapter of People to People organized a visit to a Buddhist temple for American GIs' stationed in Korea, as an integral part of its annual local event to expose GIs to Korean culture (*Maeil Shinmun*, October 23, 2006).

50. *Segye Times*, February 28, 2005. The government tries to develop Korea as a major stopover site for European tourists headed to Australia, New Zealand, and the Pacific area. Among such tourists, women and retirees are targeted for their interests in health and food, and they are provided with specialty Korean food like temple food, herbal medicine, and royal court cuisine.

51. *Dong-A Ilbo*, December 7, 1997.

52. Jogyesa temple, Bongeunsa temple and Hwagyesa temple in the Jogye Order were selected, and Bongwonsa temple in the Taego Order was selected (*Munhwa Ilbo*, August 6, 1999).

53. *Hankook Ilbo*, February 8, 2002.

54. *Seoul Shinmun*, March 10, 2004; *Korea Economic Daily*, December 23, 2004.

55. The local rule was initially introduced in South Korea in 1952 but suppressed until the early 1990s. The revival of local assembly elections was followed by that of governors and mayors in 1995.

56. *Hankyoreh*, October 11, 1996; *Munhwa Ilbo*, September 19, 1997; *Kukmin Daily*, October 9, 2002; *Dong-A Ilbo*, October 1, 2005.

57. Hankook Ilbo, April 5, 2004; Korea Herald Business, April 7, 2004; Financial News, May 24, 2005; *Munhwa Ilbo*, July 7, 2006. In 2005, this tourism industry increased the aggregate rural household income to 2.7 billion won from 600 million won in 2004.

58. See Bak (2005), Yu et al. (2005), Kim (2006), and Kang (2006).

59. *Dong-A Ilbo*, September 21, 2006.

60. *Hankyoreh*, October 3, 2002.

61. *Seoul Shinmun*, January 5, 2006.

62. *Segye Times*, July 29, 2004; *Hankook Ilbo*, June 24, 2005.

63. *Hankyoreh*, May 17, 2007.

64. *Korea Economic Daily*, September 26, 2007.

65. *Kyunghyang Daily News*, October 6, 2007.

66. *Financial News*, May 16, 2003.

67. *Korea Economic Daily*, March 8, 2006; *Seoul Shinmun*, March 9, 2006.

68. *Hankyoreh*, August 30, 2006.

69. *Hankyoreh*, January 31, 2007; *Kyunghyang Daily News*, May 31, 2007.

70. *Dong-A Daily*, May 12, 1996.

71. *Korea Economic Daily*, May 17, 2007.

REFERENCES

Appadurai, A. (1981). Gastro-politics in Hindu South Asia. *American Ethnologist*, *8*(3), 494–511.

Appadurai, A. (1988). How to make a national cuisine: Cookbooks in contemporary India. *Comparative Studies in Society and History*, *30*(1), 3–24.

Appadurai, A. (1996). *Modernity at Large: Cultural Dimensions of Globalization*. Minneapolis, London: University of Minnesota Press.

Bak, J. (2005). *Hallyu, geullobeol sidae-ui munhwa gyeongjaengnyeok [The Korean Wave, Cultural Competitiveness in the Age of Globalization]*. (3rd ed.). Seoul: Samsung Economic Research Institute.

Bhabha, H. (1994). *The Location of Culture*. London, New York: Routledge.

Buswell Jr., R. (Ed.). (1992a). *The Zen Monastic Experience: Buddhist Practice in Contemporary Korea*. Princeton, NJ: Princeton University Press.

Buswell Jr., R. (1992b). *Tracing Back the Radiance: Chinul's Korean Way of Zen.* Honolulu: University of Hawaii Press.

Buswell Jr., R. (2005). *Currents and Countercurrents: Korean Influences on the East Asian Buddhist Traditions.* Honolulu: University of Hawaii Press.

Chang, K. (Ed.) (1977). *Food in Chinese Culture: Anthropological and Historical Perspectives.* New Haven, London: Yale University Press.

Davidson, A. (2006). *The Oxford Companion to Food.* (2nd ed.). Oxford: Oxford University Press.

Daean. (2003). *Maeum-ui sal-kkaji ppaejuneun sachal eumsik daieoteu [Buddhist temple food diet].* Seoul: JoongAng M&B.

Daean. (2008). *Siktak wi-ui myeongsang [Meditation on a Dining Table].* Seoul: Ancient Future.

General Affairs Office. (2006). *Sachal eumsik-ui ususeong mit daejunghwa bangan [Benefits of Temple Food and a Plan for Its Popularization].* Proceedings of the Seminar on Temple Food, Jogye Order, Seoul, Korea.

Goody, J. (1982). *Cooking, Cuisine, and Class: A Study in Comparative Sociology.* Cambridge: Cambridge University Press.

Gusfield, J. (1967). Tradition and Modernity: Misplaced Polarities in the Study of Social Change. *The American Journal of Sociology, 72,* 351–362.

Hobsbawm, E., & Ranger, T. (Eds.) (1983). *The Invention of Tradition.* Cambridge: Cambridge University Press.

Home Economics Department (HED). (2006). *Sachal eumsik joribeop jeongni: jaryo mit joribeop tongil [Temple food recipes collection: Unifying ingredients and recipes].* Seoul: Dongguk University.

Hongseung. (2003). *Nokcha-wa chaesik [Green Tea and Vegetarian Food].* Seoul: Uri Chulpansa.

Jeokmun. (2000). Jeontong sachal eumsik [Traditional temple food]. *Public Nutrition, 25.*4(238), 26–33.

Jeong, S. (2000). *Sansa-e gamyeon teukbyeolhan sikdan-i itta [There are Special Menus in Mountainous Temples].* Seoul: Mosaek.

Kang, C. (2006). *Hallyu jeon munga gangcheolgeun-ui hallyu iyagi: hally-ui geunwon-eseo miraekkaji [A Story of the Korean Wave: From its Origin to Its Future].* Seoul: Ichae.

Khare, R. (Ed.). (1992). *The Eternal Food: Gastronomic Ideas and Experiences of Hindus and Buddhists.* Albany: State University of New York.

Kim, S. (Ed.). (2006). *Hallyu-wa 21 segi munhwa bijeon: yonsama-eseo munhwa jeongchaek-kkaji [The Korean Wave and a Cultural Vision for the 21st century: From "Yonsama" to cultural politics].* Seoul: Cheongdong Geoul.

Kim, Y. (1987). *Sanchae yori [Mountain Vegetables Cuisine].* Seoul: Hakwonsa.

Kim, Y. (1995). Sachal eumsik-ui oesik sangpumhwa bangan-e gwanhan yeongu [A study of a plan to develop Buddhist temple food for the restaurant business] (Doctoral dissertation). Chung-Ang University, Seoul, Korea.

Kim, Y. (1997). *Hanguk sachal eumsik [Korean temple food].* Seoul: Uri Chulpansa.

Kim, Y. (2002). *Nun-euro meongneun jeol eumsik [Buddhist temple food eaten with eyes].* Seoul: Uri Chulpansa.

Klein, N. (1999). *No Logo: Taking Aim at the Brand Bullies*. New York: Picador.

Korea Buddhist Culture Enterprise Group (KBCEG). (2006). *Hanguk sachal jeontong eumsik siltae josa saeop gyeolgwa bogoseo [Research Report on Traditional Korean Temple Food]*. Seoul: KBCEG.

Korean Employers Federation (KEF), & *Chosun Ilbo*. (2007). *Jayeongeopja hyeonhwang gukje bigyo mit jeongchaek gwaje [The Current State of the Self-employed: International Comparison and Policy Issues]*. Seoul: KEF.

Petrini, C. (2001). *Slow Food: The Case for Taste*. (W. McCuaig, Trans.). New York: Columbia University Press.

Reinders, E. (2004). Blessed are the meat eaters: Christian anti-vegetarianism and the missionary encounter with Chinese Buddhism. *Positions: East Asia Cultures Critique, 12*(2), 509–537.

Seonjae. (2000). *Seonjae seunim-ui sachal eumsik [Nun Seonjae's Temple Food]*. Seoul: Design House.

Sterckx, R. (2004). *Of Tripod and Palate: Food, Politics and Religion in Traditional China*. New York: Palgrave-MacMillan Press.

Ulrich, K. (2007). Food fights: Buddhist, Hindu, and Jain dietary polemics in South India. *History of Religions, 46*(3), 228–261.

Wilk, R. (2006). *Home Cooking in the Global Village: Caribbean Food from Buccaneers to Ecotourists*. New York: Berg Publishers.

Yi, Y. (2002). *Jayeon geongang sachal eumsik [Natural Health Buddhist Temple Food]*. Vol. 2. Seoul: Yeollin Sowon.

Yu, S., Ahn, H., Jeong, H., Kim, J., & Jeong, K. (Eds.). (2005). *Hallyu-ui bimil [Secret of the Korean Wave]*. Seoul: Thinking Tree.

Chapter 6

The Reinvention of Traditional Cuisine as Counterculture

Jeehee Kim

Barugongyang[1] is a temple food restaurant located on the fifth floor of the Templestay Information Center. The Templestay Information Center is housed in a modern, chic, grey building. Ethnic elements are also infused in its modern architecture as we can see in figure 6.1. For instance, its front gate consists of two plates. The exterior is made of glass and is attached to a wooden frame carved into a flower motif. Inside, we can also see lamps in a lotus shape.

On the first floor of the Templestay Information Center, one can find brochures on temple stay in several languages. There are also two restaurants in this building. Entering *Barugongyang* on the fifth floor, one can see a picture of Richard Gere on the reception desk. Some may find this too vulgar, whereas others might share the pride of the restaurant in attracting a Hollywood star and proving the competitiveness of Korean food. In Seoul, photographs of celebrities who have visited are often hung on restaurant walls to attract customers; and, in the use of this tactic, temple food restaurants are no exception. Monastic cuisine *Barugongyang Kong* (bean) is on the second floor and is more casual than Monastic cuisine *Barugongyang* on the fifth floor. The Education Center and the office are located in between the two restaurants.

This building serves a different purpose from the Buddhist temple across the street. Whereas the temple is a place for religious events, the Templestay Center serves a more commercial purpose. For example, there are information center, gift shop and restaurants in this building. Figure 6.2 may suggest that most people are heading toward the temple, but in fact the Templestay Center can be more inviting and open for those who are from other countries. The most noticeable difference is the way that food is consumed. Whereas people can get lunch at the temple for 2,000 won,[2] a relatively cheap price,

117

Figure 6.1 **Templestay Information Center.** *Source*: Copyright © 2014 Jee Hee Kim.

they need to pay almost double the price if they go to the restaurants in the Templestay Center.

An air of sophistication permeates *Barugongyang*, which is on the fifth floor of the Templestay Information Center. There is a sheet on each table, where four guidelines from the Dharmagupta Vinaya are printed: "to eat proper food at the right time," "to eat food in season," "to have a balanced diet," and "not to overeat and to abstain from meat." This might seem a little didactic to some people. However, considering that there is a general understanding that the culture of temple food embodies the philosophy of Buddhism, it is not surprising that customers are led to meditate on the act of choosing and having meals at this place.

Figure 6.2   Jogyesa Temple in Seoul. *Source*: Copyright © 2014 Jee Hee Kim.

For lunch, there are four sets of course meals starting with the ten-course option. The more the number of courses, the more expensive the meal. The most expensive menu has seventeen courses. The interesting thing is the name of each course option. The cheapest set menu, which offers only ten courses, is named the "Paramita (婆羅蜜) Course." Here, *paramita* means "the state of perfection." The fifteen-course meal, in contrast, is called the "Englishtenment Course." And the seventeen-course meal is named "Barugongyang Course." Since *barugongyang* refers to "a formal monastic meal," it may feel like there is a slight decline in the degree of spiritual enlightenment as the course gets expensive. Nevertheless, the price and the number of courses demonstrate that the temple food has been transformed into gourmet food (see figures 6.3 and 6.4).

In recent years, traditional food has gained popularity in Korea as people have come to regard what they eat as being closely related to their lifestyle. For this reason, an individual's choice of food is now considered as a form

Figure 6.3   Main Course. *Source*: Copyright © 2014 Jee Hee Kim.

Figure 6.4   Dessert. *Source*: Copyright © 2014 Jee Hee Kim.

of self-expression. People now read political and spiritual messages in the food products available in the food market. Meanwhile, it is important to note that contemporary Korean food culture has been largely shaped by capitalist ideology and pop culture. For example, during the time when South Koreans considered their nation to be developing, western food was received more favorably than today. People associated western cuisine with affluence and a level of sophistication that they want to emulate. However, nowadays they are becoming more critical about the eating culture associated with the West, which I interpret as a sign that signals changing attitudes toward capitalist culture and lifestyle.

People recognize that their spiritual and physical health is endangered especially when it comes to the safety of food. For instance, after the outbreak of Bovine Spongiform Encephalopathy (BSE) and other food safety issues surrounding "*kimchi* containing parasites, and rotten dumpling and bird flu" (Food Bank 2005 as cited in Suh, Eves, and Lumbers 2012), there is a growing suspicion within the country about the safety of food products. Ethical issues related to the production, circulation, and consumption of food products have become important in the shaping of eating habit in Korean culture.

The revival of traditional cuisines suggests that consumers try to have a sense of belonging by consuming the food that is associated with the idea about the past. In this respect, the current study aims to examine how the *nostalgic desire*, which Fredric Jameson (2009) discusses in his seminal essay *Postmodernism and Consumer Society*, operates in the production and consumption of traditional cuisine in Korea. Therefore, the chapter will seek out the reasons for the contemporary demand for *nostalgia* products (Jameson 2009). The rise of traditional cuisine in contemporary Korean culture suggests that people seek a sense of belonging and continuity in their choice of food, showing resistance to the rapidly changing lifestyles in capitalist society.

(RE)INVENTION OF TRADITION

Hobsbawm (2012) draws our attention to the fictionality of so-called traditions and memories of the past when they write, "traditions which appear or claim to be old are often quite recent in origin and sometimes invented" (1). He also illuminates why people tend to invent traditions; it is because in a set of practices, people find a sense of continuity with the past (Hobsbawm 2012). In other words, where there is a demand for this sense of *continuity*, traditional culture could play a crucial role in the society providing a sense of membership to its people (Hobsbawm 2012). Posed in this way, the revival of traditional cuisines as trendy choices suggests that people often try to compensate for a contemporary sense of confusion and discontinuity by consuming those foods that are associated with the ideas about the past. And they also try to attain a sense of belonging to their nation by consuming the products that embody the national history. This chapter argues that consumers try to attain membership to "pseudo-communities" by consuming traditional food (Hobsbawm 2012, 10).

In this chapter, I will explore the history of temple food and Andong food, focusing on the changes that took place in the process of institutionalization of the traditional foods. Also, by looking at how temple food is being reinvented in the contemporary culture, I will also attempt to show that there is an irony in consuming a culture that has already been manufactured in the first place. The first question that I raise is whether these cuisines that are believed to embody certain ideologies are truly related to the traditions or traditional values of Korea. In order to find out the way that tradition is being discovered in the food market, a case study of Buddhist cuisine and Andong food was carried out. These products are believed to be associated with particular ideologies, namely Buddhism and Confucianism. I argue that Buddhist temple food and the local food of Andong are receiving more attention from the media and the food industry because there is a growing demand for traditional cuisine, which evokes people's nostalgia. At the same time, these food trends express people's dissatisfaction with current eating habits, which are fostered by capitalist ideology and pop culture.

The Invention of Tradition

There are many overlapping features between Buddhist temple food and traditional food in Korea. Local food is often viewed as traditional food in Korea. Temple food and traditional food in Korea are credited for their fermenting skills and their use of vegetables, which makes them relatively healthy compared to other meat-based cuisines. In this section, I am going to talk about the circumstance that led to the diversification of temple food during the Joseon Dynasty. I also want to note that even though one makes a distinction and confine temple food to a range of foods that are cooked and shared at Buddhist temples, it should not be neglected these temples were located in mountains, limiting the food supply. Later in this section, I am going to make a comparison between temple food and Andong food, to show how temple food is being reinvented.

Buddhism was introduced to Korea from China during the Three Kingdom period (300s–600s). During the Goryeo Dynasty, which preceded the Joseon Dynasty, Buddhist cuisine took its form with the patronage of the royal court, which recognized Buddhism as the state religion (Moon 2008). The fermenting skills, which became the characteristic of temple food, were developed in this period (Moon 2008). Buddhism began to decline in the Joseon Dynasty while Confucianism was endorsed by the government as a state religion. Moon Seungsook (2008) points out that during this time, "as Buddhism lost its wealthy and powerful patronage by royal court and nobility, opulent Buddhist ceremonies accompanied by luxurious temple food disappeared" as well (154). As a result, it adapted to the material condition of its environment, which became the basis for "rustic vegetarian cuisine" (Moon 2008, 154) that we find in temple food today.

According to Moon (2008), it was during the Japanese colonization that debates flared over the celibacy of its monks, which eventually split the Korean Buddhism into the Jogye Order and the Taego Order. And the division in Buddhism has hindered its growth until now. In addition, she points out that there are "heterogenous views" on temple food. Moon (2008) writes:

Two factors were significant to the emergence of temple food as an integral part of the monastic culture. First unlike Buddhist temples in South Asia that were built in residential neighborhoods, temples in Korea were mostly located in mountains away from populous residential areas due to the history of the persecution of Buddhism. Hence, while monks in South Asia obtained their daily food through alms collections form local villagers, monks and nuns in Korea cultivated or collected their own food. Second, as mentioned above, Korea Buddhism stressed meditation as the vehicle to achieve enlightenment, and monks and nuns devoted their lives to meditative training (*suhaeng*). (155)

We should understand the historical background of temple food that Buddhism was oppressed by the state since the Joseon Dynasty. To avoid the persecution, the temples were located in mountains, which eventually led to the localization as well as diversification of temple food. Moon's observation allows us to discuss two important aspects of temple food today. One is the culinary diversification of temple food as a result of isolation and adaptation to its material condition. The second feature is that despite its diversification temple food is understood as the "vehicle to achieve enlightenment" (Moon 2008, 155).

On the other hand, temple food is becoming a brand with strong attributes as a healthy food for physical and spiritual nourishment. These days, one can easily come across cookbooks on temple food written by Buddhist monks, and there are temple food restaurants run by these experts as well. Naming plays a central role in this process. For example, *baru* is used as a brand name for a temple food restaurant run by a Buddhist organization. Meanwhile, one could also find that Buddhist organizations are actively participating in commercializing the temple food culture. For instance, visitors to the Templestay Information Center could see *baru* set is on sale. Despite its original meaning, "special bowls made for the monks" (Han 2010), *baru* bowls are made into commodities in the gift shops affiliated with the Buddhist organization.

According to the monk Dae An (2012), the term *baru* comes from the story that tells how Buddha was offered a first meal by two merchants, whose names were Tapussa and Bhallika, using a *baru*, a special bowl for offering food. Dae An (2012) also notes that it can also be explained differently; the word *baru* is made of two foreign words. Its first syllable *ba* (鉢) comes from the Sanskrit word *patra*, and its second syllable is the Chinese letter "盂" (bowl). As the words show, in the formation of Korean temple food, both Indian and Chinese Buddhism have played significant roles.

There are numerous orders in the Buddhist organization, suggesting that it would be hard to have a unified view on the practice and discipline of temple food. In ancient China, the vegetarian diet was implemented into the Buddhist food culture under the guidance of political leaders (emperors). In this way, Buddhist doctrine functioned as a binding force of the nation, placating people who had been forced to eat vegetables only as a result of material conditions. The history of temple food suggests that food used to be a vehicle for circulating and implementing the ruling ideology in the ancient societies of China.

Scholars have not reached agreement on when Buddhism first entered China (Tan 2012), since Buddhism was introduced through many channels. In fact, most scholars agree that the stories concerning the arrival of Buddhism in China are fictions, as they were invented later, and their purpose was to legitimize the authority of Buddhism in Chinese society. For example, one story tells that the Emperor Ming dreamed of "a golden Buddha flying over his palace" (as cited in Tan 2012). When we consider that this story was invented while Buddhism had growing influence, we can see that attempts were made to integrate Indian Buddhism into Chinese history. Yet, Indian Buddhism and Chinese Buddhism differ from each other in their views on meat eating, as Huang (2008) argues.

A view on meat-eating of Indian Buddhism manifests the traditional ideas of respecting life and the purity of Buddha's teaching. It shows that traditional Chinese ideas such as filial piety, care of health of evolution of nature and mankind have permeated into Sakyamuni's doctrines (Huang 2008). On the other hand, there are evidences that in the early days of Buddhism in India, meat was not strictly prohibited. Some records suggest that in the old days, it was fine to eat meat as long as a person did not participate in killing animals. Hopkins (1906) even suggests that Buddha might have "died of eating pork, the flesh of a wild boar":

> The words silkara-imaddava, "boar-tender" (-loin?) was interpreted either as a sauce or as a vegetable eaten by a boar; some said bamboo- sprouts, other said

a kind of mushroom, although no sauce or vegetable is known by the name of "boar-tender." (458)

Although Hopkins's view may need more support, Huang (2008) also argues that the tradition of not eating meat was established in the Emperor Wu period and was passed down to the next generations. We have to take into account that while agriculture developed in China, there was a huge gulf between the ruling and the ruled class in their economic powers, which distinguished their eating habits. The ruled, who were mostly farmers, ate only a small amount of greens, whereas the ruling class was able to afford meat. In this way, whether a person ate meat or not was closely related to his or her social class.

The Reinvention of Tradition

It is not surprising that people seem more conscious of their choice of food in developed countries. Many people recognize that ethical issues are involved in the consumption of food. Moon points out that temple food took on importance in the media from the mid-1990s as the public grew dissatisfied with the food supply chain, believing it to be simply serving the commercial interests of the multinational corporations. Also, in South Korea, in the past ten years, eating meat has become both morally and politically problematic since the South Korean government decided to resume the import of US beef despite the risk of mad-cow disease.

Moon has noted that temple food arose in the culture of Korea due to the growing concern for a healthy diet (Moon 2008). In Korea, there are many overlapping features between Buddhist temple food and other traditional foods. In fact, they share the characteristics of *hansik* (Korean cuisine) with their use of fermenting properties and also the fact that they are regarded as representative of Korean culture. Consumers find the national class and cultural identities reflected in the kinds of food they eat. In this respect, the rise of temple food and Andong food as an important culinary trend in contemporary Korea is being framed as if it were a show of resistance against consumerism and globalism. But the idea that traditional food embodies certain ideas or traditions may in fact be simply a myth or sweet lie invented by the food industry to satisfy middle-class consumers.

In *Millennial Capitalism and the Culture of Neoliberalism*, Comaroff and Comaroff (2001) point to the reversed relationship between consumption and production. For them, "the emergence of consumption as a privileged site for the fabrication of self and society, of culture and identity" sheds light on this process (Comaroff and Comaroff 2011, 9). Temple food is closely related to the formation of the middle class in the food market. It also suggests that food is a site for the negotiation of identities and desires. In this respect, it is important that the commercialization of temple food first became an issue in the late 1990s with a growing demand for more traditional, healthier food. Similarly, Andong food arose in the wake of the commodification of Korean tradition, along with the rise of the tourism industry. In other words, traditional foods were invented as their value as cultural products and alternative choices for sophisticated consumers were first recognized.

THE DECONTEXTUALIZATION OF ANDONG FOOD

The culture of Andong food demonstrates the fact that food culture provides middle-class consumers with the fantasy that they can regain a meaningful attachment to a forgotten past. However, it is important to discuss the dynamics between economic growth and consumer food preferences. There have been some changes in the reception of fast food brands, such as McDonald's and Burger King, and this reflects how people feel about the capitalist culture and their roles as consumers.

The traditional cuisine of Andong shows that local food is consumed with a strong reference to its cultural heritage. Andong, where historical sites are preserved, is being promoted as "the capital of the Korean spirit" (Andong City 2004). On the other hand, Bae (2004) contends that the local food of Andong was not regarded as unique or distinctive until the early 1970s. Besides, as spiritual aspect of Andong food has been increasingly important, Andong steamed chicken was invented in the 1990s, targeting college students around the area of Andong. As Hobsbawm (2012) notes, this is a kind of food that is "deliberately invented and constructed by a single initiator" (4). By establishing a tie with its local culture and therefore becoming a medium, which social and cultural significance are transferred, the local cuisine of Andong became a *symbolate*, which helped separate its image from that of other food (Hobsbawm 2012). Without the idea of Andong as the home of Confucianism and a place where traditional life is preserved, the traditional cuisine of Andong could not have been so successfully commercialized. In this respect, it suggests to us why and how temple food is gaining attention.

Bae (2004) also points out that "the major driving force of the commercialization of Andong's traditional food is the activation of tourism, though each item has a slightly different background" (332). He examines how the traditional food gets *decontextualized* by tracing the way that Andong *soju*, *hut-jesa bab* (a mock ancestoral memorial service meal), *gunjin* noodle (Andong handmade knife-cut noodle), Andong mackerel, and Andong steamed chicken are promoted as local foods outside Andong. For instance, *hut-jesa bab* did not exist until a particular restaurant owner came up with the name. There was a tradition of having meals when people got hungry at night in winter, usually mixing rice with seasoned vegetables, which was called *hut-jisin-bap* (mock food for the spirits of the terrain). Despite these similar names, *hut-jisin-bap* was very different from the notion of *jesa bap* (memorial service meal for ancestors), which uses a specific way of setting up the dishes. In this way, this was invented by someone who had the intention of going along with the municipal policy that promoted traditional food.

Arguably, decontextualization is closely related to the local food commercialization. Changes have been made to make the traditional food more appealing to those who wish to consume an authentic ethnic culture. Jameson (2009) points out that "the informational function of the media would thus be to help us forget, to serve as the very agents and mechanisms for our historical amnesia" (11). Here, the term *historical amnesia* is important, since it is possible to see that there is a kind of *amnesia* taking place in the commercialization of traditional food (Jameson 2009). It is often emphasized that eating is a pseudo-religious practice and a vicarious form of meditation for Buddhist monks.

Just as the media associates Andong food with Confucianism because of its association with Andong, even when Confucian doctrine plays no role in its practice, temple food is identified with Buddhism. Also, the temple food movement is supported by the government, which recognizes its value as a cultural product to generate tourism in Korea. Like Andong food, decontextualization may be detected in the representation of temple food. For example, each menu or course item is named after a Buddhist doctrine without bearing any reference to this idea. Also, the fact that temple food is practiced outside Buddhist temples also suggests that it is being decontextualized in the process of becoming a commodity in capitalist society.

THE PRACTICE OF TEMPLE FOOD: NOSTALGIA FOR *JANGAJJI*

Yun Dae-nyeong (2006), a South Korean novelist, writes about his encounter with temple food in his essay titled *Eomeoni-eui Soojeo (Mom's Spoon)*. *Jangajji* is the name for the side dish made of pickled vegetables. He writes about a year he spent at a Buddhist temple. One day, the head monk discovered that Yun ate chicken and punished him by restricting the number of dishes that were served at his table. Yun was served only one type of *jangajji* as a side dish with his meal. Eventually, however, he began to enjoy his meal and felt as if he had been purified. He confesses that the experience gave him a taste for simple meals. The following passage is from the chapter on *jangajji*:

As strange as it may sound, they say that they "decimate living cells." If vegetables are not completely dry, the paste and the *jangajji* may go bad. With the digestive process of the enzymes in the paste, the ingredients of the *jangajji* no longer function as their original cells but turn into delicious food with a richer flavor. They came out from the enlightenment while being secluded in a jar. So they carry a different gravity and presence from other foods. (Yun 2006)

Here, the writer is making an allusion to the Buddhist monks with his description of *jangajji*. He is implying that there is an analogy between *jangajji* and Buddhist monks because they are both blessed by their secluded lives, which leads them to spiritual enlightenment. As Yun (2006) suggests, in the culture of Buddhist temple food, eating can be a form of religious practice; it promises spiritual growth to people. His story ends with a later episode in which he fails to purchase some real *jangajji* at a traditional market. The item he buys turns out to be a fake, which he renames *jangji*. I suggest that we can read this story as an allegory of how the food industry fails to satisfy today's consumers. This explains the demand for more authentic food. At the same time, Yun's desperate search for the taste of temple food appears to contribute to the process of commercialization.

Comaroff and Comaroff (2011) state that "consumption" is "the moving spirit of the late twentieth century" (4). With this in mind, we can go back to Yun's essay on *jangajji*, in which he romanticizes his experience at the Buddhist temple and expresses disappointment in the kind of *jangajji* he discovered at one of the traditional markets in Seoul. When he laments over the poorly made, low quality, un-authentic *jangajji*, the readers are made to share his nostalgia for the past and the tradition that has been lost in the course of Korean industrialization. At the same time, however, I want to point out that this is also the lamentation of a consumer and in a way, a demand for traditional food. Simply put, making *jangajji* is not impossible. What Yun needs to do, if he really misses its taste, is to buy white radish and preserve it with soy sauce for a while. Instead, he searches the entire market to check if they are selling what he wants. His story shows what kind of *consumerist spirit* dominates the lives of Koreans.

Another point that we can make from Yun's account is that *jangajji*, which for Yun is a pseudo-product of *jangajji*, is abhorrent to the writer. There is a comic element in his reaction to this *jangajji* because of the discrepancy between the Buddhist temple and the market. Ironically, the traditional market is the closest place where he can try to find the food, which once healed and purified him. In a sense, he is making an effort to revisit his memory by going to the market and tasting the food he found most similar to that he previously experienced. Without the element of "tradition," these two places are in fact antithetical, and readers find Yun trapped in between two realities that cannot be equated with or substituted with each other. Is his story what Jameson (2009) called "a pointless satire?" (5) While discussing the *nostalgia* films, Jameson (2009) explains that pastiche "satisfies a deep (might I even say repressed?) longing to experience them again" (5). In Yun's essay, *jangajji* works as a metonymy of the past, which cannot be retrieved in capitalist society. And the writer finds it hard to believe that the market fails to satisfy him by providing him with the perfect imitation of *jangajji*.

CONCLUSION

If Buddhist cuisine has made it easier for ordinary people to accept a vegetarian diet and accept their roles as subjects in the past, nowadays it is accommodating itself to the needs of consumers. The reference to Jameson (2009) substantiates our understanding of the reinvention of traditional cuisines as capitalizing on the *nostalgia* of consumers. However, one needs to take into account the fact that *nostalgia* is inevitably a vague word, because it only shows how people feel about the past. It is possible that the products that are said to embody traditional values are not necessarily realistic in their representations of tradition. In his essay *Postmodernism and Consumer Society*, Jameson (2009) points out that films such as *Chinatown* and *Star Wars* use certain images that resonate with what people imagine about the past. Here, he also points out how the film embodies "false realisms" (10) by showing clips of images or texts that have no meanings after all.

Temple food is still a product of capitalist ideology. It is bought as an alternative option by middle-class consumers. These people previously mobilized politically around the issue of imported beef from the United States, but afterward dispersed and returned to their roles as consumers. In fact, the popularity of temple food shows how religious organizations are working closely with the food market in trying to cater to middle-class consumers. Visitors to the temple food restaurants buy the fantasy that they have chosen traditional food instead of manufactured food at a franchise restaurant. In the end, temple food has become trendy not as a political gesture but as a luxury good that reflects the middle-class desire to stay healthy while enriching their lives with spiritual training. In this process, it has been decontextualized in a similar fashion to the way that Andong food has become a trendy choice for consumers.

The decontextualization of Andong food shows how local cuisine can be turned into a saleable commodity. People give more meaning to food when they recognize their choice as a form of expression. The local cuisine of Andong is attached to the name "Andong," which mystifies the act of eating. People believe they have become more meaningful when they eat other foods. In fact, when the food is presented with a certain name, people give it more respect. In this light, there is a demand for renaming food so that it can carry spiritual significance, in order to cater to the taste of the middle class. This middle class is making the demand that there should be more alternatives, even though the demands are to be fulfilled within the capitalist system. For instance, some people go to a traditional food restaurant and think that they found an alternative to franchise restaurants. At the same time, temple food is often promoted as a possible solution to the current culture of consumption, as its ideological charge creates the hope that people can change their eating habit by adopting the state of mind and attitude required of the Buddhist monk. These discussions are taking place side by side with a growing criticism of Western traditions. Temple food attracts consumers who have been disappointed by the current food industry. They refuse to endorse the fast food culture represented by Coca-Cola and McDonald's. Instead, the consumers of temple food regard temple food as an alternative choice or counterculture within contemporary capitalist culture.

NOTES

1. This chapter was previously published with the same title in *Journal of the Korea Contents Association*, *14*(11), 944–954.
2. This lunch, which is served at the temple, is called *Manbalgongyang*, a ritual whose aim is to feed as many people as possible. This lunch ticket is available for those with membership cards for the Jogye Order.

REFERENCES

Andong City. (2004). Andong tourism. Retrieved from http://www.tourandong.com/.
Bae, Y. (2004). 안동 지역 전통 음식의 탈맥락화와 상품화: 1970 년대를 중심으로 [The decontextualization and commercialization of the traditional cuisine of Andong]. *사회와 역사* [*Journal of Korean Social History Association*], *66*, 35–68.
Comaroff, J., & Comaroff, J. (2001). Millennial capitalism: First thoughts on a second coming. In J. Comaroff & J. Comaroff (Eds.), *Millennial Capitalism and the Culture of Neoliberalism* (pp. 1–57). Durham: Duke University Press.
Dae An. (2012). *(대안스님의) 마음설레는 레시피: 비움의 그릇에 자기 한 스푼으로 차려낸 사찰음식과 친해지는 법* [*(Dae An's) Heartening Recipe: The Way to be Familiar with Temple Food Prepared with a Bowl of Blank and a Spoonful of the Self*]. Paju: Gimm-Young Publishers.
Han, B. (2010). *사찰음식* [Temple food]. *한국민족문화대백과사전* [*Encyclopedia of Korean Culture*]. Seongnam: The Academy of Korean Studies. Retrieved from

https://encykorea.aks.ac.kr/Contents/SearchNavi?keyword=%EC%82%AC%EC%
B0%B0%EC%9D%8C%EC%8B%9D&ridx=0&tot=1.

Hobsbawm, E. (2012). Introduction: Inventing traditions. In E. Hobsbawm & T. Ranger (Eds.), *The Invention of Tradition* (pp. 1–14). Cambridge: Cambridge University Press. (Original work published 1983).

Hopkins, E. (1906). The Buddhistic rule against eating meat. *Journal of American Oriental Society*, *27*, 455–464.

Huang, X. (2008). View on a meat diet of 'Sammesucham': Regarding the view of the Chinese Emperor Wu of the Liang Dynasty on a meat diet. 불교학보 *[Journal of Buddhism Studies]*, *50*, 99–130.

Jameson, F. (2009). *The Cultural Turn: Selected Writings on the Postmodern 1983-1998*. London, Brooklyn: Verso. (Original work published 1998).

Moon, S. (2008). Buddhist temple food in South Korea: Interests and agency in the reinvention of tradition in the age of globalization. *Korea Journal*, *48*(4), 147–180.

Suh, B., Eves, A., & Lumbers, M. (2012). Consumers' attitude and understanding of organic food: The case of South Korea. *Journal of Foodservice Business Research*, *15*(1), 49–63.

Tan, S. (2012). The spread of Buddhism to China: Re-examination of the Buddhist interactions between ancient India and China. *China Report*, *48*(1–2), 11–27.

Yun, D. (2006). 어머니의 수저 *[Mom's Spoon]*. Seoul: Woongjin Thinkbig.

Chapter 7

Taste of Korea

Governmental Discourse on National Cuisine and Its Articulation of Nation-ness

Jaehyeon Jeong

On[1] February 25, 2008, MyungBak Lee, the seventeenth president of South Korea, announced the globalization of *hansik* (Korean cuisine) as a national project. One month later, the minister of food, agriculture, forestry, and fisheries (MFAFF) declared 2008 the "Year of Korean Food Globalization." He announced that the Korean government would promote the sustained growth of the food and agriculture industry, establish a national food cluster, and make Korean food one of the five most popular cuisines in the world by 2017.

The Korean government's increasing interest in Korean cuisine was primarily based on an awareness of the enlarging size of the global food industries. It was also interlocked with Lee's presidential election pledges to improve the domestic agriculture and fishery industries, as well as his policies on foreign affairs and national security. For a better understanding of this phenomenon, however, we should take into consideration the role of food in cultivating a sense of national belonging. As demonstrated by various sociological and anthropological studies, food is critical to (re)making social identities and group boundaries (Appadurai 1981; Belasco 2008; Bell and Valentine 1997; Ceccraini 2010; Cwiertka 2006; Holtzman 2006; Mintz and Du Bois 2002). In particular, national cuisine strongly ties collective identity to food, and functions as a central part of gastronationalism and other nationalist projects (Bell and Valentine 1997; Cwiertka 2006; DeSoucey 2010). In Korea, the government and its associated organizations have fostered a large number of discussions on Korean food to sustain the binding force of the nation-state since 2008, using public announcements, festivals, exhibitions, forums, media outlets, and organizational magazines.

The purpose of the current study is to understand the growth of governmental discourse on national cuisine as a struggle for nation-ness. Due to its incomplete nature (Bhabha 1990), a nation requires a constant symbolic process of "the naturalization of arbitrariness," which imbues it with "an aura of factuality" (Foster 1991, 237). Here, I argue that the Korean government utilizes national cuisine to narrate *Korea* and establish its cultural boundaries, which, in turn, obscures the temporality and indeterminacy of the nation (Bhabha 1990). To make this argument, I first discuss the anthropological notion of food as *deep play* and the invented nature of national cuisine, which underlie the research agenda of this article. Then, I elucidate the economic and political backgrounds of the Korean government's increased interest in food matters to contextualize my analysis. To offer detailed properties of the governmental discourse on Korean cuisine, I then analyze *The Taste of Korea*, the official newsletter of the Korean Food Foundation, focusing on the cover page of each volume, which features photographic images of *traditional* Korean food.

FOOD, NATIONAL CUISINE, AND
NATIONAL IDENTITY

Food as *Deep Play*

In our everyday lives, we tend to take culinary practices and traditions for granted. The ubiquitous nature of food-related practices particularly makes their ideological and political relevance almost invisible (Parasecoli 2008). Yet, food means more than just *what we eat*; indeed, people use food to speak with one another, establish rules of behavior, and reveal *what they are* (Belasco 2008); moreover, our foodways are embedded in economic, political, emotional, and ideological relationships among people (Cwiertka and Walraven 2001). Thus, the study of food-related practices can signal the material structure and symbolic boundary politics of a given society across time and space (DeSoucey 2010).

The *culinary* turn in academia began in the late 1970s as a result of work by anthropologists, sociologists, folklorists, and historians who understood food as a multilayered and multidimensional subject (Holtzman 2006). They see food as a vantage point for examining various issues concerning theory and research methods (Mintz and Du Bois 2002). For example, scholars have discussed food as a system of communication and symbolic value creation, a key component of rituals and social distinction, or a site of memory and meaning construction (Barthes 1979; Holtzman 2006; Mintz 1985; Munn 1986; Sutton 2010). In particular, Appadurai (1981) utilizes Clifford Geertz's anthropological notion of deep play and argues that "food can signal rank and rivalry, solidarity and community, identity or exclusion, and intimacy or distance" (494).

Drawing on these seminal studies, researchers have addressed issues of identities, memories, and boundaries through the subject matter of food. These inquiries have often been explored with such expressions as *you are what you eat* (Scholliers 2001), *we are what we ate*, and *we are where we eat* (Belasco 2008; Bell and Valentine 1997; Gabaccia 1998). This close relationship between food and identity has been evident in an increasing number of recent sociological, anthropological, ethnographical, and geographical studies (see Belasco 2008; Bell and Valentine 1997; Gabaccia 1998; Kanafani-Zahar 1997; Korsmeyer 1999; Lentz 1999; Leitch 2008; Wilk 2008).

Discussions on food and belonging have not been limited to companions, villages, or kin groups. Researchers have extended their discussions to the intertwined relationships between food practices and the nation. To take an example, Preston-Werner (2009) notes that eating *gallo pinto* (rice and beans) arouses a nostalgic image of lived culture and a sense of national belonging in Costa Rica. Within East Asian contexts, Tam (2001) examines how Hong Kong people establish their national identity by eating *yumcha* (several small courses of dim sum and Chinese tea); additionally, Ohnuki-Tierney (1993) argues that rice, as the staple of the Japanese diet, plays a central role in constructing Japanese national identity. By examining transformations in Belizean food practices from colonial times to the present, Wilk (2008) demonstrates that food practices are firmly linked to the ways people identify and experience their nationhood. In this sense, Bell and Valentine (1997) write, "Food and the nation are so commingled in popular discourses that it is often difficult not to think one through the other" (168).

National Cuisine as a Vehicle of National Identity

The relationship between food and national identity is strongly tied to the development of national cuisine. Despite its seemingly essential nature, however, national cuisine is a modern construct (Belasco 2008). Indeed, the proliferation of culinary nation-making was a distinguishing feature of the nineteenth and twentieth centuries (Cwiertka 2006). As other modern traditions conceal their invented nature (Hobsbawm and Ranger 1983), national cuisine also hides its short-lived origins and complex histories of hybridity—trade links, cultural exchange, and colonialism—as well as its history of negotiation between local and foreign, private and public, and high and low (Bell and Valentine 1997; Cwiertka 2006). In so doing, national cuisine naturalizes a clear continuity with the past and ethnic cores, provides the illusion of a common history, and constructs intra-national sameness. Additionally, its emphasis on a shared past and ethnic cores makes what we eat a reservoir of both personal recollection and collective memories (Belasco 2008; Holtzman 2006).

National cuisine serves two opposed semiotic functions—the homogenization and heterogenization of actors (Appadurai 1981). Through the study of the creation of Indian national cuisine, Appadurai (1981) argues that Indian cookbooks from the 1960s to 1980s condensed regional and local culinary diversity to a single dish in order to construct *the taste of India.* Consequently, cultural, religious, and ethnic differences of Indian people were reduced, while the unity of Indian society was enhanced. In a similar vein, Cwiertka (2006) claims that in the course of inventing Japanese national cuisine, the diversity of local food practices was replaced by a peculiar set of food practices and tastes with which the majority of Japanese people would willingly identify. On the other hand, national cuisine speaks of *difference.* The Jewish dietary law *kashrut* is a semantic system that enables Jewish people to classify foods as either *clean* or *unclean*, and therefore distinguishes themselves from others (Douglas 1966). Such distinctions clearly identify those who belong to particular cultural norms and practices, and those who do not (Palmer 1998). Specifically, at times of national crisis, national cuisine gains enhanced symbolic values and evokes strong nationalism in confronting "filthy foreign food" (Bell and Valentine 1997, 167); furthermore, it becomes a medium of cultural politics that demarcates national boundaries to defy the homogenizing force of globalization (DeSoucey 2010).

Additionally, the ubiquity and unconsciousness of food maintain nationhood as an integral part of ordinary life. Moreover, as significant element of the material world (Palmer 1998), food functions as a "banal flag" of national identity (Billig 1995, 181). This culinary flagging may be unconsciously displayed, but constantly reminds people of the nation on a daily basis, and serves to keep people aware of where they belong and what they believe. However, most studies that approach nations through the lens of food have explored the limited dimensions of food practices, such as food production and consumption. Though food discourses are intertwined with the organization of everyday conduct and function as a "biological device" that links individuals to a multitude of governing bodies (Hiroko 2008, 9), the discursive dimension of food has hardly been studied.

Due to the rise of food television within the past two decades, scholars have begun to pay more attention to the discursive dimension of food in order to investigate such issues as class, gender, age, and ethnicity (Adema 2000; de Solier 2005; Hansen 2008; Kelly 2017; Ketchum 2005; Oren 2013; Parasecoli 2008; Swenson 2009; Wright and Sandlin 2009). Yet, there is still a shortage of academic research on the conjuncture of food discourse and the nation. It is also noteworthy that the tendency to protect national cuisine as representative of national traditions is a transnational phenomenon;

particularly, in the face of open-market structures various nation-states have asserted national claims of cultural patrimony for foods to carve out their global position (DeSoucey 2010).[2] It is within this context that the current study critically examines the Korean government's discourse of national cuisine and its articulation of nation-ness.

RESEARCH METHODS

This chapter explores both the social contexts and concrete examples of the Korean government's discursive practices. To offer detailed properties of the governmental discourse on Korean cuisine, I examined *The Taste of Korea*, an online newsletter of the Korean Food Foundation (hereafter, KFF), which had been published twice a month from August 2011 to February 2014. Although other government institutions, such as the Ministry of Culture, Sports and Tourism, and the Ministry of Health and Welfare, have implemented their own food-related policies, KFF has functioned as the only official organization of Korean food globalization. KFF has manifested itself as a private, nonprofit, and nonpartisan organization; however, its policies and directions have been determined by governmental agencies. For instance, WoonCheon Jeong, a former Minister of MFAFF, was appointed as the first president of the foundation (Lee 2010, March 17); YoonOk Kim, the first lady, was appointed as an honorary president of the Korean Food Globalization Committee—the initial form of KFF. In addition, its status became legally secured due to the enactment of the Food Industry Promotion Act and the amendment of the Enforcement Decree of the Food Industry Promotion Act.[3] Thus, KFF provides a vantage point for observing how the Korean government has promoted Korean food, and its newsletter, *The Taste of Korea*, provides a good window through which government discourse on Korean food can be observed, although it is not a popular magazine that retains significant circulation or readership in Korea.[4]

Given that discourse includes not only written and spoken texts, but also visual images (Fairclough 1995), this chapter analyzes the cover page of twenty-seven volumes of *The Taste of Korea* published from August 2011 to September 2012. As noted earlier, the newsletter was published between August 2011 and February 2014, including sixty-two volumes. However, since the twenty-eighth volume, it used either an image that would signify the organization's mission or paintings that could symbolize Korea in general. For this reason, I focused on the first twenty-seven volumes, which provide a photographic representation of *traditional* Korean food on the cover page. Through an analysis of these images, I aimed to discover the patterned themes that the newsletter seeks to convey with regard to Korean food, as well as the representational strategies used to justify these particular themes. Specific attention was paid to how the newsletter produces connotative meanings and transforms them into factual systems. As Barthes (1972) writes, the meanings of cultural texts in a second signification order—connotation—are constructed through the use of other sign systems. These sign systems can be loosely or tightly connected, and the relations within them can vary (Manning and Cullun-Swan 1994). Yet, it is through these relations with other sign systems that particular cultural texts generate mythical value and meaning. With that in mind, I explored the following inquiries: (1) What food practices are represented as *Korean* food practices?; (2) How are particular food practices visualized as *tradition*?; and (3) How is regional and class-specific culinary diversity negotiated in the construction of the *taste of Korea*?

As Fairclough (1992) points out, discourse analysis—even a textually-oriented discourse analysis—should address not only concrete texts, but also the social contexts in which the texts are embedded. Thus, before answering the aforementioned questions, I will explain the economic and political contexts of the Korean government's strong intention to globalize Korean food. For doing this, I searched news articles on *hansik segyehwa* (Korean food globalization) published before and during the early MB (MyungBak Lee) administration via KINDS (Korean Integrated Newspaper Database System), which is provided by the Korea Press Foundation. After an initial reading of 1,618 news articles published from May 2007 to April 2012, I removed articles that did not offer a meaningful coverage of Korean food globalization, ending up with 394 articles on Korean food and 163 articles on Korean food globalization. In order to uncover the implicit and multilayered social conditions of the Korean government's increased interests in Korean food, I applied other search words that often appeared on the initial search results, such as President Lee's campaign pledges (eighty-two articles) and the Korea-United States Free Trade Agreement (sixty-seven articles). The analysis of news articles was done through the researcher's careful reading rather than a systematic analysis, as its goal was not to identify journalistic discourse on Korean food, but to contextualize and nuance the analysis of *The Taste of Korea*. In my presentation, the main focus will be on the semiotic analysis of the newsletter; news articles will be used to historically situate my analysis, and thus avoid textual reductionism.

THE ECONOMIC AND POLITICAL CONTEXTS
OF THE GOVERNMENT'S INTEREST IN FOOD

The Korean government's focused attention to food matters was initiated by its awareness of the increasing size of the global food industry, and its awareness of other countries' efforts to make their own food culture global. In his writing for *Seoul Economic Daily*, Young Man Kim (2007, October 12), director of the Bureau of Agricultural Marketing, stressed that the scale of the global food industry was much larger than that of the auto and IT industries. Indeed, the market breadth of the global food industry in 2008 was US$4,800 billion; IT, $1,500 billion; and auto, $1,000 billion (Lee 2008, October 1). He pointed to the Dutch and Danish cases that nurtured the food industry as a driving force of the national economy by establishing food clusters, such as the Food Valley and Öresund Clusters. Kim (2007, October 12) also referred to the efforts of Thailand, Japan, and Italy to globalize their national cuisine, with examples being Thailand's "Kitchen to the World" project, Japan's "TRY Japan's Good Food," and Italy's "Ristorante Italiano Certificate."

Based on this awareness, WoonCheon Jeong, Minister of MFAFF, announced that MFAFF would promote the food industry, establish a national food cluster, and make Korean food one of the world's best five cuisines (Jeong 2008, July 28). *The Taste of Korea* also introduced other countries' efforts to globalize their food and food culture as valid grounds for Korean food globalization. In January 2012, KyuYong Seo, the new Minister of MFAFF, said:

> Our goal of globalizing Korean food is being achieved in enterprising ways: to apply sustainability to our food, agriculture, forestry, and fishery industries. . . . Other countries renowned for their culinary culture, such as Japan, Italy, and France, are devoting considerable public and private resources to make their own food culture global. (Seo 2012, 4)

As described earlier, the economic grounds and references to other countries' successful cases have been at the center of the governmental and journalistic justification of the Korean Food Globalization project. However, its implicit relation to President Lee's economic and foreign policy initiatives, which required the ratification of KORUS FTA (The Free Trade Agreement between the United States of America and the Republic of Korea),[5] should not be ignored. The market-oriented economic policy of MyungBak Lee was called MBnomics, and his stated goals were expressed in the 747 Plan: 7 percent annual growth in the GDP, US$40,000 per capita, and making Korea the world's seventh-largest economy (Hwang 2008, February 23). When he was a presidential candidate, Lee associated his economic policies with foreign and security policies, claiming that Korea had to strengthen its national security and foreign relations for a 7 percent annual growth in the GDP (Nam 2007, August 23). Particularly, Lee's foreign policy initiative, the MBdoctrine, advocated tightening the US-Korea alliance. He stated that he would rebuild better relations with the United States through a greater emphasis on free market solutions (Kim 2008, August 20). For example, at the open forum of presidential candidates held by the Korean Advanced Farmers Federation on November 6, 2007, Lee defined the KORUS FTA as an unavoidable reality. He said, "You may say that you do not want the KORUS FTA, but you are the person who will overcome FTA," and, "Do you think you can go easy with the current farm management? You can't" (Jang 2007, November 7).

Considering the ratification of the KORUS FTA as one of the critical factors in implementing MBnomics and the MBdoctrine, Lee sought a way to justify his policies and obtain the consent of those who would suffer losses caused by the KORUS FTA. Specifically, in order to reduce opposition from farmers and fishermen and compensate the putative loss of rural areas, Lee announced that he would transform the Ministry of Agriculture and Fisheries into the Ministry of Food, Agriculture, Forestry, and Fisheries (Jeong 2008, July 28). On December 20, 2007, the day after he was elected president, Lee claimed that his attempt to reorganize these ministries reflected his plan to change the concept of agriculture from a primary industry to secondary and tertiary industries that would include food processing, distribution, and service (Jeong 2007, December 20). At a public meeting with representatives of farmers and fishermen on January 21, 2008, he also stressed that the goal to combine the food industry with agriculture and fisheries was to create added value and to avoid a potential crisis resulting from the expansion of agricultural product importation (Yim 2008, February 14).[6] Although the economy was foregrounded, Lee's governmental reorganization was not irrelevant to his attitude toward the KORUS FTA. Within this context, the Korean government began to address food as an industry and implemented the Korean Food Globalization project as a tool for improving the national economy. This close, but implicit relationship between the KORUS FTA and Korean food globalization is properly described on the weblog of the Ministry of Foreign Affairs and Trade (MFAT), which is designed to provide an easy explanation of the government's foreign policies to ordinary people:

> Korean food globalization will be rapidly developed as the age of FTA has arrived. Korean food globalization is the best opportunity for agriculture and fisheries, which may suffer a loss because of the FTA. Once Korean food globalization is begun by the FTA, the export of Korean agricultural products will be innovatively increased. The fear that Korean agriculture will be damaged by the FTA is groundless. Rather, due to the FTA, we will be able to expand our market and our agri-food all over the world. (The Ministry of Foreign Affairs and Trade [MFAT] 2012, February 21)

FEATURES OF THE GOVERNMENTAL PALATE

Within the aforementioned economic and political contexts, *The Taste of Korea* emphasized three repetitive themes when visually representing Korean food: (1) the homogeneity of Korean food, (2) the uniqueness of Korean food, and (3) Korean food as a primordial tradition. To legitimize the homogeneity of Korean food, newsletter employed three strategies, each of which is not exclusively distinguished. First, it reduced the class diversity of Korean food. When the newsletter portrayed *hanjeongsik* (the traditional Korean set menus that are spatially developed) in its first volume,[7] it presented *chilcheop bansang* (a table setting composed of seven dishes, including rice and side dishes) as the standard *bansang* (table setting). However, in Korea, the number of dishes varied in the past, depending on socioeconomic class, such as ordinary people, noble families, and royal families: *chilcheop bansang* was not a trans-class food practice. In other words, *The Taste of Korea* represented the food practices of a specific class as the representative and traditional food practices of Korea. Secondly, *The Taste of Korea* strategically removed the local diversity of Korean food. Through the color tone of soup (Vol. 11-1), one can recognize that the soup of *tteokguk* (rice cake soup) is made of *sagolgukmul* (beef bone stock). While people in the mid- and inland provinces of Korea enjoy beef stock, people in the southern regions, especially the coastlines, tend to cook rice cake soup with *myeolchi* (anchovy) broth. Additionally, salt is presented as the main seasoning for *kongguksu* (a cold soybean noodle soup) (Vol. 20). Yet, in *Jeollado* (Jeolla province), people often season cold soybean noodle soup with sugar. Given that food preparation and flavor principles are important elements of a national cuisine (Belasco 2008), these examples show how regional culinary differences are replaced by a single dish to construct a national taste (Appadurai 1981; Cwiertka 2006).

The last strategy, albeit overlapped with the two other strategies, was to standardize Korean food. For example, *bibimbap* has different stories regarding its origins: royal cuisine, the king's refugee food, *eumbok* (partaking of sacrificial food), temple food, and marketplace food (Lee 2006). Also, there are various ways to cook *bibimbap,* according to different regions in Korea, such as *Seoul, Ahndong, Jinju, Haeju,* and *Jeonju.* Yet, the photo of *bibimbap* in the second volume represents *Jeonju-* and the royal cuisine-style as a traditional way of preparing *bibimbap.* This particular food preparation is *anchored* as a norm or tradition by its caption, which speaks of the main ingredients of *bibimbap*: "Rice topped with various cooked vegetables such as zucchini, mushroom, and bean sprouts, plus beef and a fried egg. Served with *gochujang* (red chili paste), which should be mixed in thoroughly" (KFF 2011, August, 1). By concealing the different origins and styles of *bibimbap,* the newsletter removed the diversity of taste in favor of *decent* taste.

The second theme, the uniqueness of Korean food, was justified by two strategies: hiding the hybrid nature of Korean food and assimilating other food cultures. As Pieterse (2009) puts it, all cultures are historically mixed. The national cuisine is also a mixture of the old and new, and of the local and foreign (Cwiertka 2006). For instance, *shinseonro* (a brass chafing dish), featured in the seventh volume, was developed as a highbrow food in Korea with the import of the Chinese *huoguo* (Chinese hot pot) in the sixteenth century. Though it was invented as a symbol of Korean cuisine by the Japanese in the early twentieth century, it was an outcome of the cultural exchange between Korea and China (Joo 2013).

Also, the modern form of *japchae* (a mixed dish of boiled bean threads, stir-fried vegetables, and shredded meat) (Vol. 8) could not have been developed without the import of *dangmyeon* (glass noodle) from China in the late nineteenth century, and of brewed soy sauce from Japan in the early twentieth century (Lee 1985; Joo 2013). In other words, *japchae*, which has occupied an important position on Korea's feast table since the 1930s, is a joint work of the Korean, Chinese, and Japanese, which is inseparable from Japanese colonization. In addition, although the newsletter presents *gochu* (red hot pepper) as a distinctive type of Korean seasoning, it is said that red hot pepper was introduced by Japan during the *Imjin* war (Japanese invasion of Korea in 1592) (Kwon, Jeong, and Yang 2011). However, *The Taste of Korea* did not speak of this hybridized and short-lived origin of Korean food when it introduced the aforementioned foods. According to Fairclough (1995), discourse is constitutive both in conventional and creative ways. de Cillia, Reisigl, and Wodak (1999) further develop this idea, distinguishing four types of discursive strategies—constructive, perpetuating, transformational, and destructive. By concealing the hybrid nature of Korean food, the newsletter prevented people from recognizing significant others or other food cultures involved in the development of Korean cuisine. In so doing, it perpetuated existing myths about the uniqueness and purity of Korean cuisine, and eventually enhanced a sense of continuity to ethnic cores, whether imagined or experienced.

Another strategy is constructive rather than perpetuating. It is constructive in that it incorporates other food cultures into the features of Korean cuisine. For example, chopsticks were often horizontally placed below food on the newsletter's cover page (see figure 7.1). However, this table setting represents the Japanese style: chopsticks and spoons are vertically placed in Korea. Nevertheless, *The Taste of Korea* portrayed it as a distinctive manner or *protocol* (Barthes 1979) of Korean food culture. While the first strategy reinforces the uniqueness of Korean cuisine by hiding its modern and hybrid nature, the second one constructs or reinvents it by taking advantage of others' food practices.

Figure 7.1   Cover Photo of *The Taste of Korea*, Vol. 3. *Source*: Courtesy of Korean Food Foundation.

To portray Korean cuisine as a primordial tradition, the newsletter emphasized the embodiment of national culture in Korean food. Most food images in *The Taste of Korea* consist of five colors: yellow, blue, red, white, and black (see figure 7.1).[8] These five colors imply the philosophy of Yin-Yang and the Five Elements, which had provided Korean people with an epistemological and ontological basis in the past (Dong-A Ilbo Publication Team 2010). In order to materialize the five colors, the newsletter occasionally added unnecessary ingredients to the food. For instance, when presenting *neobiani* (slices of seasoned roast beef) (Vol. 4), it portrayed *kim* (seaweed) as a garnish, which is an unusual way of food preparation and is unnecessary for flavor. More frequently, it directly used other traditions with a longer history, such as traditional ornaments, architecture, and fabrics, to complete the five colors when the food itself did not complete all of them (see figure 7.2). Additionally, *The Taste of Korea* represented a certain food as traditional through metaphorical relations

Figure 7.2   Cover Photo of *The Taste of Korea*, Vol. 5. *Source*: Courtesy of Korean Food Foundation.

with signs of other symbolic systems (Manning and Cullun-Swan 1994). For instance, the image of *songi-sanjeok* (pine mushroom shish kebab) is designed to arouse the imagery of Korean painting and calligraphy (see figure 7.3).

Not surprisingly, most traditions that are directly or metaphorically called for do not include *low* culture; only high culture was formulated as a cultural reference in *The Taste of Korea*, as Gellner (1983) notes. Such a practice implies that not all ethnic cores or cultural practices are selected as traditions: some are brought together, while others are neglected or expunged for the present purpose (Edensor 2002). This visual strategy supports Smith's (2003) following argument: "[Ethnic cores] will only survive and flourish as part of the repertoire of national culture if they can be made continuous with a much longer past that members of that community presume to constitute their 'heritage'" (279).

Figure 7.3   Cover Photo of *The Taste of Korea*, Vol. 27. *Source*: Courtesy of Korean Food Foundation.

By representing Korean food in a peculiar way, *The Taste of Korea* reinforced the homogeneity of the Korean people and culture. As referred to earlier discussion, images of Korean food strategically serve to reduce class and local diversity in Korea. This discursive strategy of assimilation contributes to the construction of intra-national sameness (de Cillia, Reisigl, and Wodak 1999), bridging and homogenizing regional and class differences. In the meantime, as van Dijk (1993) explains, the discursive construction of the self always accompanies the construction of others. Within the governmental discourse of Korean food, the representation of other groups is absent, whether positive or negative. However, it does not mean that those discourses do not draw a boundary between *us* and *them*. Rather, they reinforce a boundary fetishism (Pieterse 2009) by hiding the boundaries according to which Korean people identify themselves. Specifically, through deliberate representational acts, the newsletter concealed the mixed origins of Korean food and consequently reproduced a fantasy about the ethnic and racial purity of the Korean people and culture, which has been a tenet of the Korean nation since its emergence. As Smith (1991) notes, every nation-state contains civic (political) and ethnic (cultural) elements in different forms, producing a distinctive form of nationhood. In Korea, the notion of nation emerged in the early twentieth century in response to Japanese colonialism (Youn 2013), defining the Korean nation as an "ethnically homogeneous and racially distinctive collectivity" (Shin, Freda, and Yi 1999, 469). In particular, the term *minjok* was developed in 1907 in order to call for strong ethnic nationalism (Chang 2010). Since then, there has been a substantial overlap among race, ethnicity, and nation in Korea: race has functioned as a "marker" of ethnic identity and has played an "instrumental role" in defining the Korean nation (Shin, Freda, and Yi 1999, 469). This conflation of race, ethnicity, and nation is connoted in the representational practices of *The Taste of Korea*.

Additionally, visual emphasis on the philosophy of Yin-Yang and the Five Elements represents Korean people as those who share ethnic cores and traditional values. For instance, the discourse of Korean food stresses the group-oriented characteristics of Korean people by presupposing shared traditional values, such as *johwa* (balance) and *hwahap* (harmony), which are connotatively manifested in the below images (see figure 7.4). Korean food is also portrayed as a *tradition* through the juxtaposition with other cultural traditions that have a longer history. This strategy legitimizes the continuity of Koreanness to the past and enhances a sense of shared collective memories. Yet, the process of recollection is always selective: only the idealized past is recalled and reconstituted. Through the selective reproduction of "the pattern of values, symbols, memories, myths, and traditions" (Smith 2001, 30), *The Taste of Korea* constructed the distinctive national heritage of Korea, which, in turn, would be used for each individual's identity construction. Further, visual emphasis on the idealized past and a distinctive heritage arouses a sense of Korean supremacy. Particularly, the false analogy between Korean food and a noble or royal culture shapes a belief in the superiority of Koreanness.

Figure 7.4   Cover Photo of *The Taste of Korea*, Vol. 2, 7, and 24. *Source*: Courtesy of Korean Food Foundation.

CONCLUSION

Drawing on the anthropological notion of food as deep play, this chapter aimed to investigate the Korean government's discourse on Korean food and its articulation of Koreanness. My analysis shows that the newsletter has constructed three different discursive themes in relation to Korean food: the homogeneity of Korean food, the uniqueness of Korean food, and Korean food as a primordial tradition. These patterned themes demonstrate that the Korean government, through the discourse of national cuisine, seeks to stress intra-national sameness and unity of Korean society, as well as the ethnic and racial purity of Korean people and culture. The findings of the discursive strategies used to legitimize these themes support two claims of ethno-symbolists: the nation is constructed through the use of primordial ethnic quality; and only the idealized past is called for the present purpose (Smith 1991). This study also shows that national cuisine, as an invented tradition, contributes to the (re)construction and perpetuation of nation-ness, strengthening the cultural boundary between national *we* and *others*.

Before addressing these issues, I provided the economic and political contexts of the Korean government's increased interest in Korean cuisine. Through an analysis of news articles, I argue that the growth of the government's attention to Korean food was initiated not only by awareness of the increasing size of the global food industry but also by efforts to maintain the national unity of Korean society, which would be weakened by the KORUS FTA. This finding enhances an understanding of the mutually formative relationship between the discourse of national cuisine and the discourse of the nation. In other words, food discourse in Korea functions as a "biological device" that tethers individuals to the nation, as Hiroko (2008, 9) notes.

The Korean government's involvement with gastronationalism is not specific to the MB administration. During the government-led national festival *Gukpung 81* (National Customs 81), the eleventh and twelfth president of South Korea, Doohwan Chun, utilized national cuisine to diminish citizens' political awareness and spread statist discourse on tradition and national subjectivity. Specifically, the Chun administration sought to arouse a sense of nostalgia and a desire for traditional culture by emphasizing *hyangto eumsik* (local food). When South Korea underwent a rapid globalization process in the late 1980s due to the worldwide sport events and international agreements, such as Asian Game in 1986, Trade Liberalization of Foreign Processed Food in 1987, the Seoul Olympics in 1988, and Liberalization of Overseas Trip in 1989, the Roh administration largely promoted a superiority of Korean cuisine and the diversity of local foods. In a similar vein, the Youngsam Kim administration (1993–1998) circulated the discourse of *shintoburi* (body and land are inseparable) in the face of global force of economic liberalization. As the Eighth Multilateral Trade Negotiations—the Uruguay Round—pushed the Korean domestic agricultural industry into the global economy system and forced market-opening of agricultural products, President Kim promoted the consumption of domestic agricultural products and strengthened the linkage among body, food, and nation while he declared globalization as one of his key policies.

The MB administration's discursive practice regarding Korean cuisine, which is exemplified by KFF's newsletter, is in line with these preceding examples in that it promoted the superiority and uniqueness of Korean food, as well as it utilized national cuisine to arouse a sense of national belonging. This discursive practice is still continuing although tactics of each regime have slightly changed depending on the historical circumstances. Indeed, KFF's initial goals, such as fostering global appreciation of Korean food culture, spurring the growth of related industries, and improving Korea's national image, are reflected in the objectives of the Korean Food Promotion Institute (KFPI), which replaced KFF in 2017 (KFF 2012, January).[9] The MB administration stood apart from previous governments by promoting the global expansion of Korean food, particularly through the standardization of Korean cuisine and the commodification of prestige traditions, which are demonstrated in the newsletter's removal of local/class diversity and emphasis on royal cuisine. As noted earlier, this shift took place due to the MB administration's plan to use national cuisine as a driving force of national economy, as well as efforts to reduce opposition from farmers and fishermen and sustain the national unity of Korean society, which would be weakened by the KORUS FTA. While President Chun took advantage of food as part of cultural events to justify the legitimacy of his regime, President Lee attempted to globalize Korean food in order to legitimize neoliberal market-opening and keep people from realizing the putative loss.

Given the limited sources of research materials, it is too soon to generalize the government's discourse on Korean food and Koreanness from these findings. Nevertheless, this chapter, as an instrumental case study, helps us understand the interplay between national cuisine and nation-state, and makes three broad contributions to the literature of the nation, food, and discourse. First, by showing the continuous efforts of the Korean government to (re)construct national cuisine as a *tradition* and to perpetuate a national/ethnic boundary, the current study suggests that it is premature to confirm the "death throes" of the nation-state (Marden 1997, 37); it rather demonstrates that the nation-state, as a strategic actor, still plays a significant role in producing a sense of belonging in the era of globalization. Indeed, a number of countries—Croatia, Mexico, France, Japan, Turkey, and—have designated their national cuisine as the Intangible Cultural Heritage of Humanity in order to carve out their global position through national cuisine. Second, while most food-focused

communication studies have addressed the limited dimensions of food practices, such as food classification and consumption, this article (by looking
into the discursive dimension of food matters) contributes to expanding the
range of food-communication studies and diversifying the research objects of
discourse analysis. Finally, while this study is rooted in the Korean context,
it encourages comparative work on the reflective and formative roles of food
discourse with regard to a discourse of the nation.

NOTES

1. This chapter was previously published with the same title in *Ewha Journal of
Social Sciences*, *35*(1), 153–186.
2. Those who designated their national cuisine as the Intangible Cultural Heritage
of Humanity include Croatia (2010), Mexico (2010), France (2010), South Korea
(2013), Japan (2013), Georgia (2013), Cyprus/Croatia/Spain/Greece/Italy/Morocco/
Portugal (2013), Turkey (2011; 2013), Armenia (2014), North Korea (2015), and the
UAE/Saudi Arabia/Oman/Qatar (2015).
3. Article 17 (Globalization of Traditional Food and Dietary Culture) of the Food
Industry Promotion Act states, "In cases where deemed necessary to globalize traditional food under paragraph (1), the State and local governments may subsidize
expenses incurred in advertising the Korean traditional food and dietary culture,
assisting Korean restaurants opening branches overseas and food industry opening
overseas markets, improving competitiveness of the food industry operating overseas,
etc." (Ministry of Food, Agriculture, Forestry, and Fisheries, 2008, March 21). In
addition, Article 39 of the Enforcement Decree of the Food Industry Promotion Act
entrusts authority to KFF as follows: "The Minister of Agriculture, Food and Rural
Affairs shall entrust the affairs related to the globalization of the traditional food and
dietary culture provided for in Article 17 of the Act to the institutions for Korean food
globalization projects designated under Article 17-2 of the Act" (Ministry of Food,
Agriculture, Forestry, and Fisheries, 2012, July 22).
4. Although the newsletter attempts to reach a global audience, it is targeted at
domestic people. Indeed, the first ten volumes do not have an English translation.
5. Korea and the United States reached an agreement on FTA in April 2007, under
the MooHyun Roh administration. The KORUS FTA was passed in the National
Assembly of Korea in November 2011, and became effective in March 2012.
6. Drawing on Lee's pledges and plans, the MFAFF also established "Making-
Money Agriculture and Fisheries, Rural Areas Worth Living In" as a new goal of
agricultural administration so as to enhance the competitiveness of Korean agriculture
and to face market-opening, which would be followed by the KORUS FTA (Baek
2008, March 19; Woo 2008, March 16). Yet, the focus of the MFAFF was on promoting the agri-food industry rather than stabilizing rural household incomes (Baek 2008,
March 19).
7. In this chapter, I used the English translation of Korean food menus made by the
Korean Food Foundation to deliver the organization's intention as it is. For example,

there has been an ongoing controversy over the origin of *hanjeongsik*, as the term *jeongsik* came from the Japanese expression *teshoku*. According to a food historian and anthropologist, Youngha Joo (2011), there was no such expression as *hansik* or *hanjeongsik* before Japanese colonization. Rather, Japanese colonialists coined the term *Joseon eumsik* (food of the Joseon Dynasty) in order to distinguish it from their mainland food; additionally, it was replaced by *hansik* (Korean food/cuisine) for administrative purposes when the modern form of the Korean nation-state was established. Nevertheless, the Korean Food Foundation represents *hanjeongsik* as a cultural tradition, featuring it in the first volume.

8. At times, each color is replaced by analogous color. For example, red is replaced by pink, which is next to red on the color wheel; black, brown; blue, green.

9. KFPI's major initiatives include: (1) Korean food legitimacy research, (2) traditional Korean food discovery, (3) establishment of Korean food culture, and (4) define the excellence of Korean food (KFPI n.d.).

REFERENCES

Adema, P. (2000). Vicarious consumption: Food, television and the ambiguity of modernity. *The Journal of American Culture, 23*(3), 113–123.

Appadurai, A. (1981). Gastro-politics in Hindu South Asia. *American Ethnologist, 8*(3), 494–511.

Baek, M. (2008, March 19). Nongrimsusansikpumbu jeongchaek mokpyo jesi [MFAFF suggested a goal of policy]. *Seoul ShinMun*, p. 6.

Barthes, R. (1972). *Mythologies* (A. Lavers, Trans.). New York: Hill and Wang.

Barthes, R. (1979). Toward a psychosociology of food consumption. In R. Forster & O. Ranum (Eds.), *Food and Drink in History* (pp. 166–173). Baltimore, MD: Johns Hopkins University Press.

Belasco, W. (2008). *Food: The Key Concepts*. Oxford, New York: BERG.

Bell, D., & Valentine, G. (1997). *Consuming Geographies: We Are Where We Eat*. London, New York: Routledge.

Bhabha, H. (1990). Introduction: Narrating the nation. In H. Bhabha (Ed.), *Nation and Narration* (pp. 1–7). London, New York: Routledge.

Billig, M. (1995). *Banal Nationalism*. London: SAGE.

Ceccraini, R. (2010). Food studies and sociology: A review focusing on Japan. *Journal of Area-Based Global Studies, 1*, 1–17.

Cwiertka, K. J. (2006). *Modern Japanese Cuisine: Food, Power and National Identity*. London: Reaktion Books.

Cwiertka, K. J., & Walraven, B. (Eds.). (2001). *Asian Food: The Global and the Local*. Honolulu: University of Hawaii Press.

de Cillia, R., Reisigl, M., & Wodak, R. (1999). The discursive construction of national identities. *Discourse & Society, 10*(2), 149–173.

de Solier, I. (2005). TV dinners: Culinary television, education and distinction. *Journal of Media & Cultural Studies, 19*(4), 465–481.

DeSoucey, M. (2010). Gastronationalism: Food traditions and authenticity politics in the European Union. *American Sociological Review, 75*(3), 432–455.

Dong-A Ilbo Publication Team. (2010). *Korean Food, the Originality.* Seoul: Dong-A Ilbo Publication.

Douglas, M. (Ed.). (1966). *Purity and Danger: An Analysis of Concepts of Pollution and Taboo.* London: Routledge & Kegan Paul.

Edensor, T. (2002). *National Identity, Popular Culture and Everyday Life.* Oxford, New York: BERG.

Fairclough, N. (1992). *Discourse and Social Change.* Cambridge: Polity Press.

Fairclough, N. (1995). *Media Discourse.* London, New York: E. Arnold.

Foster, R. J. (1991). Making national cultures in the global ecumene. *Annual Review of Anthropology, 20,* 236–260.

Gabaccia, D. (1998). *We are What We Eat: Ethnic Food and the Making of Americans.* Cambridge, London: Harvard University Press.

Gellner, E. (1983). *Nations and Nationalism.* Oxford: Blackwell.

Hansen, S. (2008). Society of the appetite. *Food, Culture & Society, 11*(1), 49–67.

Hiroko, T. (2008). Delicious food in a beautiful country: Nationhood and nationalism in discourses on food in contemporary Japan. *Studies in Ethnicity and Nationalism, 8*(1), 5–30.

Hobsbawm, E., & T. Ranger (Eds.). (1983). *The Invention of Tradition.* Cambridge: The Press Syndicate of the University of Cambridge.

Holtzman, J. D. (2006). Food and memory. *Annual Review of Anthropology, 35,* 361–378.

Hwang, M. (2008, February 23). Saejeongbu chumbeom edo kyeongjejeongchaekeun dangbunkan 'honseon.' [Despite the new government was launched, the economic policy would be confusing for a while]. *Nocut News.* Retrieved from http://www.nocutnews.co.kr/show.asp?idx=756380.

Jang, K. (2007, November 7). Daeseonjuja nongeupjeongchaek gongyak [The agriculture pledges of the presidential candidates]. *DongAh IlBo,* p. 8.

Jeong, Y. (2007, December 20). Lee Myung-Bak dangseonja nongeup jeongchaek [The president-elect, Lee's agriculture policy]. *Naell ShinMun,* p. 16.

Jeong, Y. (2008, July 28). Sikpumjonghapjeongchaek seongkong woihae byeonshinjung [Change for the success of a comprehensive plan for food industry]. *Naell ShinMun,* p. 14.

Joo, Y. (2011). *Eumsik inmunhak [Humanities of Food].* Seoul: Humanist.

Kanafani-Zahar, A. (1997). Whoever eats you is no longer hungry, whoever sees you becomes humble: Bread and identity in Lebanon. *Food and Foodways, 7*(1), 45–71.

Kelly, C. (2017). *Food Television and Otherness in the Age of Globalization.* Lanham, MD: Lexington Books.

Ketchum, C. (2005). The essence of cooking shows: How the Food Network constructs consumer fantasies. *Journal of Communication Inquiry, 29*(3), 217–234.

KFF. (2011–2012). The Taste of Korea, Vol. 1-27. Retrieved from https://www.hansik.org/en/article.do?cmd=html&menu=PEN4060100&lang=en.

KFPI. (n.d.). Purpose of establishment. Retrieved from http://www.hansik.org/en/article.do? cmd=html&menu=PEN6010100&lang=en.

Kim, M. (2008, August 20). "747" plan kongsupyo…daewoonha jwacho… minyeong-hwa jjilddeum [747 Plan ended in an empty pledge…the Grand Korean Waterway project failed…privatization, just a little]. *Seoul ShinMun*. Retrieved from http://www.seoul.co.kr/news/newsView.php?id=20080822009004&spage=1#.

Kim, Y. (2007, October 11). Sikpum saneopeun sae seongjang dongryeok [Food industry as a new driving force of growth]. *Seoul Economic Daily*. Retrieved from https://news.naver.com/main/read.nhn?mode=LSD&mid=sec&sid1=110&oid=011&aid=0000202243.

Korsmeyer, C. (1999). *Making Sense of Taste: Food and Philosophy*. Ithaca, London: Cornell University Press.

Kwon, D., Jeong, K., & Yang, H. (2011). *Gochu iyagi [The Story of Red Hot Pepper]*. Seoul: HyoIl.

Lee, H. (2006). *Hangukeui matkwameot [The Taste and Style of Korea]*. Seoul: ShinKwang.

Lee, M. (2010, March 17). 'Hansik jaedan' chulbum, saegyewha bonkyeok chujin [Korean Food Foundation starts, seeking globalization seriously]. *Munhwa IlBo*, p. 37.

Lee, S. (1985). *Hangukyori munhwasa [The History of Korean Food Culture]*. Seoul: KyoMunSa.

Lee, Y. (2008, October1). 2009 nyeon yesan kikeum pyeonseongan [The budget plan for 2009]. *Seoul ShinMun*, p. 6.

Leitch, A. (2008). Slow food and the politics of port fat: Italian food and European identity. In C. Counihan & P. Van Esterik (Eds.), *Food and Culture* (pp. 381–399). New York: Routledge.

Lentz, C. (1999). (Ed.). *Changing Food Habits: Case Studies from Africa, South America and Europe*. Amsterdam: Harwood Academic Publishers.

Manning, P. K., & Cullum-Swan, B. (1994). Narrative, content, and semiotic analysis. In N. K. Denzin and Y. S. Lincoln (Eds.), *Handbook of Qualitative Research* (pp. 463–477). Thousand Oaks, London, New Deli: SAGE Publications.

Marden, P. (1997). Geographies of dissent: Globalization, identity and the nation. *Political Geography, 16*(1), 37–64.

Ministry of Foreign Affairs and Trade. (2012, February 21). FTAro panro yeonda. Alkishiun hanmi FTA [FTA expands market. Easy KORUS FTA]. Retrieved from http://blog.naver.com/smilevirus12/150132234064.

Mintz, S. W., & Du Bois, C. M. (2002). The anthropology of food and eating. *Annual Review of Anthropology, 31*, 99–119.

Mintz, S.W. (1985). *Sweetness and Power: The Place of Sugar in Modern History*. New York: Penguin.

Munn, N. D. (1986). *The Fame of Gawa: A Symbolic Study of Value Transformation in a Massim (Papua New Guinea) Society*. Cambridge: Cambridge University Press.

Nam, S. (2007, August 23). Hannara daeseon hubo Lee Myung-Bak seonchul yihu/kongyakbunseok [After the election of Myung-Bak Lee/Analysis of a presidential election pledge]. *SeGye IlBo*, p. 6.

Ohnuki-Tierney, E. (1993). *Rice as Self: Japanese Identities through Time*. Princeton, NJ: Princeton University Press.

Oren, T. (2013). On the line: Format, cooking and competition as television values. *Critical Studies in Television, 8*(2), 20–35.

Palmer, C. (1998). From theory to practice: Experiencing the nation in everyday life. *Journal of Material Culture, 3*(2), 175–199.

Parasecoli, F. (2008). *Bite Me: Food in Popular Culture.* Oxford: Berg.

Pieterse, J. N. (2009). *Globalization & Culture: Global Mélange.* Lanham, Boulder, New York, Toronto, Plymouth: Rowman & Littlefield Publishers, INC.

Preston-Werner, T. (2009). Gallo pinto: Tradition, memory, and identity in Costa Rican foodways. *Journal of American Folklore, 122*(483), 11–27.

Scholliers, P. (Ed.). (2001). *Food, Drink and Identity: Cooking, Eating and Drinking in Europe since the Middle Ages.* Oxford, NY: Berg.

Seo, K. (2012). Nongshipumsaneopkwa hansikeui dongbanseongjangeul wuihae [For the growth of agri-food industry and Korean food]. *The Taste of Korea,* 11, p. 4.

Shin, G., Freda, J., & Yi, G. (1999). The politics of ethnic nationalism in divided Korea. *Nations and Nationalism, 5*(4), 465–484.

Smith, A. (1991). *National Identity.* Reno: University of Nevada Press.

Smith, A. (2001). Interpretations of national identity. In A. Dieckhoff & N. Gutierrez (Eds.), *Modern roots: Studies of National Identity* (pp. 21–42). Burlington, VT: Ashgate.

Smith, A. (2003). Towards a global culture? In D. Held & A. McGrew (Eds.), *The Global Transformations Reader* (pp. 278–286). Cambridge: Polity Press.

Sutton, D. E. (2010). Food and the senses. *Annual Review of Anthropology, 39,* 209–223.

Swenson, R. (2009). Domestic Divo? Televised treatments of masculinity, femininity and food. *Critical Studies in Media Communication, 26*(1), 36–53.

Tam, S. M. (2001). Lost, and found?" Reconstructing Hong Kong identity in the idiosyncrasy and syncretism of Yumcha. In D. Y. J. Wu & T. Chee-beng (Eds.), *Changing Chinese foodways in Asia* (pp. 49–70). Hong Kong: Chinese University Press.

van Dijk. (1993). Principles of critical discourse analysis. *Discourse & Society, 4*(2), 249–283.

Wilk, R. (2008). "Real Belizean food": Building local identity in the transnational Caribbean. In C. Counihan & P. Van Esterik (Eds.), *Food and Culture* (pp. 308–326). New York: Routledge.

Woo, S. (2008, March 16). Nongrimsusansikpumbu daetongryeong eopmubogo [MFAFF reported to President Lee]. *SeGye IlBo,* p. 6.

Wright, R., & Sandlin, J. (2009). You are what you eat!?: Television cooking shows, consumption, and lifestyle practices as adult learning. *Proceedings of the Adult Education Research Conference,* Chicago, IL.

Yim, J. (2008, February 14). Nongeupkwa sikpumsaneup convergence shidae yeolja [Let's open the era of convergence between agriculture and food industry]. *SeGye IlBo,* p. 29.

Youn, D. (2013). Hangukminjokjueuieui jaengjeon - Minjokjueuireul baraboneun yanggajeok shiseone daehan jajoneui byeonmyeong [An issue of Korean nationalism: The apology of self-respect on ambivalent recognition]. *Korean Studies Quarterly, 6*(2), 30–365.

Part III

FOOD PRACTICES IN
MULTICULTURAL KOREA

Chapter 8

Globalization of Halal Food

A Study on Its Diffusion into *and* *Export* from *South Korea*

Hyunseo Park and Youngmin Lee

As[1] the Muslim population worldwide continues to grow steadily, the global demand for halal food, the Islamic way of eating, has also been increasing. The global Muslim population is expected to rise from 1.7 billion in 2014 to 2.2 billion by 2030 (26.4 percent) (Pew Research Center 2015). Halal food stems from the religious practice for Muslims, but in many countries, it is considered to be easily accessible and well known to non-Muslims as well (Mathew et al. 2014; Muhammad 2007). Contrary to its popularity in many parts of world, Halal food is not well known in South Korea because of its limited exposure to the Islamic culture and Muslims. However, the number of visiting Muslims to South Korea as their long-term or short-term stay for the purpose of studying abroad, tourism, and medical care has been increasing over 980,000 in 2016 (Korea Tourism Organization [KTO] 2016). Muslim influence on Korean food and restaurant markets is expected to grow as a result, and the Korean government is paying attention to the halal food industry for Muslims visiting or staying in Korea.

A significant amount of research has been conducted on the modern production and consumption of food surrounding globalization and has highlighted many ways in which the food we eat links us to peoples from all parts of the world (Friedmann 1999; McMichael 1991). In many societies, religion plays one of the most influential roles in food choice (Dindyal and Dindyal 2003; Musaiger 1993). In particular, Muslims have a high proportion of food items in taboo, and Muslim food is, therefore, an important part of religious practice (Cho et al. 2008). Halal food in Islam means *permitted food* that Muslims should practice in significant ways, and food produced according to the Qur'anic religious law. For instance, halal signifies *pure food* with

157

regard to meat, such as ritual slaughter and pork avoidance.[2] In the modern
and globalized industry, a number of Muslim requirements have been met
to be setting new standard for production, preparation, handling, storage,
and certification (Fischer 2015). The halal certification system, which means
reviewing the halal integrity and verifying compliance with the halal standard
(Park 2017), has made a great contribution to the systematic institutionalization of halal food.

The purpose of this chapter is to examine the institutionalization process
of the halal food market in South Korea and the consequent globalization
process of the halal food industry. It analyzes the formation of the global
halal market, development of the halal food system on the global scale, and
the impact that the global halal market has on the institutionalization of the
domestic halal market in South Korea. The following questions are proposed:
(1) How is the globalization of the halal food market progressing at the transnational level?; (2) What is the impact of the globalization of halal food on
the halal market in Korea?; (3) What is the role and influence of the diverse
actors in the process of development in the Korean halal market?

TREND OF HALAL FOOD GLOBALIZATION

The size of the global halal market, including food, tourism, pharmaceuti-
cals, and cosmetics, was US$1.9 trillion in 2015, and by 2021, it is expected
to grow annually by 8 percent and reach US$3 trillion (Thompson Reuters
2016). The growth of the halal market is explained not only by the increase in
the Muslim population but also by the development of the Islamic economy
and the influx of Western culture. Increase in disposable income due to the
rise of oil prices in the Gulf Cooperation Council (GCC), Westernization of
food consumption patterns, and awareness of well-being, hygienic and safe
foods have led to the heightened interest in halal food (Mathew et al. 2014).
The word halal was mainly confined to usage in meat products in the past but
its usage is expanding to cosmetics, medicines, and tourism products and the
logistics industry.

Specifically, the food market is expected to grow from US$1,173 billion
to US$1,914 billion by 2021 with an annual increase of 8.5 percent—about
27 percent of the global food market and 63 percent of the total halal market
(Thompson Reuters 2016). The global markets for imported halal food are
worth US$145 billion, and the exports of halal-certified food are primarily led
by non-Muslim countries such as Brazil, India, the United States, China, and
Australia (KOTRA 2016). Among the halal exporters, Brazil has the highest percentage of 10.7 percent, followed by India with 9 percent, the United
States with 4.9 percent, and China with 4.6 percent (Thompson Reuters 2015)

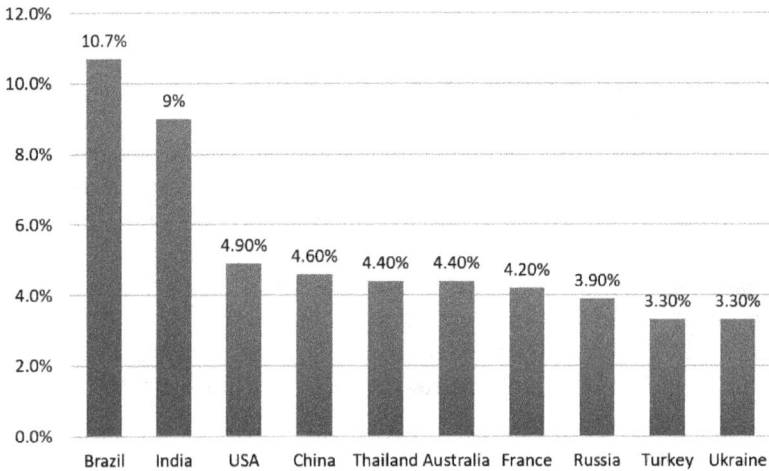

Figure 8.1   Top Halal Food Exports by Country. *Source*: Adapted from KOTRA (2016).

(see figure 8.1). Turkey is the only Islamic country among the top-ten halal exporters. The products are mainly the meats, such as beef, poultry, and mutton (Salaam Gateway 2017).

Malaysia, Turkey, and the UAE are actively taking steps to lead the Islamic halal market among the Islamic countries (Thompson Reuters 2016). Malaysia, which has a high percentage of Muslims, has been developing the processed halal food industry at the government level, leading the halal market with the certification system (Fischer 2015). In particular, the Halal Industry Development Corporation (HIDC) in Malaysia is promoting halal standards and a representative from Jabatan Kemajuan Islam Malaysia (JAKIM), Malaysia's halal state certification body. Turkey is the second-largest halal food market after Indonesia, as a country with a high proportion of Muslim population and a major producer of food, having ample potential to develop into a halal hub in the Middle East. The Association for the Inspection and Certification of Food and Supplies (GIMDES) and the Turkish Standards Institution (TSE) began issuing halal certificates respectively in 2009 and 2011. Despite the relatively small size of the food market and high reliance on food imports, the UAE government has constructed a halal cluster in Dubai Industrial City (6.7 million s/f) to support the companies producing halal products such as food and cosmetics (Gulf News 2014, February 23). Those Islamic countries where most of the people are Muslims have been actively responded to the halal market, such as spreading policies on halal foods.

On the contrary, the leading multinational companies (MNCs) in the global halal market are Nestlé in Switzerland, Carrefour in France, and

American Halal in the United States (KOTRA 2016), the representatives of non-Muslim countries. McDonald's, Nestlé, and KFC, among other food outlets with global reach and production plants, have consistently striven to meet the local demands and international diversity of their consumers through building of separate lines for halal and non-halal products in order to attract their customers (Adams 2011). Nestlé is a European food company, and since the 1980s, it has recognized the importance of the halal market and has set up a halal dedicated part. Considering that 1994 was the year in which the Malaysian government (Fischer 2015), which was leading the halal certification market, began issuing the halal certification, it can be seen that Nestlé's movement to create the halal department was a very early attempt. Nestlé (2016) reported that in 2015, among its 468 factories, 159 were exclusively engaged in producing halal products, being exported to fifty countries. It also revealed its planning to invest US$120 million in establishing a factory in Dubai to enter Middle East coffee and food market. Nestlé has also pursued halal food research and production hubs around Malaysia.

The global institutionalization of certification systems enables the globalization of halal foods. The halal certification system includes halal integrity, which means that the product remain halal from the upstream to downstream supply chain, free from any activities that might breach the halal status, intentionally or unintentionally (Zulfakar et al. 2012). There are around 300 halal certification bodies all over the world (Salaam Gateway 2016), so far no unified international certification system has been established for standard halal accreditation standards in all Muslim countries. Thus, Muslim countries are implementing halal certification schemes with different standards. Halal Certification Authorities Certified organizations worldwide include Jabatan Kemajun Islam Malaysia (Malaysia, JAKIM), Majelis Ulama Indonesia (MUI), and Majelis Ulama Islam Singapura (Singapore, MUIS). Since the standards for halal certification are not integrated worldwide, and certification bodies are fragmented, MNCs such as Nestlé, a leader in the Halal food industry, have used the glocalization strategy to obtain the most recognized halal certification in the region to respond to the worldwide fragmented halal certification.

Therefore, the globalization of halal foods means the process of industrialization of halal foods. In this modern society, halal foods have industrialized that the evaluation of halal foods often have functional and materialist interpretations, as halal is recognized as a brand element (Wilson and Liu 2010). As mentioned earlier, building a brand for halal food is a process of globalization; halal food products are produced by MNCs, including receiving halal food certification through national or transnational institutions for halal foods.

INCREASE OF KOREAN MUSLIMS
AND HALAL MARKET

The distribution of halal food to Korea in earnest became the occasion of the settlement of migrant workers and small merchants from all over Asia and Africa for the *Korean Dream*. As Muslims lived in Seoul Central Masjid since the end of the 1980s, they began establishing halal grocery stores in Itaewon, Hannam-dong, and Bokwang-dong (Song 2011). In order to solve the labor shortage problem in the early 1990s, the foreign industrial trainee system was introduced, and foreign workers began to move into South Korea. Industrial trainees were mainly from Southeast Asia, South Asia, Central Asia, and other Muslim countries, so these immigrants mostly constituted the Muslim community in the early days of Muslim immigration (Ministry of Justice 1998). They did not return home countries after the contract ended, as in the case of Germany's early migrant labor, instead stayed illegally in South Korea and worked in 3D industries avoided by the domestic workers (Song 2011).

Since then, Muslims have continued to flow, and the population has grown rapidly since the mid-1990s. In 2016, the number of South Korean Muslims staying in South Korea was calculated to be 47,200, and the number of foreigners was 154,000, and the total of 201,000 Muslims lived in the country,[3] increased 1.5 percent from 2015 (Park 2017). The number of foreign Muslim in South Korea was highest from the Central Asia (60,055) next to Southeast Asia (55,117) (Ministry of Justice 2017). In addition, over the past five years, the number of domestic residents has increased by an average of 6 percent, and the number of tourists grew by an average of 18.6 percent with 980,000 tourists visiting South Korea in 2016 (KTO 2016) (see figure 8.2). Those

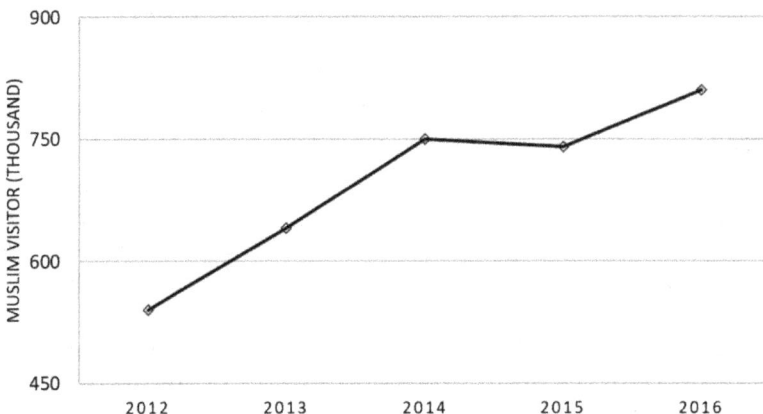

Figure 8.2 Muslim Visitors to South Korea. *Source*: Adapted from KTO (2016).

long-term or short-term staying Muslims have become key consumers or producers in the Korean halal market.

Demand for halal foods has been rising because of the establishment of a community in major cities in Korea. Halal food in Korea began to circulate as migrant workers and small merchants from Asia and Africa came to Korea. Since the end of the 1980s, Muslims have lived in Itaewon-dong, Hannam-dong, Bokwang-dong, and Yongsan-gu, mainly in Seoul Central Masjid in Itaewon—Itaewon Antique Furniture Street—and Usadan-ro (Kang 2010). Since then, the Muslim population has continued to flow, and the number has increased rapidly since the mid-1990s. In 1993, Korean industrial training system for foreign labors became an opportunity to increase its Muslim population. On November 24, 1993, Korea decided to introduce 20,000 foreign industrial trainees first, who entered the country on May 31, 1994 (Kim 2000). As the number of industrial trainees from Islamic countries such as Pakistan, Bangladesh, Indonesia, and Uzbekistan increased, they started to settle in Itaewon (Kang 2010).

They have settled in Itaewon due to the location as the Islamic center and low rents. In addition, it was important for foreign workers from Muslim countries to eat halal food because they are mostly Muslims who believe in Islam and religion was not an abstract faith but a life in itself (Lichtenstadter 1958). Thus, Itaewon, a district of Muslim central where merchants sold goods such as halal food for Muslims, became a good place to live in for them.

The Itaewon recession and the Newtown Urban Renewal District designation, which began in the 1990s, have resulted in lower rents for housing around Seoul Central Masjid (Kang 2010). Due to the decline of the Itaewon entertainment industry from the early 1990s, the number of vacancies increased and the rent began to decline. When Hannam-dong and Bokwang-dong were selected as Newtown district in 2003 and the speculative capital purchased buildings there, the buildings in Itaewon became more aged and slumped, prolonging the decline in the rent (Kang 2010). For the migrant workers, the cheap rental housing of Bokwang-dong and Hannam-dong was an excellent residence that was hard to find in the center of Seoul where rent prices are soaring, and it was also a place where many other foreigners lived, which allowed them to avoid unwelcoming gaze on the foreigners. Since 1990, it has become a major residential area of black Africans (Nigerians, Ghanaian), and Muslims from various countries have gathered here (Han 2005).

In the 2000s, many Muslim foreign workers began to gather around the Central Masjid (Kang 2010). As the number of foreign Muslims in Itaewon increased, the demand for daily necessities for Muslims increased, and the places near the Central Masjid changed. When the number of

Figure 8.3 Muslim Restaurant Makkan on the Islamic Street in Itaewon. *Source:* Copyright © 2017 Hyunseo Park.

foreign Muslims settling around the central Muslim community and foreign Muslims visiting the worship service increased from 2000, restaurants and food shops for the Muslims began to grow around the Islamic center. At that time, Itaewon had many vacant stores due to the depression and the new town development, the malls around the Islamic center were quite fitting for the Muslims to rent. Therefore, it was possible to open Muslim-related shops without any resistance (Song 2011). The streets from Bokwang Elementary School to Islamic Central Branch were gradually filled with Muslim-related restaurants, butcher shops, bookstores, travel agencies, and so on (see figure 8.3). As the streets developed, more Muslims began to flock to the Islamic street to worship at Seoul Central Masjid on Friday, and eat halal foods. After the mid-2000s, the area has formed the Muslim commercial district. The streets were called Islamic street in the media (Hwang 2010) and the visitors who came to experience Islamic culture and food also increased.

DIVERSIFICATION OF HALAL FOOD DISTRIBUTION NETWORK IN SOUTH KOREA

As the number of foreign Muslims in the country increased and their nationalities became more diverse, their food and beverage trade network tended to be divided by nationality (Song 2011). In other words, workers from Pakistan, Bangladesh, and Indonesia gradually created shops that specialized in spices and ingredients from their countries and the workers tended to gather at the stores of their nationality. From the mid-1990s to the early 2000s, there were grocery stores and restaurants serving Muslim immigrants of various nationalities under the name of "Islamic Restaurant" and "Halal Mart (Song 2011)." In the early days, the demand was relatively large compared to the supply, and the number of suppliers was limited, so the initial participants earned considerable profits. The market was not so large or small, so food-related conglomerates did not participate in the market.

In the early days, halal chicken has been produced by migrant workers but without an official market (Jang and Cho 2014). Many Southwest Asian foreign workers who entered Korea in the late 1980s and early 1990s were Muslims who believed in Islam. In the early days of their stay in Korea, halal ingredients needed by the early settlers were not distributed in the food supply chain, and the official market for halal foods was not formed yet. Bangladesh, Pakistan, and other South East Asian Muslims resorted to eating poultry. Then the idea came out to prepare halal poultry on individually by handling live poultry in Korea. The idea evolved to cooperating in handling live poultry and eating together (Civitello 2007). In particular, on weekends, it became a regular event for South Asian Muslim workers to buy poultry from a market and cook together in the Islamic way. Our interviewee Patwan, an international referee of *taekwondo* (a Korean traditional martial art) from Pakistan,[4] stated that he sometimes got the freshly slaughtered chicken for the consumption of halal meat.

Some Muslims made the halal poultry slaughtered. For example, they would contact a poultry house to reserve about 100 poultries, and about a dozen Muslims would go to the house to pray and prepare the poultry (Song 2011). Unofficially, some retailers ordered chickens at poultry farms, arranged them according to halal's rule, and then sold them to migrant workers. The production developed into a form of slaughtering poultry while playing prayer voices in a tape (Song 2011). The halal chicken is made in this way one or two times a month, usually supplying 10,000 to 20,000 poultries each time. Some large distributors are said to provide between 50,000 and 100,000 poultries a month (Jang and Cho 2014). Therefore, halal poultry has been able to be mass-produced in this country leading to commercialization of halal meat.

Since the 2000s, the domestic halal food distribution network has been structured in earnest and at the same time has been forming an official network to export the overseas halal market. After September 11, 2001, the Korean government had restricted the entry of immigrants from major Islamic cultures such as Pakistan and Bangladesh, and raised the percentage of the entry rate of Indonesian workers who are perceived to be relatively less religious (Song 2011). This shift is due to the belief that migrant workers from these countries are less likely to be Islamic fundamentalists. As a result, the distribution network that supplied halal food went through a significant change. Pakistan and other halal food wholesalers have been relatively reduced in size, and Korean retailers gradually expanded the area of halal food supply (Hwang et al. 2015). Korean companies have involved in the halal food industry for the reasons that they could deal with various countries at the same time, and they were relatively advantageous to receive bank loans from the local banks, as well as in negotiating imports and exports with the government authorities (Song 2011).

There have been ethnic changes in food wholesalers, but the biggest change in the halal food distribution network was that MNCs have significantly increased their market share (Hwang et al. 2015). As multinational food companies dominated the global processed foods, wholesale and retail stores displayed imported food products from highly reliable food brands. As mentioned earlier, the development of standardization and certification systems for halal foods has led multinational food companies to occupy the global halal market. For instance, Nestlé's manufacturing facilities are 100 percent halal, and the Group produces and exports halal products to more than fifty countries across the globe (Nestlé 2016), and Nestlé Halal products are sold at large retail outlets in Korea such as Lotte Mart (KOTRA 2016). The imported halal products of MNCs have an important place in the food consumption market of foreign Muslims in Korea.

New types of consumption are emerging alongside the development of the internet and traffic communication. In the past, foreign Muslims working in relatively remote areas of foreigner-occupied settlements visited the food supply stores using the holidays. There was a periodic cycle of movement for food purchases. Recently, however, grocery stores begin to provide delivery services for consumers who are far from ethnic enclaves. This service has made it easier for Muslim consumers to purchase halal foods.

Furthermore, as the age and type of Muslim migrants have changed, new distribution networks have emerged. The number of international Muslim students (college students) from Muslim countries increased by 44.6 percent in Uzbekistan, 15.2 percent in Indonesia, 10 percent in Pakistan, 7.7 percent in Malaysia, and 19.7 percent in Bangladesh (Ministry of Justice 2016). The majority of international students are comfortable using online shopping in Korea. They use smartphones to purchase foods from vendors such as *Coupang* and *SSG*, where goods are delivered in one day. In particular, consumption patterns for halal foods shows that meat and spices are purchased using online halal food sales site (e.g., *Yes! Halal*[5]) (see figure 8.4). Muslim consumers can easily buy Islamic products online regardless of their residence, using the delivery services provided by existing retail stores.

The expansion of halal food industry in Korea has been led by the presence of the unofficial domestic halal market. Although the dominant role of market development by the government and essential food companies has been emphasized, it can be seen that the expansion of the actual market has led to the formation and development of the market by the Muslim immigrants who moved to Korea. As focusing on this point of halal food production and its consumption, Muslim migrants' life seems to have remained the Islamic

Figure 8.4 Online Halal Food Website Yes! Halal (http://www.yeshalal.com). *Source*: Courtesy of Yes! Halal.

foodways from the country of origin as an example of the term cultural diffusion. On the contrary, from the perspective of halal itself, halal food products today seek to brand themselves as halal and prepare for the cultural transformation of identity in Korea. Many products within Muslim countries have previously taken their halal status as a given (Wilson and Liu 2010). In this non-Islamic country, the government has announced the halal food exports in 2015.[6] Halal often represents something *lucrative factor*, and thus presents itself as a potential *globalization of Korean food*.

EXPORTS OF HALAL FOOD FROM SOUTH KOREA: ITS STRATEGY GRAFTED WITH KOREAN WAVE

As the influence of Korean dramas and Korean pop has been unprecedented, the demand for Korean food in the Islamic market has increased due to the Korean Wave including K-pop. The South Korean Ministry of Agriculture Food and Rural Affairs (MAFRA) has been participating in the major international expositions of the Islamic market since 2015 and has been expanding the local market for exporting agricultural products and expanding its exports through halal seminars, export conferences, and consumer experience events (Park 2017). K-Food Fair and other exhibitions will be the space where MAFRA's export of Korean food is maximized. Domestic halal foods, which have already obtained national and international accreditation, gave an opportunity for foreign buyers to focus on the Korean market, and further promoted to the Islamic market.

Since 2010, Korean food companies are actively pursuing halal certification to enter the halal market (Hwang et al. 2015). The number of local enterprises and products that have obtained KMF certification in Korea grew from 404 items from 133 companies in 2014 to 501 items from 167 companies in 2015 (Hwang et al. 2015) and to 562 items from 197 companies in May 2016 (Park 2017). On the other hand, no foreign company has yet obtained KMF certification. There are some cases in which domestic companies acquired non-Korean certification, such as JAKIM (Malaysia) and MUI (Indonesia). In the event of a company promoting localization policy, obtaining overseas certification is beneficial for expanding sales through local production and brand localization.

With Halal Food Industry Development and Export Promotion Policy in 2015, the South Korean government has been focusing on building infrastructures through the construction of an information center, a slaughterhouse for poultry and a production complex. To expand the halal export market, the government has enlarged its support for halal certification fee, established the Korean halal certification standard and guided domestic institutions. To increase the agricultural products exports in the halal market, the government put forth plans to expand overseas marketing such as holding export conferences. The government has registered domestic halal certification standards as national industry standards, increased cross certification with overseas certification agencies. For the current supply chains and distribution centers of domestic halal ingredients, the government has financed the refurbishment of slaughterhouses. Furthermore, it opened the halal industry lectures for professional training.[7]

Many Korean food companies are pursuing policies to export to the Southeast Asian market. *Daesang* first entered the Southeast Asian market and established a halal food factory in Indonesia in 1973 (Choe et al. 2003). It is considered as the first-generation halal food company. It received the halal-certified MUI from Indonesia and sold only 30 billion KRW worth of halal food produced locally. *Cheil Jedang (CJ)* obtained JAKIM Halal certification for forty-three items including pre-cooked rice, seasoned laver, and Kimchi. They aim for sales worth 100 billion KRW by 2018 through aggressive marketing. *Nongshim* acquired eight kinds of KMF halal certifications, including Shin Ramen and six cup noodles for export to the Middle East.

In the first half of 2013, Shin Ramen increased its salary by 54 percent to US$1 million (approximately, 1.1 billion KRW), which was the largest increase in its export.

With the popularity of K-Culture, for example, exports of Korean confectionery to Southeast Asia and the Middle East surged. Therefore, confectionery companies are planning to expand their investment in the Southeast Asian market. Exports of confectionery in 2015 were US$251.61 million, up 785 percent from US$140.93 million in 2011 (aT 2017). The export from Korea to Southeast Asian countries such as Singapore (316.7 percent), Malaysia (297.7 percent), the Philippines (194.8 percent), Saudi Arabia (141.8 percent), and the UAE (60.7 percent) have also increased their exports (aT 2017). As a result, exports of confectionery, especially in Southeast Asia and the Middle East, will increase rapidly, boosting the interest in the confectionery sector as a market for halal food exports.

Therefore, the Muslim food culture diffused to the South Korea has changed into a brand of the halal food. Halal-certified Korean food serves as part of the national cultural promotion project. To export halal Korean food is a policy of globalizing the K-food according to the current of Korean Wave.

CONCLUSION

As the global Muslim population grows, the halal food industry is growing at a rapid pace to meet the growing demand of Muslims. The size of the global halal market was US$1.9 trillion in 2015 (Thompson Reuters 2015). In many countries, attention has been paid to the growth potential of the halal food market as a new economic growth engine, and the Korean government announced the halal Food Measure in June 2015 to expand its entry into the halal food market. The government has implemented a variety of detailed policies to build an industrial base for the global halal food market to allow domestic agricultural products to be halal certified, to revitalize product distribution, and to supply halal foods to hospitals and restaurants for Muslim tourists.

Not only to follow the global economic trend (Thompson Reuters 2016) but also to spread the Islamic culture to Korea and the spread of Islamic culture due to the increase of Muslim migration, the Korean halal food market was formed and developed in the late 1980s, and halal restaurants and grocery stores have appeared in Muslim ethnic enclaves (Jang 2006), as a grocery store plays a significant role in choosing where to live, work, and attend religious services for Muslims. Halal meat, especially chicken, was slaughtered by individual Muslims, but now supplies a certain level of domestic production farms. In the early days, the food network that had been distributed through individual packers was diversified and developed. In particular, halal food distribution is being actively carried out by food MNCs. Recently, online food transaction is actively taking place with the development of information communication network. This study reviewed the government's halal food policy, which is strategically pursued by the global market development. However, the Korean halal market has evolved gradually since the 1990s and developed independently from the recent government's halal food policy.

As the food culture of Muslims spreads in Korea, Korean companies are increasingly entering the overseas halal market by Korean Wave. Korean food companies are producing food according to the halal food certification system to enter the halal food market targeting Muslim consumers. By acquiring various certification systems of KMF as well as overseas institutions, the competitiveness in the foreign market has become higher. The government has implemented the policies to enhance the competitiveness of Korean food. The halal food is a multifaceted crossing between the sects of science, economy, and politics.

The globalization of halal food takes place in the transformation of the identity of culture spread by transnational migrants. This chapter describes the changes in Korean food by halalization and materialization through the entry of major food companies in overseas markets. Moreover, it examined the government's export promotion strategy regarding food companies as part of the link with the globalization policy of Korean food actively promoted since 2010. Halal foods play a multiplicative role in linking the Muslim and non-Muslim domains in that they encourage the export of Korean food and further improve its brand value. Halal foods play a multiplicative role in linking the Islamic and non-Islamic regions in that the government promotes Korean food exports and its brand values using the halal certification system.

NOTES

1. This chapter was previously published with the same title in *Journal of the Korean Urban Geographical Society*, *20*(3), 131–142.

2. Halal meat is mainly confined to permitted meats, such as sheep, cows, and chickens, and allowed meats are only slaughtered in a halal manner, slaughtering the veins in a single knife after a prayer called "Bis Milah (In the name of Allah)."

3. The annual report "Korea Immigration Service Statistics 2016" is to provide raw data of foreign residents. In order to calculate more accurately the population of Muslims in South Korea, the status of foreigners in 2016 has been categorized by nationality from the Organization of Islamic Cooperation (OIC). The number of Muslims staying in South Korea was estimated based on the percentage of Muslims in each country found in CIA World Factbook. In the case of married immigrants, eleven

Muslim countries, such as Indonesia, Uzbekistan, and Pakistan where Koreans find their spouses most commonly, were included. As for the naturalization analysis, only thirty OIC member countries from which naturalization occurred most often were included.

4. Patwan continues to state, "I sometimes visit the poultry farm near Gyeonggi province with my friends. . . . We pray and make halal poultry. Even though it's cumbersome to visit, we can get the fresh halal poultry . . . and I can make the chicken *karahi* taste similar to the one from my hometown" (personal interview). He often visits Korea for a short stay and returns to his hometown in Pakistan. In 2016, Patwan stayed with his wife for several months in Seoul. Though chicken *karahi* is one of his favorites, it is not easy to find a chicken that is slaughtered in halal in Korea.

5. *Yes! Halal*, a company headquartered in Korea, has built an online platform for halal products since 2016, and dozens of halal suppliers are using the platform. The number of products registered on the website is 554, as of April 2017.

6. The South Korean Ministry of Agriculture Food and Rural Affairs has announced, in June 2015, the Halal Food Industry Development and Export Promotion Measures as a growth engine for the domestic food industry.

7. Those are to raise halal industry specialists—Korea Trade-Investment Promotion Agency (KOTRA) and Korea Agro-Fisheries Trade Corporation (aT)—and halal consulting companies such as Korea Institute of Halal Industry (KIHI). They provide information on halal certification, procedures for acquiring the halal certification, and information on the oversea halal market. Halal training courses provide the concept of halal food and its religious background.

REFERENCES

Adams, I. (2011). Globalization: Explaining the dynamics and challenges of the halal food surge. *Intellectual Discourse*, *19*(1), 123–145.

aT. (2017). Korean processed food market 2016. Retrieved from www.atfis.or.kr.

Cho, H., Kim, D., Ahn, J., Oh, J., & Kim, H. (2008). Muslim communities in the Korean Society: Focusing on the influx, adaptation, and social network of Muslim Immigrants in Korea. *Journal of the Institute of the Middle East Study*, *27*(2), 81–124.

Choe, S., Lee, C., & Chung, T. (2003). PT Miwon Indonesia: Its thirty years' business in the Asian market. *Korean Academic Society of Business Administration*, *6*(2), 67–89.

Civitello, L. (2007). *Cuisine and Culture: A History of Food and People*. Hoboken, NJ: John Wiley and Sons.

Dindyal, S., & Dindyal, S. (2003). How personal factors, including culture and ethnicity, affect the choices and selection of food we make. *Internet Journal of Third World Medicine*, *1*(2), 27–33.

Fischer, J. (2015), *Islam, Standards, and Technoscience: In Global Halal Zones*. London: Routledge.

Friedmann, H. (1999). Remaking traditions: How we eat, what we eat and the changing political economy of food. In D. Barndt (Ed.), *Women working the NAFTA food chain: Women, food, and globalization* (pp. 35–60). Toronto: Sumach Press.

Gulf News. (2014, February 23). Halal cluster launched at Dubai Industrial City. Retrieved from http://gulfnews.com/business/ economy/halal-cluster-launched -at-dubai-industrial-city-1.1294870.

Han, G. (2005). Understanding of African workers migration to Korea: Migration system, process and social network. *Korean Association of African Studies, 21,* 215–239.

Hwang, Y., Lee, K., Kim, S., & Choi, J. (2015). A study on the domestic market for halal food. *Korea Rural Economic Institute,* 1–121.

Jang, G., & Cho, S. (2014). Demand and supply status and estimation of equilibrium quantity for halal chicken industry in Korea. *Journal of The Korean Association of The Islamic Studies, 24*(1), 107–136.

Jang, Y. (2006). Growth of the business area for migrant workers and ethnic networks: In case of Wongok-Dong, Ansan. *Journal of The Korean Association of Regional Geographers, 12*(5), 523–539.

Kang, H. (2010). *Itaewon.* Seoul: Seoul Art History Museum.

Kim, S. (2000). Activation plan of industrial training system for foreign labors (Master's thesis). Graduate School of Honam University, South Korea.

Korea Tourism Organization (KTO). (2016). Muslim-friendly restaurants in Korea. Retrieved from https://kto.visitkorea.or.kr/kor.kto.

KOTRA. (2016). Global halal market trend and certification system (KOTRA 16-046). Retrieved from https://www.kotra.or.kr/biz/.

Lee, H., & Lee, S. (2013). An exploratory study of Korean food globalization through Diffusion of the Korean food to Islamic country. *Korean Association of Islamic Studies, 23*(2), 115–138.

Lichtenstadter, I. (1958). *Islam and the Modern Age: An Analysis and An Appraisal.* New York: Bookman Associates.

Mathew, V., Abdullah, A., & Ismail, S. (2014). Acceptance on halal food among non-Muslim consumers. *Procedia–Social and Behavioral Sciences, 121*(Supplement C), 262–271.

McMichael, P. (1991). Food, the state, and the world economy. *International Journal of Sociology of Agriculture and Food, 1*(1), 71–85.

Ministry of Culture, Sports and Tourism. (2017). International visitor survey 2016. Retrieved from https://www.mcst.go.kr/kor/main.jsp.

Ministry of Justice. (1998). Korea immigration service, Statistics related to foreign immigrants. Retrieved from http://search-home.moj.go.kr/search.jsp#.

Ministry of Justice. (2017). Korea immigration service statistics 2016. Retrieved from http://search-home.moj.go.kr/search.jsp#.

Muhammad, R. (2007). Branding halal food as safe, healthy and clean. *Halal Journal, 2*(3), 32–34.

Musaiger, A. (1993). Socio-cultural and economic factors affecting food consumption patterns in the Arab countries. *Journal of the Royal Society of Health, 113*(2), 68–74.

Nestlé. (2016). Nestlé's annual review. Retrieved from https://www.nestle.com/si tes/default/files/asset-library/documents/library/documents/annual_reports/2016-annual-review-en.pdf.

Park, H. (2017). Food globalization and culture war: The case of the halal food complex in South Korea (Master's thesis). Graduate School of Ewha Womans University, South Korea.

Pew Research Center. (2015). The future of the global Muslim population projections, 2010-2050. Retrieved from https://fronteirasxxi.pt/wp-content/uploads/2018/11/The-Future-of-World-Religions_-Population-Growth-Projections-2010-2050-_-Pew-Research-Center-1.pdf.

Salaam Gateway. (2016). UAE Cabinet approves establishment of International Forum for Halal Certification Bodies. Retrieved from https://www.salaamgateway.com/en/story/UAE_Cabinet_approves_establishment_of_International_Forum_for_Halal_Certification_Bodies-SALAAM11012016051840/.

Salaam Gateway. (2017). The OIC's current and potential role in the global halal food trade. Retrieved from http://repository.salaamgateway.com/images/iep/galleries/documents/201702260610175356.pdf.

Song, D. (2011). Cultural interpretation on the patterns of consumption and supply system of Islamic (halal) food in Korea. *Korean Journal of The Middle East Studies*, *32*(1), 217–249.

Thompson Reuters. (2015). State of the global Islamic economy 2015-2016 report. Retrieved from http://www.halalbalancing.com/Downloads/Events/2015/SGIEReport2015.pdf.

Thompson Reuters. (2016). State of the global Islamic economy 2016-2017 report. Retrieved from https://www.slideshare.net/EzzedineGHLAMALLAH/state-of-the-global-islamic-economy-report-201617.

Wilson, J., & Liu, J. (2010). Shaping the halal into a brand? *Journal of Islamic Marketing*, *1*(2), 107–123.

Zulfakar, M., Jie, F., & Chan, C. (2012). *Halal food supply chain integrity: from a literature review to a cosnceptual framework*. Paper presented at the 10th ANZAM Operations, Supply Chain and Services Management Symposium, Australia.

Chapter 9

Intrahousehold Discrepancy Regarding Food Insecurity within Intermarried Couples of Vietnamese Wives and Korean Husbands in South Korea

Haney Choi, Hye Won Chung,
Ji-Yun Hwang, and Namsoo Chang

The[1] number of female immigrants arriving in Korea through marriage has been increasing rapidly since 1990, especially more recently, with the number of marriages between Korean men and foreign women increasing by 362 percent between 2000 and 2009 (25,142 cases) (Korea National Statistical Office 2009b). Our previous studies have revealed the inadequate nutritional status of Vietnamese female marriage immigrants as well as their Korean spouses (Hwang et al. 2010; Kim et al. 2009; Lyu et al. 2009), who account for the second-highest rate of intermarriage after Chinese women (Korea National Statistical Office 2009; Ministry of Justice 2009).

Food insecurity is defined as "limited or uncertain availability of nutritionally adequate and safe foods resulting from financial resource constraints" (USDA 2000, 6). The World Food Summit of 1996 defined food security as existing "when all people at all times have access to sufficient, safe, nutritious food to maintain a healthy and active life" (World Food Summit 1996). Therefore, both financial and access constraints should be considered when addressing food insecurity. In the United States, households with immigrants were more likely to have food insecurity than households in which all members were born in the United States (Borjas 1999; Kaiser et al. 2002, 2004; Kasper et al. 2000; Kersey, Geppert, and Cutts 2007; Quandt et al. 2004, 2006). Furthermore, the prevalence of food insecurity in the United States was higher among female immigrants (35 percent) than among economically underprivileged females (16 percent) (Chilton et al. 2009). In Korea, the rate of household food insecurity in rural areas (9.9 percent) is about two times higher than the national average (5.4 percent) (Kim and Kim 2009; Kim, Kim, and Shin 2009). Most Korean men who are married to Vietnamese women have a low socioeconomic status and live in rural communities (Hwang et al. 2010; Kim et al. 2009; Lyu et al. 2009). Therefore, these intermarried couples and their heightened economic difficulties are far more susceptible to food insecurity than their non-intermarried counterparts. In addition, new immigrant wives have an impaired ability to gain access not only to nutritionally adequate foods but also to culturally acceptable foods, partly due to a lack of adjustment to unfamiliar Korean foods and limited access to Vietnamese foods. At the same time, Korean spouses may not have sufficient access to Korean foods because their Vietnamese wives, who are mainly responsible for preparing meals, are not familiar with Korean foods and cooking (72.2 percent) (Kim et al. 2009). Therefore, both Korean husbands and their Vietnamese wives may experience food insecurity, not only due to economic problems but also due to the unavailability of foods that appeal to their appetite.

While food insecurity may be a major contributor to nutritional inadequacy among intermarried couples in Korea, no study has investigated food insecurity among such couples. Most previous studies of food insecurity among immigrants have involved children (Chilton et al. 2009; Dave et al. 2009; Kersey, Geppert, and Cutts 2007) and Hispanic (Dave et al. 2009), Latino (Kaiser et al. 2004; Kuyper et al. 2006; Quandt et al. 2004, 2006), and Mexican (Kaiser et al. 2002; Kersey, Geppert, and Cutts 2007) adults participating in food-assistance programs (Kuyper et al. 2006; Nam and Jung 2008; Rush et al. 2007) in the United States, as well as adult immigrants from Colombia in Canada (Rush et al. 2007). In addition, only one previous study has investigated the discordance of thirteen food insecurity items between native Bangladeshi couples living in Bangladesh (Coates et al. 2010). Therefore, the present study investigated the prevalence of food insecurity in Korean-husband-Vietnamese-wife couples in Korea to determine whether they exhibit an intrahousehold discrepancy regarding food insecurity. In addition, we compared general characteristics, daily nutrient and food intakes, and blood profiles between the subjects with and without food insecurity.

SUBJECTS AND METHODS

Study Subjects

The participants were Vietnamese female marriage immigrants who voluntarily participated in the Cohort of Intermarried Women in Korea study, which is an ongoing, prospective, epidemiological study that forms part of the Korean Genome and Epidemiology Study (KoGES), established in

November of 2006, as described elsewhere (Hwang et al. 2010; Kim et al. 2009; Lyu et al. 2009). Those eligible for the study were female marriage immigrants from Vietnam, their Korean spouses (who had been in Korea for > six months), and their children, who were contacted regularly by local governmental health officials in centers that support families of intermarried couples. As a baseline investigation, subjects received either a telephone call or an advertisement inviting them to attend a comprehensive health screening at local clinical centers in Seoul, Busan, Daegu, Danyang, Gimhae, Gwangju, Gyeongju, Gongju, Jinju, Sangju, Masan, Okcheon, and Pohang, Korea, between May and August 2009. Among the 287 immigrant respondents, 96 subjects visited health clinics with their spouses. Of those 96 husbands, data for 12 were excluded because of insufficient information on anthropometry (n = 3), sociodemographic characteristics (n = 2), dietary intakes (n = 4), or food insecurity (n = 3). Therefore, eighty-four intermarried couples were finally eligible for this analysis. The anthropometric, sociodemographic characteristics, and food insecurity did not differ significantly between subjects with (n = 84) and without (n = 203) sufficient spouse data. The anthropometric parameters and sociodemographic characteristics did not differ significantly between subjects who were excluded and included in the analysis. The study protocol was approved by the Human Investigation Review Board of Ewha Womans University College of Medicine, and informed consent to participate was obtained from all subjects.

Food Insecurity

Food insecurity was measured using two questions regarding economic difficulty and two questions regarding lack of appetizing foods, through face-to-face interviews. The United States Department of Agriculture (USDA) household food insecurity measurements (USDA 2000) and modified USDA household food insecurity questionnaires have been validated (Kim and Kim 2009) to be applied to the Koreans, but have not been validated for Vietnamese immigrants in Korea. The following two questions from the six-item short-form of the United States Household Food Insecurity Survey Module (USDA 2000) were used to assess food insecurity due to economic problems: "Did you ever reduce the size of meals or ate less than you desired because there was not enough money for food in the last year?" (Q1), and "Did you ever skip meals because there was not enough money for food in the last year?" (Q2). In addition, we modified Q1 and Q2 to measure food insecurity due to lack of availability of foods that subjects desired to eat or because a lack of foods that appealed to their appetite: "Did you ever feel hungry because there were no foods that you wanted to eat or no foods that appealed to your appetite at home in the last year?" (Q3), and "Did you ever skip meals because there was no food that you wanted to eat or there was no food that appealed to your appetite at home in the last year?" (Q4). A food insecurity score was used to assess concordance with the degree of food insecurity between couples for each of the four questions. All items were weighted equally and scored 1 for yes and 0 for no, and each individual had scores that ranged from 0 to 1. The anthropometric parameters and sociode-mographic characteristics (household income, education level, and length of residence) did not differ significantly between respondents (95 percent) and non-respondents (5 percent) to the four food insecurity questions.

Sociodemographic Characteristics and Dietary Intakes

Each subject was individually interviewed by trained technicians and graduate students to obtain data regarding their sociodemographic characteristics, food consumption, and dietary behaviors, using standard protocols. Vietnamese translators fluent in both Korean and Vietnamese helped in the investiga-tion process. Household monthly income was classified as < US$1,000, US$1,000–1,499, US$1,500–2,000, and > US$2,000. The education level of the Vietnamese wives and their Korean husbands was categorized as ≤ elementary school, middle school, and ≥ high school. Length of residence in Korea was classified as < 1, 1–3, 4–7, and > 7 years. Food consumption by intermarried couples was assessed using a one-day twenty-four-hour recall. Food models and photographs were used to explain the portion sizes. Dietary intake data were analyzed using the Computer Aided Nutritional Analysis program version 3.0 software (CAN-Pro 3.0).

Anthropometric Parameters, Blood Pressure, and Blood Biochemical Profiles

Standing height and body weight were measured using an automatic height/ weight-measuring instrument (Dong Sahn Jenix, Seoul, Korea) by trained nurses or medical doctors. Body mass index was calculated, and waist and hip circumferences were measured with a tape measure (Anthropometric tape, Preston 5193, Seoul, Korea). Blood pressure was measured using an automatic blood pressure calculator FT0500R (Jawon Medical, Gyeongsan, Korea) after a ten-minute rest in the sitting position; the average of two measurements was used. Blood samples were drawn after an eight-hour over-night fast into EDTA tubes. The plasma samples were centrifuged at 3,500 rpm for 10 minutes at 4°C and stored at −70°C until analysis. Fasting plasma levels of glucose, total cholesterol, triglyceride (TG), albumin, hemoglobin, hematocrit, and high-density lipoprotein (HDL)-cholesterol were measured with an autoanalyzer (ADVIA 1550, Bayer Diagnostics, Tarrytown, NY,

USA); low-density lipoprotein (LDL)-cholesterol was calculated as total cholesterol-HDL-cholesterol-(TG/5) (Friedewald, Levy, and Fredrickson 1972).

Statistical Analysis

All analyses were performed using SPSS software (version 12.0) and the data are expressed as mean ± SD values (continuous variables) or as numbers and percentages (categorical variables). Student's *t*-test was used to compare anthropometric parameters and blood biochemical profiles between subjects with and without food insecurity. The Pearson's χ^2 test or fisher's exact test was used to assess whether intermarried couples reported food insecurity differently. The level of statistical significance was defined as $P < 0.05$.

RESULTS

Sociodemographic Characteristics and Nutritional Status of Intermarried Couples

The Korean husbands were aged 41.0 ± 5.6 years and 41.7 percent of them were over 50 years, and there was a large age gap within intermarried couples (mean = 16.5 years; table 9.1). About half of the Korean husbands had an education level below middle school (57.1 percent), and had a low-income level (< US$1,500, 48.8 percent; table 9.1). Most of the Vietnamese immigrants (89.3 percent) did not meet the estimated energy requirement (EER), and the proportion of immigrants whose nutrient intakes did not meet the estimated average requirement (EAR) (Korean Nutrition Society 2005) was > 50 percent for most nutrients (calcium, iron, vitamin B_2, vitamin C, and folate; data not shown). Only 10.7 percent of the Korean husbands met the EER, and the proportion of Korean husbands below the EAR for Koreans (Korean Nutrition Society 2005) was highest for folate (84.5 percent) and lowest for phosphorus (8.3 percent) and iron (8.3 percent; data not shown).

Vietnamese wives with food insecurity due to economic problems had significantly lower intake levels of fiber ($P = 0.046$), vitamin C ($P = 0.047$), and folate ($P = 0.038$). Korean husbands, whose wives reduced their meal sizes or ate less than they desired due to economic problems had significantly higher LDL-cholesterol levels ($P = 0.030$) and lower TG levels ($P = 0.017$), mean corpuscular hemoglobin ($P = 0.046$), and fruit intake ($P = 0.028$). Korean husbands, whose wives skipped the meals due to lack of foods that appealed to their appetite during the last year, had lower intakes of calcium/1,000kcal ($P = 0.004$) and vitamin C/1,000kcal ($P = 0.049$).

Table 9.1 Sociodemographic Characteristics of Intermarried Couples[a]

	Vietnamese Wives (n = 84)	Korean Husbands (n = 84)
Age (yrs)	24.5 ± 4.5	41.0 ± 5.6
Height (cm)	154.0 ± 4.6	167.6 ± 6.1
Weight (kg) 6	49.9 ± 5.7	8.3 ± 10.5
BMI (kg/m²)	21.0 ± 2.3	24.3 ± 3.2
Education		
≤ Elementary school	45.2 (38)	32.1 (27)
Middle school	29.8 (25)	25.0 (21)
≥ High school	25.0 (21)	42.9 (36)
Monthly household income		
< $1,000	16.7 (14)	
$1,000–$1,499	32.1 (27)	
$1,500–$2,000	20.2 (17)	
> $2,000	31.0 (26)	
Length of residence in Korea		
< 1 y	6.0 (5)	-
1–3 y	59.5 (50)	-
4–7 y	33.3 (28)	-
> 7 y	1.2 (1)	-
Energy intake (kcal)	1,496.2 ± 465.6	1,831.1 ± 556.5
Food insecurity due to economic difficulty		
Q1. Did you ever reduce the size of meals or ate less than you desired because there was not enough money for food in the last year?	27.4 (23)	6.0 (5)
Q2. Did you ever skip meals because there was not enough money for food in the last year?	36.9 (31)	7.1 (6)
Q1 or Q2	48.8 (41)	8.3 (7)
Food insecurity due to no food appealing to subject's appetite		
Q3. Did you ever feel hungry because there was no food that you wanted to eat or no food appealing to your appetite at home in the last year?	38.1 (32)	15.5 (13)
Q4. Did you ever skip meals because there was no food that you wanted to eat or no food appealing to your appetite at home in the last year?	22.6 (19)	10.7 (9)
Q3 or Q4	41.7 (35)	16.7 (14)

Note[a]: Values are mean ± SD or % (number).

Discrepancy Regarding Food Insecurity within Intermarried Couples

There was a marked discrepancy in the reporting of food insecurity between Vietnamese wives (22.6–38.1 percent) and their Korean husbands (6.0–15.5 percent) (see table 9.1). Five and two times as many Vietnamese wives indicated food insecurity due to economic problems and lack of foods appealing to their appetite, respectively, than their Korean spouses (see table 9.2). The discordance within intermarried couples ranged from 21.4 percent for Q1 to 39.3 percent for Q3. The reported difference was greater for food insecurity due to economic problems (40.5 percent) than for food insecurity due to a lack of foods that appealed to the subject's appetite (25 percent) (see table 9.2).

DISCUSSION

Questions about food insecurity were added to an existing questionnaire from 2009, since data from previous studies suggest that food insecurity is related to poor health and the nutritional status of intermarried couples (Hwang et al. 2010; Kim et al. 2009; Lyu et al. 2009). We found that Vietnamese female marriage immigrants in Korea had a high prevalence of food insecurity, with approximately 50 percent of them experiencing food insecurity due to economic difficulties and 46 percent due to a lack of foods that appealed to their appetite. This prevalence of food insecurity was greater than that found among the low-income elderly (22.7 percent) (Kwon and Oh 2007), but similar to that of recipients of the National Basic Livelihood Security System (42.1 percent) (Oh, Kim, Hong, and Chung 2002), which supports households with incomes below the minimum cost of living in Korea. The average age of the Korean husbands was 41.0 years, and about 40 percent of them were over 50 years. Thus, financial hardship in these households is unlikely to improve in the future, since the heads of these households will be retiring within ten to twenty years.

This high prevalence of food insecurity may be due not only to the low socioeconomic status of the subjects but also to the limited programs available supporting household food security for low-income families. Although 79 percent of our subjects had a monthly household income of $\leq$ US$2,000, most of them may not be beneficiaries of the National Basic Livelihood Security System due to its limited income eligibility (US$504 per household with one person, US$858 with two, US$1,110 with three, and US$1,363 with four) (Ministry of Health and Welfare 2008) and low coverage (reported to be 40 percent of eligible multicultural families in Chungnam province)

Table 9.2 Discordance with Food Insecurity between Korean-Husband-Vietnamese-Wife Couples (n = 84)[a,b]

	Household-Level Discordance		Discordance (% Point)	Household-Level Concordance		Sig.[c]	Population-Level Differences		Dif (% Point)
	W = FI H = FS	W = FS H = FI		W = FS H = FS	W = FI H = FI		W (% FI)	H (% FI)	
Food insecurity due to economic difficulty									
Q1	21.4 (18)	0 (0)	21.4	72.6 (61)	6.0 (5)	P = 0.001	27.4 (23)	6.0 (5)	21.4
Q2	33.3 (28)	3.6 (3)	36.9	59.5 (50)	3.6 (3)	P = 0.665	36.9 (31)	7.1 (6)	29.8
Q1 or Q2	41.7 (35)	1.2 (1)	42.9	50.0 (42)	7.1 (6)	P = 0.055	48.8 (41)	8.3 (7)	40.5
Food insecurity due to no food appealing to subject's appetite[c]									
Q3	31.0 (26)	8.3 (7)	39.3	53.6 (45)	7.1 (6)	P = 0.734	38.1 (32)	15.5 (13)	22.6
Q4	17.9 (15)	6.0 (5)	23.9	71.4 (60)	4.8 (4)	P = 0.199	22.6 (19)	10.7 (9)	11.9
Q3 or Q4	32.1 (27)	7.1 (6)	39.2	51.2 (43)	9.5 (8)	P = 0.322	41.7 (35)	16.7 (14)	25

Note[a]: Values are % (number).
Note[b]: H = Korean husbands, W = Vietnamese wives, FS = Food secure, FI = Food insecure.
Note[c]: Pearson χ^2 test or fisher's exact test (expected frequency < 5) for equality of proportions.

(Korea National Statistical Office 2009a). The Nutri Plus program (Korean supplemental nutrition program for women, infants, and children) also has strict eligibility criteria (infants and pregnant or nursing mothers with at least one nutrition risk factor such as anemia, being underweight, undergrowth, or nutritional inadequacy, and with income below 200 percent of the minimum cost of living) (Ministry of Health and Welfare 2010) and voluntary participation. Limited availability to various foods, especially Vietnamese foods, in rural communities or adaptation to new Korean foods may be another contributor toward food insecurity among this immigrant group.

We found a marked discrepancy regarding food insecurity between Vietnamese wives and their Korean husbands. This discordance was higher (30.4 percent) than that reported in Bangladesh (15 percent) (Coates et al. 2010), and about 40 percent of couples reported their food insecurity level differently, which is higher than native Bangladeshi husbands and wives living in Bangladesh found previously (Coates et al. 2010). Our relatively high discordance can be partly explained by the intermarriage status of our subjects and the wives' relatively short duration of stay in Korea. Traditional Korean culture could be another significant contributor to the high discrepancy. *Chemyon*, as one's social image, is related to certain psychological concepts such as self-esteem, influencing the formation or maintenance of social relationships in East Asian countries that follow Confucianism (Choi and Lee 2002). In Korea, males are more likely to be involved in activities to fulfill their image-related social expectations, such as *chemyon*, than in emotion (Hahn and Kim 2004). Korean spouses might feel too humiliated or disgraced to answer, "I am food insecure due to economic problems." In the present study, Vietnamese wives reported more food insecurity than their Korean husbands. It is therefore possible that the food insecurity of Korean husbands was underreported herein due to social stigma, without potential benefits such as food support programs for low-income multicultural families in Korea. Several previous studies (Wilde 2007) have found that the level of food insecurity was much higher for food-support program participants than nonparticipants who were eligible for the program.

While previous studies have found food insecurity to be negatively associated with diet quality and disturbed eating patterns (Champagne et al. 2007; Hamelin, Habicht, and Beaudry 1999; Kendall, Olson, and Frongillo 1996; Klesges et al. 2001; Tarasuk 2001; Vailas, Nitzke, Becker, and Gast 1998), no differences existed in sociodemographic characteristics and nutrient and food intakes between subjects with and without food insecurity in the present study. This could be due to the subjects' insufficiently low-nutrient intakes (Hwang et al. 2010; Kim et al. 2009; Lyu et al. 2009), regardless of food insecurity. Although it has been reported that food insecurity is associated with chronic diseases such as hypertension, hyperlipidemia, and diabetes among low-income participants (Seligman, Laraia, and Kushel 2010), our blood biochemical profiles did not differ significantly between Vietnamese wives with and without food insecurity, and most of the average values were within the normal range because most of our female subjects were in their twenties. On the other hand, husbands whose wives had reported food insecurity due to economic problems (Q1 or Q2) had significantly lower systolic blood pressure ($P = 0.045$), mean corpuscular volume ($P = 0.029$), and mean corpuscular hemoglobin ($P = 0.026$), while husbands whose wives were food insecure due to a lack of foods that appealed to their appetite (Q3 or Q4) had a lower diastolic blood pressure ($P = 0.003$; appendix table). We were unable to analyze differences in nutrient intake and blood profiles between Korean husbands with and without food insecurity because the prevalence of food insecurity among the husbands was too small to yield statistically significant differences. Some studies have found that the nutrient intakes of children in households with food insecurity were inadequate (Chilton et al. 2009; Dave et al. 2009; Kaiser et al. 2002; Kersey, Geppert, and Cutts 2007; Oh and Hong 2003). Therefore, a follow-up study is needed to determine the nutrition status of children in multicultural families.

There were several limitations in the present study. First, the USDA household food insecurity measurements (USDA 2000) and modified USDA household food insecurity questionnaires have been validated (Kim and Kim 2009) and tested (Kim and Kim 2009; Kim, Kim, and Shin 2009; Oh, Kim, Hong, and Chung 2002) for use with Koreans but have not been validated for Vietnamese immigrants in Korea. Second, the present study was a baseline, preliminary investigation, and evaluation of food insecurity and its relationship to poor health and nutritional status in intermarried couples living in low-income, rural communities; a follow-up study is needed to develop a methodologically valid and reliable food insecurity module for these intermarried couples. Third, a one-day twenty-four-hour recall may not be sufficient to assess normal daily intake due to the large intraindividual variability in food and nutrient intake. However, our study involved trained dietitians using standard protocols to help the subjects reflect on their daily diet to minimize bias, if it existed. Finally, although Vietnamese translators fluent in both Korean and Vietnamese assisted whenever needed, there were still some communication problems, especially with female immigrants who had lived in Korea for a relatively short time or had a low level of education.

On the other hand, this was the first study to analyze differences in indications of food insecurity between wives and husbands in Korea, as well as within intermarried couples. Therefore, the results of the present study may be helpful to policy makers and dietitians in the development and implementation of nutrition and health programs for multicultural families living in Korea. A follow-up study is needed to investigate why a food-insecurity discrepancy exists among female marriage immigrants and their Korean husbands living in low-income, rural communities.

NOTE

1. This chapter was previously published with the same title in *Nutrition Research and Practice*, *5*(5), 471–480. The original work was supported by a grant from the Korea Centers for Disease Control and Prevention (2009-E71003-00) and by the BK21 Project in 2010.

REFERENCES

Borjas, G. (1999). *Immigration and the Food Stamp Program*. Cambridge, MA: Harvard University Press.

Champagne, C., Casey, P., Connell, C., Stuff, J., Gossett, J., Harsha, D., McCabe-Sellers, B., Robbins, J., Simpson, P., Weber, J., & Bogle, M. (2007). Poverty and food intake in rural America: Diet quality is lower in food insecure adults in the Mississippi Delta. *Journal of the American Dietetic Association*, *107*(11), 1886–1894.

Chilton, M., Black, M., Berkowitz, C., Casey, P., Cook, J., Cutts, D., Jacobs, R., Heeren, T., de Cuba, S., Coleman, S., Meyers, A., & Frank, D. (2009). Food insecurity and risk of poor health among US-born children of immigrants. *American Journal of Public Health*, *99*(3), 556–562.

Choi, S., & Lee, S. (2002). Two-component model of Chemyon-oriented behaviors in Korea constructive and defensive Chemyon. *Journal of Cross-Cultural Psychology*, *33*(3), 332–345.

Coates, J., Webb, P., Houser, R., Rogers, B., & Wilde, P. (2010). "He said, she said": who should speak for households about experiences of food insecurity in Bangladesh? *Food Security*, *2*, 81–95.

Dave, J., Evans, A., Saunders, R., Watkins, K., & Pfeiffer, K. (2009). Associations among food insecurity, acculturation, demographic factors, and fruit and vegetable intake at home in Hispanic children. *Journal of the Academy of Nutrition and Dietetics*, *109*(4), 697–701.

Friedewald, W., Levy, R., & Fredrickson, D. (1972). Estimation of the concentration of low-density lipoprotein cholesterol in plasma, without use of the preparative ultracentrifuge. *Clinical Chemistry*, *18*(6), 499–502.

Gibson-Davis, C., & Foster, E. (2006). A cautionary tale: using propensity scores to estimate the effect of food stamps on food insecurity. *Social Service Review*, *80*(1), 93–126.

Gundersen, C., & Oliveira, V. (2001). The food stamp program and food insufficiency. *American Journal of Agricultural Economics*, *83*(4), 875–887.

Hahn, D., & Kim, K. (2004). The gender consensus and differences in understanding of Korean culture and common social values. *Korean Journal of Woman Psychology, 9*, 23–42.

Hamelin, A., Habicht, J., & Beaudry, M. (1999). Food insecurity: consequences for the household and broader social implications. *Journal of Nutrition, 129*(2S Suppl), 525S–528S.

Hwang, J., Lee, S., Kim, S., Chung, H., & Kim, W. (2010). Psychological distress is associated with inadequate dietary intake in Vietnamese marriage immigrant women in Korea. *Journal of the American Dietic Association, 110*(5), 779–785.

Kaiser, L., Melgar-Quiñonez, H., Lamp, C., Johns, M., Sutherlin, J., & Harwood, J. (2002). Food security and nutritional outcomes of preschool-age Mexican-American children. *Journal of the American Dietic Association, 102*(7), 924–929.

Kaiser, L., Townsend, M., Melgar-Quiñonez, H., Fujii, M., & Crawford, P. (2004). Choice of instrument influences relations between food insecurity and obesity in Latino women. *American Journal of Clinical Nutrition, 80*(5), 1372–1378.

Kasper, J., Gupta, S., Tran, P., Cook, J., & Meyers, A. (2000). Hunger in legal immigrants in California, Texas, and Illinois. *American Journal of Public Health, 90*(10), 1629–1633.

Kendall, A., Olson, C., & Frongillo, E. Jr. (1996). Relationship of hunger and food insecurity to food availability and consumption. *Journal of the American Dietetic Association, 96*(1), 1019–1024.

Kersey, M., Geppert, J., & Cutts, D. (2007). Hunger in young children of Mexican immigrant families. *Public Health Nutrition, 10*(4), 390–395.

Kim, K., & Kim, M. (2009). Development and validation of food security measure. *Korean Journal of Nutrition, 42*, 374–385.

Kim, K., Kim, M., & Shin, Y. (2009). Household food insecurity and its characteristics in Korea. *Health and Social Welfare Review, 29*(2), 268–292.

Kim, S., Kim, W, Lyu, J., Chung, H., & Hwang, J. (2009). Dietary intakes and eating behaviors of Vietnamese female immigrants to Korea through marriage and Korean spouses and correlations of their diets. *Korean Journal of Community Nutrition, 14*(1), 22–30.

Klesges, L., Pahor, M., Shorr, R., Wan, J., Williamson, J., & Guralnik, J. (2001). Financial difficulty in acquiring food among elderly disabled women: results from the Women's Health and Aging Study. *American Journal of Public Health, 91*(1), 68–75.

Korea National Statistical Office. (2009a). Female marriage immigrant and households of Koreans. Retrieved from http://kostat.go.kr.

Korea National Statistical Office. (2009b). Population and households of Koreans. Retrieved from http://kostat.go.kr.

Korean Nutrition Society. (2005). Dietary reference intakes for Koreans. Retrieved from http://kns.or.kr/index.asp.

Kuyper, E., Espinosa-Hall, G., Lamp, C., Martin, A., Metz, D., Smith, D., Townsend, M., & Kaiser, L. (2006). Development of a tool to assess past food insecurity of immigrant Latino mothers. *Journal of Nutrition Education and Behavior, 38*(6), 378–82.

Kwon, S., & Oh, S. (2007). Associations of household food insecurity with socioeconomic measures, health status and nutrient intake in low income elderly. *Korean Journal of Nutrition, 40*(8), 762–768.

Lyu, J., Yang, Y., Lee, S., Chung, H., Kim, M., & Kim, W. (2009). Nutritional status of Vietnamese female marriage immigrants to Korea in relation to length of residence in Korea. *Annals of Nutrition and Metabolism, 55*(4), 317–324.

Ministry of Health and Welfare. (2008). Report of the national minimum living security system. Retrieved from http://www.mohw.go.kr/react/index.jsp.

Ministry of Health and Welfare. (2010). Guidelines of the Nutri Plus Program. Retrieved from http://www.mohw.go.kr/react/index.jsp.

Ministry of Justice of Republic of Korea. (2009). *Immigration service statistics 2009.* Seoul: IT Planning & Statistics Team of Ministry of Justice.

Nam, Y., & Jung, H. (2008). Welfare reform and older immigrants: food stamp program participation and food insecurity. *Gerontologist, 48*(1), 42–50.

Oh, S., & Hong, M. (2003). Food insecurity is associated with dietary intake and body size of Korean children from low-income families in urban areas. *European Journal of Clinical Nutrition, 57*(12), 1598–1604.

Oh, S., Kim, M., Hong, M., & Chung, H. (2002). Food security and children's nutritional status of the households supported by the national basic livelihood security system. *Korean Journal of Nutrition, 35*, 650–657.

Quandt, S., Arcury, T., Early, J., Tapia, J., & Davis, J. (2004). Household food security among migrant and seasonal Latino farmworkers in North Carolina. *Public Health Reports, 119*(6), 568–576.

Quandt, S., Shoaf, J., Tapia, J., Hernández-Pelletier, M., Clark, H., & Arcury, T. (2006). Experiences of Latino immigrant families in North Carolina help explain elevated levels of food insecurity and hunger. *Journal of Nutrition, 136*(10), 2638–2644.

Rush, T., Ng, V., Irwin, J., Stitt, L., & He, M. (2007). Food insecurity and dietary intake of immigrant food bank users. *Canadian Journal of Dietetic Practice and Research, 68*(2), 73–78.

Seligman, H., Laraia, B., & Kushel, M. (2010). Food insecurity is associated with chronic disease among low-income NHANES participants. *Journal of Nutrition, 140*(2), 304–310.

Tarasuk, V. (2001). Household food insecurity with hunger is associated with women's food intakes, health and household circumstances. *Journal of Nutrition, 131*(1), 2670–2676.

USDA. (2000). Guide to measuring household food security (revised 2000). Retrieved from https://fns-prod.azureedge.net/sites/default/files/FSGuide.pdf.

Vailas, L., Nitzke, S., Becker, M., & Gast, J. (1998). Risk indicators for malnutrition are associated inversely with quality of life for participants in meal programs for older adults. *Journal of the American Dietetic Association, 98*(5), 548–553.

Wilde, P. (2007). Measuring the effect of food stamps on food insecurity and hunger: research and policy considerations. *Journal of Nutrition, 137*(2), 307–310.

World Food Summit. (1996). Report of the World Food Summit. Retrieved from http://www.fao.org/3/w3548e/w3548e00.htm.

Chapter 10

A Study on Multicultural Family Wives Adapting to Korean Cuisine and Dietary Patterns

Youngil Park, Hee Sun Jeong, and Nami Joo

Dietary[1] life itself shows how a nation has adapted to the specific region where the nation is located for thousands of years. Therefore, it is very helpful to know about the regional background of a country in order to understand a nation (Joo, Sim, Lee, and Jeong 2001; Park 1997). This means that a national dietary life is formed under social, economic, and environmental influences within a country (Helen, Marjorie, and Gail 1972) and, at the same time, it is made through the interaction with other countries (Carpo 1993).

A national dietary culture is formed by integrating long-existing traditional dietary patterns and food consumption patterns on a country's natural environment with newly introduced lifestyle (Lim, Park, and Lee 2007). Food is closely related to human life as a part of culture. Dietary culture has evolved under the various factors, including regional, racial and religious differences (Kang 2003). Most nations preserve and maintain their own dietary culture, but they witness it changing continuously over time (Chung 1995; Lee 1997; Sim, Jung, Kim, and Joo 2000). With the rising trend of globalization, foreign cultures and commodities are imported massively into South Korea. Through this expansion, Korean cuisine and dietary patterns are undergoing many changes today (Jung and Lee 2008). We may say that today we live in *one global community*, but dietary habits still express notable local and cultural characteristics as well as a strong conservative inclination (Cha 1998). With the rising economic status of South Korea and the increasing of globalization, *hallyu* (the Korean Wave) is gaining more and more popularity among people in the world. *Hallyu* was first mentioned in the 1990s and the term meant that "Korean Wave was flooding into the society." Since then, *hallyu* has been frequently used in order to refer to the boom of Korean pop culture. In particular, the term means that Korean TV dramas, fashion, and music are

187

gaining popularity among people in Asian countries, such as China, Japan, Taiwan, Hong Kong, Vietnam and Thailand, and especially among the youth of these countries (Cho Han 2002; Par 2010). In Korea, the number of foreign workers and foreign wives who are married to Korean men has risen sharply. According to data from Statistics Korea 2009, the number of interracial marriages has grown steadily since the 1990s and has reached over 10,000 per year in 1995, 24,776 in 2003, and finally showed a dramatic increase of 36,204 in 2008 (Korea National Statistical Office 2009). In this situation, exchanging traditional foods among nations helps to promote the mutual understanding and cultural exchange among nations (Chung 1995; Han, Huh, and Kim 1995; Han, Kim, Kim, and Kim 1998; Seo, Lee, and Shin 2003).

In terms of dietary attitudes and dietary behaviors of immigrant wives, Kuak (2008) said that most foreign wives who married Korean men pre-pared meals, considering their spouses and parents-in-law first, and that they chose food based on taste and volume rather than nutrition. According to the research of Jang (2009), the proportion of people who answered, "I some-times experienced shortage of food because of financial difficulties," was highest when they were asked about their dietary life patterns. This means that immigrant wives' families are likely to be low-income class. Lee (2009) said that the longer immigrants stayed in Korea; the more they felt respon-sibility for their family, the more they were stressed. Immigrant wives were under stress and the fact of being under stress put negative effects on the con-dition of nutrition, eating habits, and health of them. Kang (2007) reported that immigrant wives experienced cultural difference in Korean cuisine and dietary patterns for the first time when they started to adapt themselves to Korean society. Most of them have difficulty with taste of food, recipes, gro-ceries, and dietary patterns, which are different from their home country. As they stay longer in Korea, however, they become accustomed to Korean food culture much easier than to any other different cultural areas.

SUBJECTS AND METHODS

Subjects

For research, the questionnaires were distributed to 600 immigrant wives of 37 multicultural centers of the nationwide YWCA and 443 survey question-naires, which were answered completely, were used. For two months, from February 25th to April 22th 2009, well-trained researchers for this question-naire visited multicultural centers or questionnaires were sent out by post. Researchers distributed questionnaires, which were given in five different languages such as Korean, English, Chinese, Japanese, and Vietnamese.

The questionnaires were explained in detail before letting immigrant wives complete them.

The research examined home environmental factors of those surveyed and used multiple choice question type in which immigrant wives chose two mostly used food products while cooking. Korea National Health and Nutrition Examination Survey (KNHANEX)'s Dish-based Food Frequency Questionnaire was restructured appropriately to the study and recognition of Korean cuisine and food products was investigated (Ministry of Health and Welfare 2007). Moreover, the current study examined whether immigrant wives recognized BEST 12 dishes and knew how to cook them, the manner of table setting. BEST 12 dishes were out of *100 wonderful Korean cuisine*, which were selected by Ministry of Agriculture and Forestry and Ministry of Culture, Sports and Tourism. Finally, the frequency of eating their homeland's food, the way to cook the food, the reasons why they transform the way to cook the food, differences in table setting between their motherland and Korea, and difficult parts of Korean table manners among immigrant wives were examined.

Statistical Analysis

The data collected for the analysis of the research results was handled by using SPSS version 14.0 k. First, basic statistics (frequency, percentage, ranking, average, etc.) were calculated based on the responses from those surveyed on each item of the questionnaire. Second, cross tabulation analysis (Chi-square statistics) and one-way ANOVA were conducted on the frequency and average of the questionnaire items, which require verifying awareness-difference among groups.

RESULTS

General Factors of Those Surveyed

The findings on the general factors of those surveyed are shown on the table 10.1. The largest number of those surveyed was from Vietnam, followed by China, the Philippines, Japan, Russia, Uzbekistan, Mongol, and others. In terms of the length of residence, more than 60 percent of the total people questioned resided in Korean for less than one year and between more than one year and less than three years, followed by between more than three years and less than five years, between more than five years and less than ten years, and more than ten years. Thirty-two people answered that they lived in Korea for more than ten years.

Table 10.1   Distribution of Immigrant Wives under General Factors

Variables	Division	Frequency (n)	Percentage (%)
Country of origin	Vietnam	168	37.9
	Philippines	90	20.3
	China	110	24.8
	Japan	37	8.4
	Russia	8	1.8
	Uzbekistan	8	1.8
	Mongol	3	0.7
	Others	19	4.3
Residential area	Seoul	38	8.6
	Gyeonggido	83	18.7
	Chungchungdo	86	19.4
	Gangwondo	14	3.2
	Gyungsangdo	189	42.7
	Junlado	33	7.4
Length of residence	Less than 1 year	140	31.6
	1–3 years	137	30.9
	3–5 years	79	17.8
	5–10 years	55	12.5
	More than 10 years	32	7.2
Total		443	100

Food Products Used in Cooking Based on the General Factors

The findings on food products used in cooking based on the general factors are shown in table 10.2. There were noticeable differences depending on the country of origin ($P < 0.01$) and residential area ($P < 0.05$) while there were not obvious gaps depending on the length of residence among immigrant wives. In particular, the research showed the high level of use of grains in all of the countries of origin, while in terms of meat only four Japanese housewives (6.35 percent) said that they use meat, which was a significantly low level. Fish was highly used among housewives from Southeast countries such as Vietnam and the Philippines where people eat seafood frequently.

Status of Recognition and Usage of Korean Cuisine and Food Products

Recognition of Korean Cuisine and Food Products

The awareness level of foods depending on the country of origin is shown in table 10.3. In terms of grain, there were noticeable distinctions among immigrant wives from different countries in the way they recognize rice ($P < 0.05$), barley/multigrain ($P < 0.01$), *ramen* or instant noodles ($P < 0.01$), noodles (P

Table 10.2 Food Products Used in Cooking Based on the General Factors

Division		Food Products N (%)							
		Grain	Meat	Fish	Vegetable	Fruit	Others	Total	χ^2 (P)
Country of origin	Vietnam	102 (30.7)	66 (19.8)	74 (22.2)	77 (23.1)	11 (3.3)	3 (0.9)	333 (100.0)	45.458[a] (0.001)
	Philippines	52 (29.1)	30 (16.8)	33 (18.4)	50 (27.9)	14 (7.8)	0 (0.0)	179 (100.0)	
	China	69 (32.4)	44 (20.7)	19 (8.9)	70 (32.9)	9 (4.2)	2 (0.9)	213 (100.0)	
	Japan	25 (39.7)	4 (6.4)	10 (15.9)	23 (36.5)	1 (1.6)	0 (0.0)	63 (100.0)	
	Others	31 (41.3)	17 (22.7)	7 (9.3)	15 (20.0)	5 (6.7)	0 (0.0)	75 (100.0)	
Residential area	Seoul	16 (22.2)	19 (26.4)	11 (15.3)	24 (33.3)	2 (2.8)	0 (0.0)	72 (100.0)	40.823[b] (0.024)
	Gyeonggido	65 (39.2)	26 (15.7)	14 (8.4)	45 (27.1)	15 (9.0)	1 (0.6)	166 (100.0)	
	Chungchungdo	58 (33.7)	36 (20.9)	32 (18.6)	42 (24.4)	4 (2.3)	0 (0.0)	172 (100.0)	
	Gangwondo	4 (14.3)	7 (25.0)	6 (21.4)	11 (39.3)	0 (0.0)	0 (0.0)	28 (100.0)	
	Gyungsangdo	118 (32.4)	64 (17.6)	70 (19.2)	92 (25.3)	16 (4.4)	4 (1.1)	364 (100.0)	
	Junlado	18 (29.5)	9 (14.8)	10 (16.4)	21 (34.4)	3 (4.9)	0 (0.0)	61 (100.0)	
Length of residence	Less than 1 year	85 (30.9)	63 (22.9)	36 (13.1)	81 (29.5)	7 (2.6)	3 (1.1)	275 (100.0)	31.254 (0.052)
	1-3 years	92 (34.3)	48 (17.9)	49 (18.3)	66 (24.6)	12 (4.5)	1 (0.4)	268 (100.0)	
	3-5 years	41 (26.1)	31 (19.8)	31 (19.8)	39 (24.8)	14 (8.9)	1 (0.6)	157 (100.0)	
	5-10 years	38 (35.2)	13 (12.0)	22 (20.4)	31 (28.7)	4 (3.7)	0 (0.0)	108 (100.0)	
	More than 10 years	23 (41.8)	6 (10.9)	5 (9.1)	18 (32.7)	3 (5.5)	0 (0.0)	55 (100.0)	
	Total	279 (32.3)	161 (18.7)	143 (16.6)	235 (27.2)	40 (4.6)	5 (0.6)	863 (100.0)	

Note[a]: $P < 0.05$.
Note[b]: $P < 0.01$.

Table 10.3 Awareness Level of Grains Depending on the Country of Origin

	Country of Origin	Never Heard	Never Eaten	Eaten	Total	χ^2(P)
				N(%)		
Rice	Vietnam	1 (0.6)	0 (0.0)	167 (99.4)	168 (100.0)	19.57(0.012)[a]
	Philippines	0 (0.0)	0 (0.0)	90 (100.0)	90 (100.0)	
	China	0 (0.0)	2 (1.8)	108 (98.2)	110 (100.0)	
	Japan	0 (0.0)	0 (0.0)	37 (100.0)	37 (100.0)	
	Others	2 (5.3)	0 (0.0)	36 (94.7)	38 (100.0)	
Total		3 (0.7)	2 (0.5)	438 (98.8)	443 (100.0)	
Barely/	Vietnam	7 (4.2)	34 (20.2)	127 (75.6)	168 (100.0)	33.878(0.00)[b]
multigrain	Philippines	7 (7.8)	10 (11.1)	73 (81.1)	90 (100.0)	
	China	2 (1.8)	4 (3.6)	104 (94.6)	110 (100.0)	
	Japan	0 (0.0)	4 (10.8)	33 (89.2)	37 (100.0)	
	Others	6 (15.8)	3 (7.9)	29 (76.3)	38 (100.0)	
Total		22 (5.0)	55 (12.4)	366 (82.6)	443 (100.0)	
Noodle	Vietnam	19 (11.3)	15 (8.9)	134 (79.8)	168 (100.0)	31.435(0.00)[b]
	Philippines	0 (0.0)	4 (4.4)	86 (95.6)	90 (100.0)	
	China	2 (1.8)	3 (2.7)	105 (95.5)	110 (100.0)	
	Japan	0 (0.0)	2 (5.4)	35 (94.6)	37 (100.0)	
	Others	2 (5.3)	0 (0.0)	36 (94.7)	38 (100.0)	
Total		23 (5.2)	24 (5.4)	396 (89.4)	443 (100.0)	
Rice cake	Vietnam	17 (10.1)	27 (16.1)	124 (73.8)	168 (100.0)	39.113(0.00)[b]
	Philippines	0 (0.0)	8 (8.9)	82 (91.1)	90 (100.0)	
	China	0 (0.0)	11 (10)	99 (90)	110 (100.0)	
	Japan	0 (0.0)	0 (0.0)	37 (100)	37 (100.0)	
	Others	1 (2.6)	2 (5.3)	35 (92.1)	38 (100.0)	
Total		18 (4.1)	48 (10.8)	377 (85.1)	443 (100.0)	
Beef	Vietnam	6 (3.6)	16 (9.5)	146 (86.9)	168 (100.0)	15.955(0.043)[a]
	Philippines	0 (0.0)	2 (2.2)	88 (97.8)	90 (100.0)	
	China	1 (0.9)	8 (7.3)	101 (91.8)	110 (100.0)	
	Japan	0 (0.0)	2 (5.4)	35 (94.6)	37 (100.0)	
	Others	0 (0.0)	0 (0.0)	38 (100.0)	38 (100.0)	
Total		7 (1.6)	28 (6.3)	408 (92.1)	443 (100.0)	
Chicken	Vietnam	3 (1.8)	12 (7.1)	153 (91.1)	168 (100.0)	13.122(0.108)
	Philippines	1 (1.1)	1 (1.1)	88 (97.8)	90 (100.0)	
	China	3 (2.7)	3 (2.7)	104 (94.5)	110 (100.0)	
	Japan	0 (0.0)	0 (0.0)	37 (100.0)	37 (100.0)	
	Others	0 (0.0)	0 (0.0)	38 (100.0)	38 (100.0)	
Total		7 (1.6)	16 (3.6)	420 (94.8)	443 (100.0)	
Pork	Vietnam	3 (1.8)	12 (7.1)	153 (91.1)	168 (100.0)	12.86(0.117)
	Philippines	3 (3.3)	3 (3.3)	84 (93.4)	90 (100.0)	
	China	2 (1.8)	1 (0.9)	107 (97.3)	110 (100.0)	
	Japan	0 (0.0)	0 (0.0)	37 (100)	37 (100.0)	
	Others	1 (2.6)	0 (0.0)	37 (97.4)	38 (100.0)	
Total		9 (2.0)	16 (3.6)	418 (94.4)	443 (100.0)	

(Continued)

Table 10.3 Awareness Level of Grains Depending on the Country of Origin (*Continued*)

	Country of Origin	Never Heard	Never Eaten	Eaten	Total	$\chi^2(P)$
				N(%)		
Chinese cabbage	Vietnam	8 (4.7)	9 (5.4)	151 (89.9)	168 (100.0)	14.431(0.071)
	Philippines	3 (3.3)	8 (8.9)	79 (87.8)	90 (100.0)	
	China	4 (3.6)	1 (0.9)	105 (95.5)	110 (100.0)	
	Japan	0 (0.0)	0 (0.0)	37 (100.0)	37 (100.0)	
	Others	1 (2.6)	0 (0.0)	37 (97.4)	38 (100.0)	
Total		16 (3.6)	18 (4.1)	409 (92.3)	443 (100.0)	
Radish	Vietnam	7 (4.2)	21 (12.5)	140 (83.3)	168 (100.0)	21.133 (0.007)[b]
	Philippines	0 (0.0)	4 (4.4)	86 (95.6)	90 (100.0)	
	China	5 (4.5)	4 (3.6)	101 (91.8)	110 (100.0)	
	Japan	0 (0.0)	1 (2.7)	36 (97.3)	37 (100.0)	
	Others	1 (2.6)	0 (0.0)	37 (97.4)	38 (100.0)	
Total		13 (2.9)	30 (6.8)	400 (90.3)	443 (100.0)	
Red pepper	Vietnam	14 (8.3)	24 (14.3)	130 (77.4)	168 (100.0)	31.867(0.00)[b]
	Philippines	3 (3.3)	7 (7.8)	80 (88.9)	90 (100.0)	
	China	0 (0.0)	5 (4.5)	105 (95.5)	110 (100.0)	
	Japan	0 (0.0)	0 (0.0)	37 (100.0)	37 (100.0)	
	Others	0 (0.0)	2 (5.3)	36 (94.7)	38 (100.0)	
Total		17 (3.8)	38 (8.6)	388 (87.6)	443 (100.0)	

Note[a]: $P < 0.05$.
Note[b]: $P < 0.01$.

< 0.001), and rice cake ($P < 0.01$). In terms of barley/ mixed grains, females from Southeast countries such as Vietnam and the Philippines showed low level of awareness because those countries mainly plant rice. In terms of noodle, South Korean noodle, which is made of flour, was not well known to the females from Vietnam, for whom noodle is staple food along with cooked rice and both of them are made of rice (Kim 1996).

In terms of meat, there was a clear distinction in terms of beef ($P < 0.05$), but there were almost no differences in terms of chicken and pork. South Asian countries including Vietnam and the Philippines showed lower level of awareness than Japan and China. This seems that the belief on doctrine of reincarnation and the idea of charitable deeds in South East Asia's Buddhist society has affected the Buddhists' awareness of meat. In particular, the lowest level of awareness of beef in South East Asian countries demonstrates that people do not kill water buffalos recklessly, which are indispensable animals for farming, compared to common livestock such as chickens and pigs. In other words, pigs, which were started to be raised 3,000 B.C. at the latest, have been an important main source of meat in tribal society in jungle and farming areas from the beginning, except Islamic regions (Bae and Jinlin 2003; Cho 2000).

In terms of vegetables, there was obvious differences in terms of radish ($P < 0.01$) and red pepper ($P < 0.01$), unlike Chinese cabbage. In particular, most immigrant wives answered that they knew Chinese cabbage cuisine on the questionnaire. Chinese cabbage is highly recognized among them because it is grown and cooked in Vietnam, the Philippines, China, and Japan.

Recognition of Korean Cuisine, Possibility of Cooking Korean Food, and Table Setting Styles

The findings on the recognition of Korean cuisine, possibility of cooking Korean food, and table setting styles are shown in table 10.4. According to the results, most immigrant wives answered that they knew all Korean cuisine on the questionnaire. Therefore, Korean cuisine is highly recognized among them. Bae and Jinlin (2003) discovered that *kimchi, bibimbab,* and *bulgogi* gained higher level of awareness through the survey on Korean food among foreigners residing in the United States. This result shows again that *bibimbab, kimchi, bulgogi, samgyetang,* and *kimbab* enjoy higher level of awareness over 80 percent among Korean food. However, many of them answered that they could not cook the Korean cuisine. Seo, Lee, and Shin (2003) found that students with cooking experiences of Korean food showed higher level of preference for Korean food than those without the experiences through the research on Korean Food Preference and the Improvement of Korean Restaurants for Japanese and Chinese Students in Korea. Han (2010)

Table 10.4 Recognition of Korean Cuisine, Possibility of Cooking Korean Food, and Table Setting Styles

Variables	To Know N (%) Yes	No	To Cook N (%) Yes	No	Table Setting Styles N (%) Staple	Side Dish	Snack	Total
Bibimbab	407 (91.9)	36 (8.1)	320 (72.2)	123 (27.8)	384 (86.7)	22 (5.0)	5 (1.1)	443 (100.0)
Samgyetang	365 (82.4)	78 (17.6)	237 (53.5)	205 (46.3)	242 (54.6)	139 (31.4)	26 (5.9)	443 (100.0)
Galbi	320 (72.2)	123 (27.8)	177 (40.0)	260 (58.7)	81 (18.3)	307 (69.3)	14 (3.2)	443 (100.0)
Kimbab	392 (88.5)	51 (11.5)	224 (50.6)	219 (49.4)	154 (34.8)	187 (42.2)	65 (14.7)	443 (100.0)
Spicy soft tofu stew	314 (70.9)	129 (29.1)	178 (40.2)	263 (59.4)	63 (14.2)	319 (72.0)	17 (3.8)	443 (100.0)
Fried seafood pancake	284 (64.1)	159 (35.9)	153 (34.5)	290 (65.5)	40 (9.0)	260 (58.7)	102 (23.0)	443 (100.0)
Pumpkin porridge	286 (64.6)	156 (35.2)	154 (34.8)	284 (64.1)	71 (16.0)	182 (41.1)	147 (33.2)	443 (100.0)
Jap-chae	341 (77.0)	101 (22.8)	197 (44.5)	245 (55.3)	34 (7.7)	345 (77.9)	29 (6.5)	443 (100.0)
Kimchi	356 (80.4)	86 (19.4)	182 (41.1)	255 (57.6)	61 (13.8)	333 (75.2)	11 (2.5)	443 (100.0)
Naeng-myeon	297 (67.0)	146 (33.0)	157 (35.4)	280 (63.2)	224 (50.6)	123 (27.8)	55 (12.4)	443 (100.0)
Bulgogi	388 (87.6)	55 (12.4)	183 (41.3)	258 (58.2)	101 (22.8)	283 (63.9)	23 (5.2)	443 (100.0)
Pumkin rice cake	227 (51.2)	216 (48.8)	68 (15.3)	369 (83.3)	29 (6.5)	65 (14.7)	304 (68.6)	443 (100.0)

found that most immigrated housewives had little confidence in their Korean food cooking skills, showing that only 17.9 percent of the respondents said their skills were "very good" and "good", meanwhile 41.1 percent said "not good" and "almost poor" through the research on Korean food cooking skills of foreign housewives. In terms of table setting, the results display that foreign wives who married Korean men understand each form of staple, side dish and snack well, and use the different forms of food appropriately.

Status of Eating Their Own National Cuisine

The findings on the frequency of eating their own national food are shown in table 10.5. There were obvious differences depending on the country of origin ($P < 0.01$), residential area ($P < 0.01$) and the length of residence ($P < 0.01$). The number of immigrant wives who answered that they eat their own national food once a month was highest, followed by once a week and almost never. Han (2010) found that 26.8 percent of immigrated housewives enjoyed their own national dishes one to three times or not at all per month through the research on the frequency of taking their own national food among foreign housewives. Jang (2009) found that the percentage of immigrated housewives who eat their own national food was only 3 percent for breakfast, 8 percent for lunch, and 13 percent for dinner through the study on dietary life of

Table 10.5   Frequency of Eating Their Own National Cuisine

Variables		Once a Day	Twice or Thrice a Week	Once a Week	Once a Month	Almost Never	Total	χ^2 (P)
Country of origin	Vietnam	23 (13.7)	15 (8.9)	45 (26.8)	54 (32.1)	31 (18.5)	168 (100.0)	61.829
	Philippines	9 (10.0)	13 (14.4)	31 (34.5)	25 (27.8)	12 (13.3)	90 (100.0)	(0.000)[a]
	China	20 (18.2)	18 (16.4)	18 (16.4)	22 (20.0)	32 (29.0)	110 (100.0)	
	Japan	0 (0.0)	1 (2.7)	3 (8.1)	12 (32.4)	21 (56.8)	37 (100.0)	
	Others	9 (23.7)	6 (15.8)	10 (26.3)	10 (26.3)	3 (7.9)	38 (100.0)	
	Total	61 (13.7)	53 (12.0)	107 (24.2)	123 (27.8)	99 (22.3)	443 (100.0)	
Residential area	Seoul	9 (23.7)	2 (5.3)	10 (26.3)	10 (26.3)	7 (18.4)	38 (100.0)	55.978
	Gyeonggido	18 (21.6)	15 (18.1)	14 (16.9)	20 (24.1)	16 (19.3)	83 (100.0)	(0.000)[a]
	Chungchungdo	8 (9.3)	11 (12.8)	34 (39.5)	15 (17.5)	18 (20.9)	86 (100.0)	
	Gangwondo	1 (7.2)	0 (0.0)	3 (21.4)	3 (21.4)	7 (50.0)	14 (100.0)	
	Gyungsangdo	15 (7.9)	21 (11.1)	37 (19.6)	67 (35.5)	49 (25.9)	189 (100.0)	
	Junlado	10 (30.3)	4 (12.1)	9 (27.3)	8 (24.2)	2 (6.1)	33 (100.0)	
	Total	61 (13.8)	53 (12.0)	107 (24.2)	123 (27.7)	99 (22.3)	443 (100.0)	
Length of residence	Less than 1 year	33 (23.6)	17 (12.1)	35 (25.0)	27 (19.3)	28 (20.0)	140 (100.0)	64.894
	1–3 years	11 (8.1)	18 (13.1)	38 (27.7)	42 (30.7)	28 (20.4)	137 (100.0)	(0.000)[a]
	3–5 years	10 (12.7)	7 (8.9)	23 (29.1)	25 (31.6)	14 (17.7)	79 (100.0)	
	5–10 years	7 (12.7)	8 (14.6)	11 (20.0)	21 (38.2)	8 (14.5)	55 (100.0)	
	More than 10 years	0 (0.0)	3 (9.4)	0 (0.0)	8 (25.0)	21 (65.6)	32 (100.0)	
	Total	61 (13.8)	53 (12.0)	107 (24.2)	123 (27.7)	99 (22.3)	443 (100.0)	

Note[a]: $P < 0.01$.

Youngil Park et al.

Table 10.6   The Way to Cook Their Own National Cuisine

| | | The Way to Cook Their Own National Cuisine N (%) | | | | | |
		Original Way	Korean Way	Do Not Cook	Others	Total	$\chi 2(P)$
Country of	Vietnam	64 (38.1)	77 (45.8)	22 (13.1)	5 (3.0)	168 (100.0)	29.677
origin	Philippines	31 (34.4)	44 (48.9)	14 (15.6)	1 (1.1)	90 (100.0)	(0.003)[a]
	China	45 (40.9)	44 (40.0)	13 (11.8)	8 (7.3)	110 (100.0)	
	Japan	10 (27.0)	15 (40.5)	12 (32.5)	0 (0.0)	37 (100.0)	
	Others	8 (21.1)	27 (71.0)	2 (5.3)	1 (2.6)	38 (100.0)	
	Total	158 (35.7)	207 (46.7)	63 (14.2)	15 (3.4)	443 (100.0)	
Residential	Seoul	11 (28.9)	20 (52.6)	5 (13.2)	2 (5.3)	38 (100.0)	40.524
area	Gyeonggido	32 (38.6)	44 (53.0)	4 (4.8)	3 (3.6)	83 (100.0)	(0.000)[a]
	Chungchungdo	24 (27.9)	49 (57.0)	13 (15.1)	0 (0.0)	86 (100.0)	
	Gangwondo	5 (35.7)	4 (28.6)	5 (35.7)	0 (0.0)	14 (100.0)	
	Gyungsangdo	64 (33.9)	87 (46.0)	30 (15.9)	8 (4.2)	189 (100.0)	
	Junlado	22 (66.7)	3 (9.1)	6 (18.2)	2 (6.1)	33 (100.0)	
	Total	158 (35.7)	207 (46.7)	63 (14.2)	15 (3.4)	443 (100.0)	
Length of	Less than 1 year	58 (41.4)	61 (43.6)	12 (8.6)	9 (6.4)	140 (100.0)	30.422
residence	1–3 years	47 (34.3)	60 (43.8)	25 (18.3)	5 (3.6)	137 (100.0)	(0.002)[a]
	3–5 years	29 (36.7)	41 (51.9)	8 (10.1)	1 (1.3)	79 (100.0)	
	5–10 years	20 (36.4)	28 (50.9)	7 (12.7)	0 (0.0)	55 (100.0)	
	More than 10 years	4 (12.5)	17 (53.1)	11 (34.4)	0 (0.0)	32 (100.0)	
	Total	158 (35.7)	207 (46.7)	63 (14.2)	15 (3.4)	443 (100.0)	

Note[a]: $P < 0.01$.

female marriage immigrants. This study reveals that the frequency of eating their own national food of foreign housewives is strikingly low.

The findings on the way to cook their own national cuisine among immigrant wives are shown in table 10.6. There are clear differences depending on the country of origin ($P < 0.01$), residential area ($P < 0.01$), and the length of residence ($P < 0.01$). The largest number of those surveyed said that they cook their national food in transformed Korean style. The second-largest number of them answered that they cook the food in their traditional way, followed by people who said that they do not cook their national food.

The reasons why they changed the way to cook their own national food are shown in table 10.7. There was a noticeable difference depending on the country of origin while there were no differences depending on residence area and length of residence. The reasons why they change the way to cook the food are, first of all, the difficulty of finding food materials, followed by family members' rejection to unique flavor or taste, rejection of family members to food products, and the impossibility of cooking in their own national manner. Already being displayed in Kuak (2008) and Sim (2008), this shows the importance of consideration and psychological support from other family members when foreign housewives adapt to Korean culture. In the research of Jang (2009), 40 percent of immigrated housewives responded they consider their husbands first and 28 percent of them said they think the

Table 10.7 The Reasons Why They Changed the Way to Cook Their Own National Food

Variables		Reasons to Change the Way to Cook Their Own National Food N (%)						
		Hard to Find Food Materials	Rejection of Family Members to Spice	Rejection of Family Members to Food Materials	Impossibility of Cooking	Others	Total	χ^2 (P)
Country of origin	Vietnam	86 (51.2)	42 (25.0)	10 (6.0)	18 (10.7)	12 (7.1)	168 (100.0)	44.178 (0.000)[a]
	Philippines	49 (57.0)	22 (25.6)	6 (6.9)	4 (4.7)	5 (5.8)	86 (100.0)	
	China	40 (36.4)	39 (35.5)	24 (21.8)	2 (1.8)	5 (4.5)	110 (100.0)	
	Japan	13 (35.2)	12 (32.4)	4 (10.8)	2 (5.4)	6 (16.2)	37 (100.0)	
	Others	21 (56.8)	8 (21.6)	3 (8.1)	1 (2.7)	4 (10.8)	37 (100.0)	
	Total	209 (47.7)	123 (28.1)	47 (10.7)	27 (6.2)	32 (7.3)	438 (100.0)	
Residential area	Seoul	17 (44.7)	12 (31.6)	4 (10.5)	2 (5.3)	3 (7.9)	38 (100.0)	20.967 (0.399)
	Gyeonggido	32 (38.6)	33 (39.8)	7 (8.4)	4 (4.8)	7 (8.4)	83 (100.0)	
	Chungchungdo	48 (59.3)	14 (17.3)	6 (7.4)	6 (7.4)	7 (8.6)	81 (100.0)	
	Gangwondo	4 (28.6)	5 (35.7)	2 (14.3)	1 (7.1)	2 (14.3)	14 (100.0)	
	Gyungsangdo	91 (48.1)	51 (27.0)	23 (12.2)	14 (7.4)	10 (5.3)	189 (100.0)	
	Junlado	17 (51.5)	8 (24.2)	5 (15.2)	0 (0.0)	3 (9.1)	33 (100.0)	
	Total	209 (47.7)	123 (28.1)	47 (10.7)	27 (6.2)	32 (7.3)	438 (100.0)	
Length of residence	Less than 1 year	65 (47.4)	39 (28.5)	13 (9.5)	14 (10.2)	6 (4.4)	137 (100.0)	20.231 (0.21)
	1–3 years	75 (55.6)	31 (22.9)	14 (10.4)	4 (3.0)	11 (8.1)	135 (100.0)	
	3–5 years	33 (41.8)	23 (29.1)	9 (11.3)	7 (8.9)	7 (8.9)	79 (100.0)	
	5–10 years	24 (43.6)	19 (34.5)	8 (14.5)	0 (0.0)	4 (7.3)	55 (100.0)	
	More than 10 years	12 (37.5)	11 (34.3)	3 (9.4)	2 (6.3)	4 (12.5)	32 (100.0)	
	Total	209 (47.7)	123 (28.1)	47 (10.7)	27 (6.2)	32 (7.3)	438 (100.0)	

Note[a]: P < 0.01.

Table 10.8   Changes in Table Setting: Before and after Immigration

Division		Before Immigration N (%)	After Immigration N (%)
Table setting	Spreading out on the table	358 (80.8)	391 (88.3)
	In time order	83 (18.7)	52 (11.7)
	Total	443 (100.0)	443 (100.0)
Type of table	Sitting on the floor	85 (19.2)	296 (66.8)
	Sitting on the chair	385 (86.9)	147 (33.2)
	Total	443 (100.0)	443 (100.0)
Eating tools	Fork & Knife	127 (28.7)	9 (2.0)
	Spoon & Chopsticks	281 (63.4)	430 (97.1)
	Hands	19 (4.3)	4 (0.9)
	Others	16 (3.6)	0 (0.0)
	Total	443 (100.0)	443 (100.0)

entire family for the inquiry of whose preference they consider first when they prepare meals. Meanwhile, only 22 percent of respondents said they consider themselves first.

Changes in Table Setting: Before and After Immigration

The findings on changes in table setting before and after immigration of wives to South Korea are displayed in table 10.8. Most foreign wives are used to spread out dishes on the table both before and after their immigration. In Japan, China, and Thailand, people use spoons and chopsticks; but in the Philippines, heavily influenced by Spain and America, most people use a knife and fork. The research, however, shows that 97.1 percent of immigrated housewives use spoons and chopsticks after their immigration. In addition, 86.9 percent of foreign housewives said they "sat on the chair to eat" before their immigration because people sit in the chair around the table to eat in Vietnam, the Philippines and China. However, 66.8 percent of foreign housewives responded that they "sit on the floor around the table when they eat" after their immigration into Korea. This demonstrates that immigrated housewives have adapted to Korean food culture well.

Difficult Korean Table Manners among Immigrant Wives Depending on the Country of Origin

The findings on difficult Korean table manners among immigrant wives depending on the country of origin are shown in table 10.9. There was a clear difference among wives in finding which Korean table manners are difficult to follow. Not to hold up a bowl with hands and to start to eat after the elderly started were revealed to be most difficult to get used to. In particular, Japanese people hold rice bowls with their left hands and eat with their right

Table 10.9   Difficult Korean Table Manners among Immigrant Wives Depending on the Country of Origin

	Korean Table Manners N (%)							
Country of Origin	*Not to Hold Up Bowls*	*The Elderly First*	*Not to Use Spoon & Chopsticks at the Time*	*Not to Use Hands*	*Not to Make a Noise*	*None*	*Total*	
Vietnam	55 (32.7)	72 (42.9)	10 (6.0)	13 (7.7)	4 (2.4)	14 (8.3)	168 (100.0)	64.182
Philippines	24 (26.7)	30 (33.3)	3 (3.3)	10 (11.1)	10 (11.1)	13 (14.5)	90 (100.0)	(0.000)[a]
China	30 (27.3)	31 (28.2)	8 (7.3)	2 (1.8)	7 (6.3)	32 (29.1)	110 (100.0)	
Japan	20 (54.1)	9 (24.3)	1 (2.7)	0 (0.0)	0 (0.0)	7 (18.9)	37 (100.0)	
Others	4 (10.5)	15 (39.5)	4 (10.5)	1 (2.6)	3 (7.9)	11 (29.0)	38 (100.0)	
Total	133 (30.0)	157 (35.4)	26 (5.9)	26 (5.9)	24 (5.4)	77 (17.4)	443 (100.0)	

Note[a]: $P < 0.01$

hands and they also bring their soup bowls to their mouths to drink soup. Therefore, more than 50 percent of immigrated housewives from Japan find it difficult "not to hold bowls with hands." A total of 11.1 percent of immigrated housewives from the Philippines feel uncomfortable with "not using hands" because it is tradition to use hands when they eat and people still eat with their hands in some parts of the country.

DISCUSSION

The largest number of those surveyed was from Vietnam, followed by China, the Philippines, Japan, Russia, Uzbekistan, Mongol, and others. In terms of the length of residence, more than 60 percent of the total people questioned resided in Korean for less than one year and between more than one year and less than three years, followed by between more than three years and less than five years, between more than five years and less than ten years, and more than ten years. Thirty-two people answered that they lived in Korea for more than ten years.

The most used food product was grains with 32.3 percent, followed by vegetables, meat, fish, and fruits. The number of those who answered that they have tried Korean food products or cuisine was significantly higher than that of those who said that they have never heard about or never tried any of Korean food. There was a noticeable difference among immigrant wives depending on their country of origin. In fact, higher number of wives from Vietnam or the Philippines answered that they have never heard about or never tried Korean cuisine and Korean food products than those from China or Japan. In addition, many of those surveyed answered that they could not cook twelve well-known Korean cuisines, except *bibimbab*. This result displays that some education is necessary. Meanwhile, immigrant wives understand the differences of each staple, side dish and snack, and applied them in an appropriate manner.

In terms of eating their own national food, the largest number of wives said that they eat the food once a month and it was as high as 22.3 percent, who said that they almost never eat their homeland's food. A total of 46.7 percent of wives answered that they cook their own national food in transformed Korean style, 35.7 percent said that they cook the food in their traditional way, and 14.2 percent said that they do not cook their own national food. The reasons why the wives put changes in their homeland's food are that it is difficult to find food materials; their family members reject the unique flavor, taste, and even food products; and the wives cannot cook the food as the way they did at their motherland.

In terms of table setting, 79.5 percent of the wives, who used to place dishes in time order before their immigration to South Korea, changed to spread out dishes on the table without considering time order. A total of 65.8 percent of the wives, who used table and sat on a chair, changed their lifestyle into sitting on the floor, and 99.2 percent, who used fork and knife before immigration, became accustomed to using spoons and chopsticks. These findings display that immigrant wives were adapted well to Korean eating tools. Out of Korean table manners, immigrant wives found it difficult not to hold up bowls with hands, to eat after the elderly started to eat and to keep pace with others.

Based on these results, the author wants to make suggestions about the research of Korean cuisine and dietary patterns among multicultural family wives. First of all, the education related to Korean cuisine and dietary patterns for multicultural family wives needs to consider differences such as the country of origin and the education should be continued. The results of the research showed differences in dietary life of immigrant wives depending on general factors such as the country of origin and the length of residence in Korea. Currently, Ministry for Health, Welfare and Family Affairs offers customized service for multicultural families, which are designed to take account of life cycle of multicultural families. The system of this service needs to be applied to the education of Korean cuisine and dietary patterns as well. In fact, they are immigrant wives who manage food life of multicultural family and they need different dietary education at different time of their life from the moment when they come to Korea to the time when they form a family and rear a child.

In addition, although the results of the research showed that immigrant wives adapt themselves to Korean cuisine and food culture quickly, the frequency of eating their own national food was low because their family members disapprove. Therefore, not only education of Korean food culture for immigrant wives but also comprehensive education of food culture for their children and spouses are essential in order to establish right dietary culture in multicultural family.

Finally, the research demonstrates that immigrant wives cook their own national food and Korean food in transformed ways. In the long-term perspective, we might face new type of food culture with growing number of multicultural families. Therefore, we should develop our cuisine and dietary patterns in a right direction through persistent and profound study on dietary culture among multicultural families.

NOTE

1. This chapter was previously published with the same title in *Nutrition Research and Practice*, 4(5), 405–413.

REFERENCES

Bae, Y., & Jinlin, Z. (2003). Marketing strategy for Korean restaurants in Florida—Through view of customers' preference, recognition and satisfaction. *Journal of Food service Management, 6,* 85–100.

Carpo, R. (1993). *Cultural Anthropology: Understanding Ourselves and Other* (3rd ed.). Guilford, CT: Dushkin Publishing Group.

Cha, M. (1998). Study on structural characteristics of Korea's food culture. *Journal of Kyonggi Tourism Research, 2*(0), 173–190.

Cho Han, H. (2002). Modernity, popular culture and East-West identity formation: A discourse analysis of Korean Wave in Asia. *Korean Cultural* Anthropology, *35,* 3–40.

Cho, H. (2000). A study on Thai food culture. *The Korean Ethnological Association,* 4, 205–233.

Chung, S. (1995). Dietary change-food habits of Koreans in new haven (doctoral dissertation). University of Connecticut, New England.

Han, J., Huh, S., & Kim, M. (1995). American's acceptance of Korean foods. *Journal of Resource Development, 14,* 93–99.

Han, J., Kim, J., Kim, S., & Kim, M. (1998). A survey of Japanese perception of and preference for Korean foods. *Korean Journal of Food and Cookery Science, 14*(2), 188–194.

Han, Y. (2010). Influential factor on Korean dietary life and eating behaviour of female marriage immigrants (master's thesis). Hanyang University, Seoul.

Helen, H., Marjorie, B., & Gail, G. (1972). *Nutrition, Behavior and Change.* Englewood Cliffs, NJ: Prentice-Hall.

Jang, B. (2009). A Study on dietary life of female marriage immigrants (master's thesis). Kyunghee University, Seoul.

Joo, N., Sim,Y., Lee, K., & Jeong, H. (2001). The perception and preference of Americans residing in Korea for Korean traditional food. *Journal of the Korea Home Economics Association, 39*(6), 19–23.

Jung, Y., & Lee, S. (2008). A Study on the application of multicultural cuisine to Korean food: Focused on western preferences. *Korean Journal of Hospitality Administration, 17,* 157–179.

Kang, D. (2003). A study for advancing into European market of Korean cuisine and the comparison between Korean cuisine culture and European cuisine culture. *The Korean Journal of Culinary Research, 9,* 88–101.

Kang, H. (2007). Immigrant Women's desire for expressing and preserving the mother culture and their identity (master's thesis). Sookmyung Women's University, Seoul.

Kim, K. (1996). A study on Vietnamese food culture. *Southeast Asia Institute,* 129–168.

Korea National Statistical Office. (2009). Woman's life based on statistics: Changes of international marriages. Retrieved from http://kostat.go.kr/portal/korea/index.a ction.

Kuak, D. (2008). Research to ingestion of food and an attitude from food and drink of Multicultural family (master's thesis). Wosong University, Seoul.

Lee, H. (1997). Food habits of Koreans in United States (doctoral dissertation). New York University, New York.

Lee, S. (2009). Association between stress, and nutritional and health status of female immigrants to Korea in multi-cultural families (master's thesis). Ewha Women's University, Seoul.

Lim, H., Park, M., & Lee, S. (2007). A study on the trends of food service culture and the direction for the development (master's thesis). Jangan University, Seoul.

Ministry of Health and Welfare. (2008). 2007 Korea national health and nutrition examination survey. Retrieved from https://knhanes.cdc.go.kr/knhanes/main.do.

Park, S. (2010). International trade of Korean Wave (master's thesis). Ewha Woman's University, Seoul.

Park, U. (1997). Factors of food adaptation and changes of food habit on Koreans residing in America. *Journal of the Korean Society of Dietary Culture, 12*(5), 519–529.

Seo, K., Lee, S., & Shin, M. (2003). Research on Korean food preference and the improvement of Korean restaurants for Japanese and Chinese students in Korea. *Korean Journal of Food and Cookery Science, 19,* 715–722.

Sim, Y. (2008). The adoption process and transnational identity of international marriage women (master's thesis). Women's Institute of Hanyang University, Seoul.

Sim, Y., Jung, B., Kim, E., & Joo, N. (2000). A survey for the international spread of Korean food from the Korean residents in the U.S. *Korean Journal of Food and Cookery Science, 16,* 210–215.

Part IV

FOOD TOURISM AND FOOD CRISIS

Chapter 11

Exploring Tourists' Korean Food Satisfaction across Culture, Gender, and Education

Using Secondary Data from International Visitor Survey

Jee Hye Lee

In[1] the past, there was a lack of interests in tourists' food consumption within the field of tourism (Cohen and Avieli 2004); however, food has recently become one of the most important elements to tourists for a few reasons. Tourists' spending on food reached to one-third of their total expenditure (Hall and Sharples 2003; Telfer and Wall 2000), and thus, tourists' food has expenditure contributes to tourism revenue significantly (Mak, Lumbers, and Eves 2012). Furthermore, food provides the easiest way to experience the destination culture and enrich travel (Chang, Kivela, and Mak 2010; Quan and Wang 2004). The attraction toward food by the tourists has developed food tourism through an increase of economic benefits (Du Rand and Heath 2006; Kim, Taylor, and Ruetzler 2008). Tourists' desire to experience authentic food cultures has changed the tourism field and attracted the attention of scholars and travel companies. Therefore, food consumption has been an important factor within tourism studies (Hall and Sharples 2003; Quan and Wang 2004).

Although a review of tourism literature reveals the important role of food consumption in tourism, little research has systematically and comprehensively explored the factors affecting tourists' food satisfaction (Mak, Lumbers, and Eves 2012). The current study is interested in the influence of tourists' demographic information on food satisfaction. Previous studies supported the association between food preference and cultural backgrounds (Khan 1981; Longue 1991), as well as the link between other demographic factors, such as gender and education, and food preference (Cooke and

Wardle 2005; Nu, MacLeod, and Barthelemy 1996). Thus, this study examined the association between tourists' demographic characteristics and tourists' satisfaction toward Korean foods at their destination.

Many studies insisted on the strong associations among consumers' satisfaction, revisit intention, and word-of-mouth intention (Barsky and Labagh 1992; Chen and Tsai 2007; Henderson 2009; Hjalanger and Corigliano 2000; Nield, Kozak, and LeGrys 2000; Rimmington and Yuksel 1998). The current study tested this strong association among the three variables, including food satisfaction, revisit intention, and word-of mouth intention, as applied to tourists' cases. In particular, the current study examined tourists' food satisfaction as a critical determinant explaining tourist's behaviors. In sum, the aims of this chapter are (1) to examine the influence of tourists' demographic characteristics (including cultural background, gender, and education) on food satisfaction; (2) to examine the influence of tourists' education on food satisfaction; and (3) to examine the influence of tourists' food satisfaction on revisit intention and word-of mouth intention.

LITERATURE REVIEW

The Role of Food Consumption in Tourism

Tourist food consumption has been neglected in the hospitality and tourism literature because it was recognized as a *supporting resource*, not a main element (Godfrey and Clarke 2000; Quan and Wang 2004). However, a number of recent studies identified food consumption as an important aspect of hospitality and tourism. In particular, researchers paid attention to the economic benefits of food consumption brought by tourists (Telfer and Wall 2000). Eating accounted for more than 20.8 percent of tourists' total daily travel expense in Korea in 2012, according to the Korea Tourism Organization (2013). Furthermore, food is necessary for body functions, so food consumption is *obligatory* in travelers' activities (Richards 2002).

As the importance of food consumption in tourism has been recognized, there has been a significant increase in food tourism research in recent years (Ahn, Baek, and Lee 2011; Kang and Lee 2010; Yu and Seo 2009). Kivela and Crotts (2006) stated that food satisfies travelers' five human senses—vision, touch, hearing, taste, and olfaction—which distinguishes it from other traveler activities and attractions. These types of sensory pleasure play an important role in the tourists' experience and their activity (Hjalager and Richards 2002). Bessier (1998) stated that traditional food and cuisine are able to fascinate tourists because consumption of food has a critical role as entertainment and as a cultural activity. Recently, gastronomic experience is considered to be an attraction for destination choices among both rural and urban tourists (Correia, Moital, Da Costa, and Peres 2008; Gyimóthy, Rassing, and Wanhill 2000; Kastenholz, Davis, and Paul 1999). Gastronomy, therefore, has been regarded as a critical confederating element in tourism policy and marketing to determine destinations for tourists (de Rojas and Camarero 2008; Kivela and Crotts 2006; Okumus, Okumus, and McKercher 2007).

While the economic significance of tourists' food consumption at destinations is recognized, little research has systematically and comprehensively explored the factors affecting their food consumption (Mak, Lumbers, and Eves 2012).

Characteristics of Traditional Korean Foods

The Korean culinary tradition has a 5,000-year-old culinary history, and it is widely known for its spicy flavors and vegetable-heavy dishes. Rice and the large number of side dishes served with meals play a vital role in Korean meals. The traditional Korean diet consists of balanced, nutritious meals that are made with a variety of healthy cooking methods. Comparing Western food and Korean food, the Korean diet consists of 70 percent of carbohydrates, 13 percent fat, 14–17 percent, and no sugar, whereas the average Western diet consists of 40 percent of carbohydrates, 30–40 percent fat, 15–20 percent protein, and sugar 5–10 percent (The Korean Foundation 2010). As the trend in health-conscious eating has increased, organic, slow food, and health have become more and more popular (Kim 2008; Noh 2010). *Kimchi*, a famous Korean food, has been chosen as one of the five healthiest foods in the world, and its benefits such as beneficial bacteria, various vitamins, and high levels of dietary fiber have been proved by researchers (Shure 2010).

The Association between Tourists' Demographic Characteristics and Food Satisfaction

Some studies suggested that demographic factors such as gender, age, and education have an effect on tourists' destination food consumption (Kim, Ng, and Kim 2009). Although there is some evidence that tourists' demographic characteristics can be considered critical variables in explaining variations in tourists' behaviors, there is a lack of research. In the current study, cultural background, gender, and education are focused on variables, associated with tourists' food satisfaction.

Cross-cultural perspective tourism research asserted that different cultural values affect tourists' service quality perception (Bowen and Clarke

2002; Crotts and Erdmann 2000; Weiermair 2000). For instance, Turner, Reisinger, and McQuilken (2002) found significant difference in travel satisfaction and stated that it may be because tourists from different countries have different levels of emphasis on the importance of service quality attributes and actual levels of service received. In the study of Reisinger and Turner (2000), more destination attributes of Hawaii were preferred with higher travel satisfaction by Japanese tourists compared to attributes of the Gold Coast of Australia.

A number of studies agreed that culture has a major influence on food preference in tourism. Kwan (1981) and Longue (1991) stated that culture is the strongest determining factor in food preference. People judge food as good or bad based on their sensory evaluation (Prescott, Young, O'neill, Yau, and Stevens 2002), and culture has an important role in sensory evaluation. According to the "flavor principle" in the study of Rozin and Rozin (1981), the sensory properties of food can be determined by three components including common ingredients, cooking methods, and distinctive seasoning combinations. In particular, distinctive seasoning combinations are developed based on the culture. Thus, culture is the main determinant for which foods are acceptable or not acceptable and delicious or not delicious. Pizam and Sussman (1995) found that the preference for local food is different between American travelers and Japanese, French, and Italian travelers. American tourists had a preference for local food, whereas Japanese, French, and Italian travelers did not. Exotic foods in destinations can be easily accepted or cannot be accepted well depending on the tourists' cultural and religious backgrounds. Therefore, nationality is a critical determinant in food satisfaction. Although there were contradictory arguments for gender as an influencing factor on food preference, ample food literature found a significant difference in food preference between males and females (Alexander and Tepper 1995; Baker and Wardle 2003; Cooke and Wardle 2005; Nu, MacLeod, and Barthelemy 1996). In addition, there were contradictory arguments for education as an influencing factor on food preference. Some researchers supported the claim that people with higher education are more positive about trying novel foods than people with lower education (Lähteenmäki and Arvola 2001; Lowenberg, Todhunter, Wilson, Savage, and Lubawski 1979), because consumers with high education are better able to understand and integrate information in their food choice. Tourists with higher education levels were found to be more concerned about health and had a stronger desire to understand and experience foreign cultures through local food consumption (Kim, Ng, and Kim 2009). On the other hand, some research argued that there is no strong association between education and food consumption behavior (Meulenberg and Viaene 1998).

The Influence of Tourists' Food Satisfaction on Revisit Intention and Word-of-Mouth Intention

Previous studies stated that food is an important tourist attraction and has a critical role in tourist decision-making (Hjalanger and Corigliano 2000; Henderson 2009; Nield, Kozak, and LeGrys 2000; Rimmington and Yuksel 1998). For example, in the study of Sparks, Bowen, and Klag (2003), tourists' dining-out has contributed to tourists' enjoyment or satisfaction with a destination and intention to revisit. Other studies assumed food as one of the critical determinants of a travel destination's image (Hjalanger and Corigliano 2000) or travel quality (Chen and Tsai 2007). Thus, it is assumed that food satisfaction also has a critical role in tourists' decision-making. In business research, many studies have revealed that consumers' satisfaction has a strong effect on future intention to revisit (Barsky and Labagh 1992; Choi and Chu 2001; Petrick 1999; Tam 2000; Yoon and Uysal 2005).

Food has received very little attention in the tourism literature (Telfer and Wall 1996). However, food has been emphasized by gastronomic tourism researchers as a critical single determiner, which motivates tourist behavior, and not a subordinate attribute in tourists' behaviors (Hall and Mitchell 2000, 2002; Hjalager and Corigliano 2000; Hjalager and Richards 2002; Richards 2002). In Maslow's hierarchy of needs (Maslow 1943), eating is the most important need among the five sets, including physiological, safety, love, esteem, and self-actualization. Many researchers supported the relation between Maslow's hierarchy and consumers' travel and tourism needs (Fodness 1944; Holloway and Plant 1988). Previous studies confirmed the positive influence of consumers' satisfaction on revisit intention and the positive influence of consumers' satisfaction on word-of-mouth intention (Kim, Ng, and Kim 2009; LaBarbera and Mazursky 1983; Ranaweera and Prabhu 2003); therefore, the current study asks whether food satisfaction has an influence on revisit intention and, in addition, whether food satisfaction has an influence on word-of-mouth (WOM) intention. Based on the literature review, we proposed the following hypotheses:

> Hypothesis 1: Tourist's food satisfaction is different depending on the tourist's demographic characteristics.
> Hypothesis 1a: Tourist's food satisfaction is different between Asian and Western tourists.
> Hypothesis 1b: Tourist's food satisfaction is different depending on the tourist's nationality.
> Hypothesis 1c: Tourist's food satisfaction is different depending on the tourist's gender.
> Hypothesis 1d: Tourist's food satisfaction is different depending on the tourist's education level.

Hypothesis 2: Tourist's food satisfaction affects revisit intention.
Hypothesis 3: Tourist's food satisfaction affects word-of-mouth intention.

METHODOLOGY

The analyses presented in this paper used secondary data from the International Visitor Survey from 2010 to 2013: the secondary data was obtained from the Korea Ministry of Culture, Sports and Tourism. A detailed description of the survey can be found on the Korea Culture and Tourism Institute website (Korea Culture and Tourism Institute 2015). International tourists' data were collected by sampling respondents who were leaving Korea after traveling in Korea. The questionnaires were distributed to international tourists at Incheon International Airport, Gimpo International Airport, Jeju International Airport, Gimhae Airport, Incheon port, and Busan port in every month during four years from 2010 to 2013. A total of 12,030 international tourists participated in the survey voluntarily. The nationalities of foreign tourists encompass more than nineteen countries, including Japan, China, the United States, Canada, Australia, India, Thai, Singapore, and German. The questionnaire used in the International Visitor Survey is quite comprehensive, including a variety of questions regarding international tourists' current trip to Korea. This study focuses attention on, first, international tourists' demographic information, including nationality (nineteen countries were listed), gender, and education; second, food satisfaction was measured based on a five-point Likert scale (1=strongly dissatisfied; 5= strongly satisfied); third, intention to revisit Korea was measured based on a five-point Likert scale (1=strongly disagree; 5= strongly agree); and fourth, revisit intention was measured based on a five-point Likert scale (1=strongly disagree; 5= strongly agree). Descriptive statistics, independent t-test, analysis of variance, and linear regression analysis were conducted to examine the proposed hypotheses using SPSS Statistics 20.

RESULTS

The respondents' demographic data were profiled in frequencies and percentages (see table 11.1). In gender category, 47 percent of respondents were male and 53 percent were female. A majority of the sample was composed of young people (33.3 percent) who reported that they were between the ages of twenty-one and thirty. A majority of the respondents were composed of Asian tourists (85.4 percent). The most frequently occurring classification group for education level was bachelor's degree (62 percent). In the occupation category, 18.3 percent of the respondents were students.

Table 11.1 Characteristics of the Respondents

Variables		Frequency	Percentage (%)
Gender	Male	5652	47
	Female	6378	53
	Total	12030	100.0
Age	15–20	653	5.4
	21–30	4011	33.3
	31–40	3237	26.9
	41–50	2231	18.5
	51–60	1298	10.8
	Over 61	566	4.7
	N/A	34	0.3
	Total	12030	100.0
Nationality	Asian	9443	78.5
	Western	1617	13.4
	N/A	970	8.1
	Total	11060	100.0
Education	High school	1821	15.1
	Bachelor's degree	7461	62.0
	Postgraduate	2124	17.7
	Etc	519	4.3
	N/A	106	0.9
	Total	12030	100.0
Occupation	Public official/Soldier	12	5.5
	Enterpriser	3	11.5
	Office job/Engineer	2	18.3
	Sales and service	2	13.2
	Profession	26	9.2
	Production employee	45	3.8
	Independent businessman	946	7.9
	Student	1718	14.3
	Housewife	689	5.7
	Retiree	198	1.6
	Not working	214	1.8
	etc.	681	5.7
	N/A	188	1.6
	Total	12030	100.0

Table 11.2 shows foreign tourists' trends from 2010 to 2013. The foreign tourists' average personal food expenditure was US$249 in 2010, US$251 in 2011, US$259 in 2012, and US$247 in 2013. Tourists' group food expenditure showed an increase from US$105 in 2010 to US$120 in 2013 during four years. In regard to foreign tourists, food satisfaction has somewhat increased from 4.14±0.77 in 2010 to 4.17±0.76 in 2013. In addition, foreign tourists' revisit intention has increased from 4.05±0.66 in 2010 to 4.34±0.63 in 2013.

In order to examine significant difference in tourists' food satisfaction between Asian and Western tourists, the Mann-Whitney U test was conducted.

Table 11.2   Foreign Tourists' Trends from 2010 to 2013

	2010	2011	2012	2013
Personnel food expenditure (US$)	249 (n = 115)	251 (n = 420)	259 (n = 1,458)	247 (n = 1,445)
Group food expenditure (US$)	105 (n = 39)	104 (n = 140)	113 (n = 418)	120 (n = 260)
Food satisfaction (Mean ± S.D.; 5-point Likert Scale)	4.14 ± 0.77 (n = 156)	4.18 ± 0.72 (n = 572)	4.16 ± 0.72 (n = 1924)	4.17 ± 0.76 (n = 1767)
Revisit intention ((Mean ± S.D.; 5-point Likert Scale)	4.05 ± 0.66 (n = 156)	4.09 ± 0.65 (n = 572)	4.21 ± 0.64 (n = 1,924)	4.34 ± 0.63 (n = 1,767)

Table 11.3   A Comparison of Food Satisfaction between Asian and Western Tourists

	N	Mean Rank	Mann-Whitney U	Z	Sig.
Asian	8,715	4,713.75	3100318.5	−14.3	0
Western	959	5,962.13			

The results of the Mann-Whitney U test (see table 11.3) indicated that the hypothesis was accepted for some of the evaluation dimensions with a probability > 0.01 in some cases. Mean rank (5962.13) of food satisfaction for Western tourists was higher than mean rank (4713.75) of food satisfaction for Asians. Therefore, Hypothesis 1a (tourist's food satisfaction is different between Asian and Western tourists) was supported.

In order to examine significant difference in tourists' food satisfaction depending on tourists' nationality, the Kruskal-Wallis H test was conducted. Tourists were grouped into three categories based on geographical regions. These categories were Asia (n = 1,821), America (n = 7,461), and Austral (n = 2,124). The Kruskal-Wallis H test revealed a significant difference among geographical region in food satisfaction (Kruskal-Wallis χ^2 = 220.73, $p < 0.001$). An additional analysis by the Mann-Whitney U test revealed a significant difference between two groups. Food satisfaction with America (mean rank = 5999.10) was higher than Asia (mean rank = 4698.33) with a Z value of −14.78 ($p < 0.001$), and food satisfaction with America (mean rank = 484.77) was higher than Austral (mean rank = 315.44) with a Z value

Table 11.4   A Comparison of Food Satisfaction Depending on Tourists' Nationalities

Category	N	Mean±S.D.	Kruskal-Wallis χ^2	Sig.
Asia	9,075	4.06±0.76	220.73	0.0001
America	863	4.40±0.75		
Austral	121	4.22±0.86		

Table 11.5   A Comparison of Food Satisfaction between Male and Female Tourists

	N	Mean Rank	Mann-Whitney U	Z	sig.
Male	4,858	5,373.25	13414165	−3.09	0.002
Female	5,705	5,204.30			

of −3.491 ($p < 0.001$). Therefore, Hypothesis 1b (tourist's food satisfaction is different depending on the tourist's nationality) was supported.

In order to examine significant difference in tourists' food satisfaction between male and female tourists, the Mann-Whitney U test was conducted. The results of the Mann-Whitney U test (see table 11.5) indicated that the hypothesis was accepted for some of the evaluation dimensions with a probability > 0.01 in some cases. Mean rank (5373.25) of food satisfaction for male tourist was higher than mean rank (5204.30) of food satisfaction for female tourists. Therefore, Hypothesis 1c (tourist's food satisfaction is different depending on the tourist's gender) was supported.

As Table 11.6 shows, the Kruskal-Wallis H test was conducted in order to examine the differences in food satisfaction among tourists' education levels. The education level was grouped into three categories. These categories were high school (n = 1,821), bachelor's degree (n = 7,461), and postgraduate (n = 2,124). Postgraduate showed the highest food satisfaction (4.20 ± 0.81), followed by bachelor's degree (4.08 ± 0.77), and then high school (4.07 ± 0.76). The Kruskal-Wallis H test revealed a significant difference among education levels in food satisfaction (Kruskal-Wallis χ^2 = 39.82, p < 0.001). An additional analysis by a Mann-Whitney U test revealed a significant difference between two groups (Z = −6.04, p < 0.01); food satisfaction for postgraduate (mean rank = 4724.79) was higher than bachelors' one (mean rank = 4352.02). Therefore, Hypothesis 1d (tourist's food satisfaction is different depending on the tourist's education level) was partially supported.

As table 11.7 shows, the results of linear regression to examine the influence of tourists' food satisfaction on revisit intention was as follows: food satisfaction accounted for 9 percent of the variance in revisit intention, F(1, 12029) = 1154.73, adjusted R2 = 0.09, 9 percent of variance. Food satisfaction showed significant beta weight. The beta weight for food satisfaction was

Table 11.6   A Comparison of Food Satisfaction by Education Levels

Category	N	Mean±S.D.	Kruskal-Wallis χ^2	sig.
High school	1,821	4.07±0.76		
Bachelor's degree	7,461	4.08±0.77	39.82	0.0001
Postgraduate	2,124	4.20±0.81		

Table 11.7 The Results of Linear Regression Analysis

Hypothesis	Independent Variable	Dependent Variable	B (S.E.)	β (t)	R2	Adjusted R2 (F)
H2	Food satisfaction	Revisit intention	0.27 (0.01)	0.30 (33.98a)	0.1	0.09 (1154.73a)
H3	Food satisfaction	WOM intention	0.28 (0.01)	0.34 (39.48a)	0.1	0.12 (1558.58a)

0.30 (t = 33.98, p <0.001). Therefore, Hypothesis 2 (tourist's food satisfaction affects the tourist's revisit intention) was supported.

The results of linear regression to examine the influence of tourists' food satisfaction on WOM intention was as follows (see table 11.5): food satisfaction accounted for 12 percent of the variance in WOM intention, F(1, 12029) = 1558.58, adjusted R2 = 0.12. Food satisfaction showed significant beta weight. The beta weight for food satisfaction was 0.34 (t = 39.48, p < 0.001). Therefore, Hypothesis 3 (tourist's food satisfaction affects the tourist's WOM intention) was supported.

CONCLUSION

The present study aimed to examine the influence of tourists' demographic characteristics on food satisfaction and explored the associations among food satisfaction, revisit intention, and WOM intention. The current study contributes to both tourism studies and tourism industry. First, this study contributes to the tourism literature by examining the association between tourists' demographic characteristics and food satisfaction at their destination and determined the influence of tourists' food satisfaction on revisit intention and WOM intention.

In the tourism literature, food has been researched as a subordinate variable, which influences tourist behaviors. However, in the current study, food has been focused on as a critical single determiner. The findings confirmed the association between demographic characteristics and tourists' food satisfaction. In particular, the influence of education on perceived image of destination (Beerli and Martin 2004) has been researched; however, the association between tourists' education and food satisfaction at travel destination has been rarely studied.

The current study emphasized food satisfaction as a critical determinant of tourist behavior. This finding was consistent with previous studies showing that food satisfaction is a critical variable in explaining revisit intention and WOM intention (Barsky and Labagh 1992; Choi and Chu 2001; Kim, Ng, and Kim 2009; LaBarbera and Mazursky 1983; Petrick 1999; Ranaweera and Prabhu 2003; Tam 2000; Yoon and Uysal 2005).

Second, based on the findings, the current study provides targeting and positioning strategies for the Korean restaurant industry to attract foreign tourists. The results showed that Western tourists were more satisfied with Korean foods compared to Asian tourists. This result was consistent with previous studies emphasizing the role of authenticity in the tourism industry. Authentic food can be attractive to foreign tourists, and restaurant operators should put more effort into developing distinctive Korean menus. The strategy of segmentation benefits restaurant operators in avoiding head-on competition in the restaurant industry by satisfying consumers' specific needs. The findings showed a higher level of Korean food satisfaction among Western and male tourists, and thus segmentation strategies for Western and male tourists are recommended.

The limitation of the current study is that variables from the secondary data on the International Visitor Survey consisted of a single item. For example, food satisfaction can be measured by dimension considering various factors such as satisfaction of food hygiene, taste, and price. It may also increase the coefficient of determination. In the regression analysis, a number of predictors can better explain the dependent variable. A multi-predictor model can have higher R-squared to a one-predictor model because the dependent variable can be explained well with more predictors. Therefore, it is recommended that this issue be re-examined using dimension-scale items considering many factors. Furthermore, the examination of the influence of the education levels of foreign tourists on ethnic food satisfaction was an important factor to research because it has been rarely studied. However, future studies are recommended to discover the reason why there was a significant difference between those with postgraduate and bachelor's degrees, and not a significant difference between those with bachelor's degrees and high school graduates.

NOTE

1. This chapter was previously published with the same title in *Journal of Tourism and Leisure Research*, *27*(5), 317–335. The original work was supported by the 2014 Research Fund of University of Ulsan.

REFERENCES

Ahn, S., Baek, M., & Lee, H. (2011). A study of the effect of the food factor on tourist's satisfaction on destination and destination loyalty in tourism industry. *Journal of Tourism & Leisure Research*, *23*(3), 63–85.

Alexander, J., & Tepper, B. (1995). Use of reduced-calorie/reduced-fat foods by young adults: Influence of gender and restraint. *Appetite*, *25*(3), 217–230.

Baker, A., & Wardle, J. (2003). Sex differences in fruit and vegetable intake in older adults. *Appetite, 40*(3), 269–275.

Barsky, J., & Labagh, R. (1992). A strategy for customer satisfaction. *The Cornell Hotel and Restaurant Administration Quarterly, 33*(5), 32–40.

Beerli, A., & Martín, J. (2004). Tourists' characteristics and the perceived image of tourist destinations: a quantitative analysis—a case study of Lanzarote, Spain. *Tourism Management, 25*(5), 623–636.

Bowen, D., & Clarke, J. (2002). Reflections on tourist satisfaction research: Past, present and future. *Journal of Vacation Marketing, 8*(4), 297–308.

Chang, R., Kivela, J., & Mak, A. (2010). Food preferences of Chinese tourists. *Annals of Tourism Research, 37*(4), 989–1011.

Chen, C., & Tsai, D. (2007). How destination image and evaluative factors affect behavioral intentions? *Tourism Management, 28*(4), 1115–1122.

Choi, T., & Chu, R. (2001). Determinants of hotel guests' satisfaction and repeat patronage in the Hong Kong hotel industry. *International Journal of Hospitality Management, 20*(3), 277–297.

Cohen, E., & Avieli, N. (2004). Food in tourism: Attraction and impediment. *Annals of Tourism Research, 31*(4), 755–778.

Cooke, L., & Wardle, J. (2005). Age and gender differences in children's food preferences. *British Journal of Nutrition, 93*(5), 741–746.

Correia, A., Moital, M., Da Costa, C., & Peres, R. (2008). The determinants of gastronomic tourists' satisfaction: a second-order factor analysis. *Journal of Foodservice, 19*(3), 164–176.

Crotts, J., & Erdmann, R. (2000). Does national culture influence consumers' evaluation of travel services? A test of Hofstede's model of cross-cultural differences. *Managing Service Quality, 10*(6), 410–419.

de Rojas, C., & Camarero, C. (2008). Visitors' experience, mood and satisfaction in a heritage context: Evidence from an interpretation center. *Tourism Management, 29*(3), 525–537.

Du Rand, G., & Heath, E. (2006). Towards a framework for food tourism as an element of destination marketing. *Current Issues in Tourism, 9*(3), 206–234.

Fodness, D. (1994). Measuring tourist motivation. *Annals of Tourism Research, 21*(3), 555–581.

Godfrey, K., Clarke, J., & South-Western, T. (2000). *The Tourism Development Handbook: A Practical Approach to Planning and Marketing*. London: Cassell London.

Gyimóthy, S., Rassing, C., & Wanhill, S. (2000). Marketing works: a study of the restaurants on Bornholm, Denmark. *International Journal of Contemporary Hospitality Management, 12*(6), 371–379.

Hall, C., & Mitchell, R. (2000). We are what we eat: Food, tourism and globalization. *Tourism, Culture and Communication, 2*(1), 29–37.

Hall, C., & Sharples, L. (2003). The consumption of experiences or the experiences of consumption? An introduction to the tourism of taste. In C. Hall, E. Sharples, R. Mitchell, N. Macionis, & B. Cambourne (Eds.), *Food Tourism Around the World: Development, Management and Markets* (pp. 1–24). Oxford: Butterworth-Heinemann.

Hall, C., Sharples, L., Mitchell. R., Macionis, N., & Cambourne, B. (Eds.). (2003). *Food Tourism Around the World: Development, Management and Markets.* Oxford: Butterworth-Heinemann.

Henderson, J. (2009). Food tourism reviewed. *British Food Journal, 111*(4), 317–326.

Hjalager, A. & Corigliano, M. (2000). Food for tourists—determinants of an image. *International Journal of Tourism Research, 2*(4), 281–293.

Hjalager, A., & Richards, G. (Eds.). (2002). *Tourism and Gastronomy.* Oxford: Routledge.

Holloway, J., & Plant, R. (1988). *Marketing for Tourism.* London: Pitman Publishing.

Kang, S., & Lee, G. (2010). The study on owner-manager's characteristics, start-up motivations and critical success factors of local food restaurants in Jeju Island. *Journal of Tourism & Leisure Research, 22*(3), 195–209.

Kastenholz, E., Davis, D., & Paul, G. (1999). Segmenting tourism in rural areas: The case of North and Central Portugal. *Journal of Travel Research, 37*(4), 353–363.

Khan, M. (1981). Evaluation of food selection patterns and preferences. *CRC Critical Reviews in Food Science and Nutrition, 15*(2), 129–153.

Kim, M. (2008). The perception of quick service restaurants and Korean foods by Los Angeles residents (master's thesis). Sejong University, Korea.

Kim, W., Ng, C., & Kim, Y. (2009). Influence of institutional DINESERV on customer satisfaction, return intention, and word-of-mouth. *International Journal of Hospitality Management, 28*(1), 10–17.

Kim, Y., Eves, A., & Scarles, C. (2009). Building a model of local food consumption on trips and holidays: A grounded theory approach. *International Journal of Hospitality Management, 28*(3), 423–431.

Kim, Y., Taylor, J., & Ruetzler, T. (2008), A small festival and its economic impact on a community: a case study, Frontiers in Southeast CHRIE. *Hospitality and Tourism Research, 12*(2), 49–52.

Kivela, J., & Crotts, J. (2006). Tourism and gastronomy: Gastronomy's influence on how tourists experience a destination. *Journal of Hospitality & Tourism Research, 30*(3), 354–377.

LaBarbera, P., & Mazursky, D. (1983). A longitudinal assessment of consumer satisfaction/dissatisfaction: The dynamic aspect of the cognitive process. *Journal of Marketing Research, 20*(4), 393–404.

Lähteenmäki, L., & Arvola, A. (2001). Food neophobia and variety seeking— Consumer fear or demand for new food products. In L. Frewer, E. Risvik, & H. Schifferstein (Eds.), *Food, People and Society* (pp. 161–175). Berlin, New York: Springer.

Longue, A. (1991). *The Psychology of Eating and Drinking: An Introduction.* New York: WH Freeman.

Lowenberg, M., Todhunter, E., Wilson, E., Savage, J., & Lubawski, J. (Eds.) (1979). *Food and People.* New York: John Wiley & Sons.

Mak, A., Lumbers, M., & Eves, A. (2012). Globalisation and food consumption in tourism. *Annals of Tourism Research, 39*(1), 171–196.

Maslow, A. (1943). A theory of human motivation. *Psychological Review, 50*, 370–396.

Meulenberg, M., & Viaene, J. (1998). Changing food marketing systems in western countries. *Environmental Science*, Corpus ID: 127827184.

Nield, K., Kozak, M., & LeGrys, G. (2000). The role of food service in tourist satisfaction. *International Journal of Hospitality Management, 19*(4), 375–384.

Noh, K. (2010). Study of preference and satisfaction degrees on the Korean food for its globalization (doctoral dissertation). Sungshin Women's University, Korea.

Nu, C., MacLeod, P., & Barthelemy, J. (1996). Effects of age and gender on adolescents' food habits and preferences. *Food Quality and Preference, 7*(3), 251–262.

Okumus, B., Okumus, F., & McKercher, B. (2007). Incorporating local and international cuisines in the marketing of tourism destinations: The cases of Hong Kong and Turkey. *Tourism Management, 28*(1), 253–261.

Petrick, J. (1999). An examination of the relationship between golf traveler's satisfaction, perceived value and loyalty and their intentions to revisit (doctoral dissertation), Clemson University, Clemson.

Prescott, J., Young, O., O'neill, L., Yau, N., & Stevens, R. (2002). Motives for food choice: a comparison of consumers from Japan, Taiwan, Malaysia and New Zealand. *Food quality and Preference, 13*(7), 489–495.

Quan, S., & Wang, N. (2004). Towards a structural model of the tourist experience: an illustration from food experiences in tourism. *Tourism Management, 25*(3), 297–305.

Ranaweera, C., & Prabhu, J. (2003). On the relative importance of customer satisfaction and trust as determinants of customer retention and positive word of mouth. *Journal of Targeting, Measurement and Analysis for Marketing, 12*(1), 82–90.

Richards, G. (2002). Gastronomy: An essential ingredient in tourism production and consumption? In A. Hjalager & G. Richards (Eds.), *Tourism and Gastronomy* (pp. 3–20). London, New York: Routledge.

Rimmington, M., & Üksel, A. (1998). Tourist satisfaction and food service experience: Results and implications of an empirical investigation. *Anatolia, 9*(1), 37–57.

Sparks, B., Bowen, J., & Klag, S. (2003). Restaurants and the tourist market. *International Journal of Contemporary Hospitality, 15*(1), 6–13.

Telfer, D., & Wall, G. (1996). Linkages between tourism and food production. *Annals of Tourism Research, 23*(3), 635–653.

Telfer, D., & Wall, G. (2000). Strengthening backward economic linkages: Local food purchasing by three Indonesian hotels. *Tourism Geographies, 2*(4), 421–447.

The Korea Foundation. (2010). *Traditional Food: A Taste of Korean life.* Seoul: Seoul Selection.

Tikkanen, I. (2007). Maslow's hierarchy and food tourism in Finland: Five cases. *British Food Journal, 109*(9), 721–734.

Turner, L., Reisinger, V., & McQuilken, L. (2002). How cultural differences cause dimensions of tourism satisfaction. *Journal of Travel & Tourism Marketing, 11*(1), 79–101.

Weiermair, K. (2000). Tourists' perceptions towards and satisfaction with service quality in the cross-cultural service encounter: Implications for hospitality and tourism management. *Managing Service Quality, 10*(6), 397–409.

Yoon, Y., & Uysal, M. (2005). An examination of the effects of motivation and satisfaction on destination loyalty: A structural model. *Tourism Management, 26*(1), 45–56.

Yu, J., & Seo, Y. (2009). Casuality model of food service quality for foreign tourists to Korea : Focusing on Chinese, American and Japanese tourists. *Journal of Tourism & Leisure Research, 46*(21), 165–182.Exploring Tourists' Korean Food Satisfaction across Culture, Gender, and Education

Chapter 12

Perceived Value, Importance of Nutrition Information, and Behavioral Intention for Food Tourism in Busan

Joung-Min Son, Eun-Jin Lee, and Hak-Seon Kim

In[1] recent years, food tourism has grown considerably and has become one of the most dynamic and creative segments of tourism. Furthermore, food tourism includes, in its discourse, ethical and sustainable values regarding territory, landscape, environment, local culture and products, and authenticity, which are in line with current trends of cultural consumption (World Tourism Organization 2012).

Today, travelers are more experienced and have more leisure time to travel, and thus, tourism allows them to escape the daily routine of their usual environment and immerse themselves in a world of freedom and novelty. Thus, more tourists are looking for concrete learning experiences, and in this endeavor, gastronomic experience, in highly diverse ways, has become a major element of tourism (An, Jeon, and Yang 2009; Kim 2012).

Several studies have found that tourists travel to those destinations that have established a reputation as a place to experiment with quality local products. Brand image is connected, with varying levels of intensity, to gastronomic values (Crompton 1979; Gedrich 2003; Kim, Lim, and Han 2013). With the growing importance and popularity of food tourism, recent years have witnessed a surge of research interest in food tourism (Bessiere 1998). Most studies firstly discovered in destination marketing and have highlighted the importance of food tourism and proposed marketing strategies for food tourism after researching the destination marketing materials (Bessiere 1998; Kim 2012; World Tourism Organization 2012). However, very few attempts have been made from the demand side to justify the importance of food tourism value and nutritional information for food tourists (Jang and Woo 2015).

Therefore, this study aims to critically assess the importance of food tourism from domestic tourists' perspectives. In particular, this study assesses the relationship between food tourists' value, nutrition information, and behavioral intention of tourists' food experiences during their travel, using SmartPLS program.

LITERATURE REVIEW

Food Tourism

Food tourism is the exploration of food as the purpose of tourism. It is now considered a vital component of the tourism experience (Long 2004). Dining-out is common among tourists and importance to tourists. Current research in food tourism is scarce and is mainly focused on wine and food festivals (World Tourism Organization 2012). Food tourism is an emerging phenomenon that is being developed as a new tourism product due to the fact that according to the specialized literature over one-third of tourist spending is devoted to food (Quan and Wang 2004). Therefore, the cuisine of the destination is an aspect of utmost importance in the quality of the holiday experience. Previous studies proposed food tourism is an experiential trip to a tour region, for recreational or entertainment purposes, which includes visits to primary and secondary producers of food, food festivals, food fairs, events, farmers' markets, cooking shows and demonstrations, tastings of quality food products, or any tourism activity related to food (Bessiere 1998; Hall and Mitchell 2000; World Tourism Organization 2012). In addition, this experiential journey is related to a particular lifestyle that includes experimentation, learning from different cultures, the acquisition of knowledge, and understanding of the qualities or attributes related to tourism products, as well as culinary specialties produced in that region through its consumption (An, Jeon, and Yang 2009; Kim 2012).

Tourism Destination Image

The tourists' perceived value of a particular destination is therefore multidimensional. The tourist's satisfaction with the purchase depends on the product's performance in relation to the tourist's expectations (Chang, Kivela, and Mak 2010; Kim 2012). It should be kept in mind that different cultures have different perceptions of satisfaction and evaluation of gastronomy and that high quality of service can result in dissatisfaction among consumers if their expectations had been too high, for example, due to exaggerated advertising (Chang, Kivela, and Mak 2011).

Satisfaction with the destination leads to customer loyalty and this, in turn, gives a higher level of intention to repeat the visit. Quality is a decisive factor in satisfaction, as it produces a lasting memory about the experience lived by the tourist (Ahn, Jun, and Kim 2015). Tourists revisit the destination due to its gastronomy. Food tourism is a local phenomenon of universal scope that is in a clear growth phase; it has a positive impact on the economy, employment, and local heritage, as tourists seek to get to know not only the local food but also to know its origin and production processes, making it an expression of cultural tourism (Ahn, Jun, and Kim 2015; Kim, Lim, and Han 2013).

Nutrition Information

The regulation of nutrition labeling has changed since it was introduced in South Korea in 1995. Nutrition information was displayed on 18.7 percent of all food products in 2001. That percentage increased in 2005 by 24.1 percent and in 2007 by 79 percent (Kwon et al. 2007). As consumer interest in health rises, their attention to nutrition information also increases (Borra 2006). However, there are still differences between nutrition label recognition and actual nutritional label use. It has been reported that consumers showed higher nutrition label recognition than the actual usage level and that they were mainly aware of calories (Kim, Oh, and No 2016). According to past studies, many consumers recognized nutrition labels, but only a few consumers used them (Hwang and Lorenzen 2008; Jennings 2008).

Motivation

A study found that 67 percent of and obtain the desired outcomes, and the personal value of all outcomes associated with that activity (Jennings 2008). Therefore, one can influence motivation by manipulating cues that define an individual's expectation concerning the consequences of action and the incentive value of the consequences produced by the action (Feather 1990). Thus, one can perceive the likely consequences of an action without being able to execute the action. A lot of studies regarding motivation follow a deliberate decision-making process to explain choice among goals and action alternatives (Boo, Noh, Kim, Kim, and Rha 2015; Crompton 1979; Joung, Choi, Lee, and Kim 2010). A person chooses a certain behavior for its expected results. From this perspective, the motivational process represents a prerequisite step to action. It can be explained as a cognitive elaboration with emotional components (Feather 1990).

METHODS

A self-reported survey was adopted in this study. The respondents were tourists who had experience dining when they traveled in Busan, Korea. Because

Busan is one of the fastest-growing tour areas in Korea, Busan was chosen. The survey questionnaire was divided into three major sections. Each section contained questions addressing the variables suit to the research objectives. Respondents' perception was required to answer on a seven type Likert scale ranging from 1 with *totally disagree* to 7 *totally agree*. The information on the anonymity and confidentiality was provided through the information sheet attached to the questionnaire. This information sheet provided the details about the researcher, the aim of the study and the purpose of the survey to be conducted. With absent of obvious problems, a total of 260 usable question-naires were obtained. Data were compiled and analyzed using the statistical analysis program SPSS 21.0 and SmartPLS. Descriptive statistics described the respondents' demographic profile in frequencies and percentages, and independent *t*-test and ANOVA were conducted to indicate the differences on demographics. Finally, multiple regression analysis was conducted in order to test causal relationships of nutritional information.

RESULTS

General Characteristics of Respondents

The importance of food tourism shows that 51.5 percent of the respondents answered, "important or very important." Close to 26 percent of the respondents reported that they utilize nutrition facts label while they purchase food product, while 44.7 percent reported that they would not use nutrition facts label frequently.

Gender does matter when it comes to the intended use/importance of Nutrition Information (NI) and dining out more frequently if NI is available. Meanwhile, women order well-being (M = 3.58, SD = 1.52; t = 2.06) and low calorie menu (M = 3.77, SD = 1.61; t = 2.52) significantly more than men (M = 3.12, SD = 1.51; M = 3.16, SD = 1.68) while dining out at a full-service restaurant. However, women less believe (M = 4.08, SD = 1.11) they can order well-being menu from full-service restaurant than men (M = 4.51, SD = 1.19; t = –2.61), but the level is still close to *neutral*. This is a noteworthy finding, as women have traditionally made a conservative decision regarding the menu when they travel.

There is not a significant correlation between age and other items regarding NI usage. They may not see it as an occasional indulgence. In all likelihoods, they are not looking for any incentives to eat out more often. Significant differ-ences were observed between the monthly income of the respondent and usage of NI if available (F = 3.686, p < 0.05). As income levels increase, so does the intended frequency of usage of the NI. This could present a business oppor-tunity for full-service restaurants, as the income level also correlates to the frequency of dining-out, and satisfying these important consumers could build loyalty. Moreover, there were significant differences between income and dining frequency if NI was provided in restaurants. High-income travelers are likely to dine out when restaurant provides NI. Dining-out could be a necessity for them when they travel; they do not see it as an occasional indulgence.

Measurement Model Evaluation

This study used the SmartPLS (Ringle, Wende, and Will 2005) implementation of partial least squares (PLS) structural equation modeling to estimate our theoretical model. As a distribution-independent method, PLS has fewer constraints and statistical conditions than covariance-based techniques, such as LISREL. The use of PLS path modeling is recommended in early stages of theoretical development to test and validate exploratory models (Hair, Hult, Ringle, and Sarstedt 2014; Henseler, Ringle, and Sinkovics 2009).

Table 12.1   Descriptive Statistics and Correlations[a]

Items	Number of Items	M	SD	α	CR	1	2	3	4
Value	3	4.72	1.20	0.75	0.88	0.62			
Importance	2	4.63	1.25	0.60	0.82	0.52	0.80		
Product	2	4.22	1.24	0.68	0.85	0.52	0.75	0.71	
Restaurant	2	4.15	1.33	0.70	0.83	0.46	0.43	0.43	0.75

Note[a]: All correlations are significant at: p < 0.001; the square root of the AVE is on the diagonal, as a test of discriminant validity; M – mean; SD – standard deviation; α – Cronbach's α; CR – composite reliability.

SmartPLS assesses the psychometric properties of the measurement model and estimates the parameters of the structural model taking into account the moderating latent constructs. The parameters converged in fewer than twenty iterations, and both the measurement model and the structural model parameters support our hypotheses. We find these composite reliability scores highly satisfactory. We estimated the Cronbach's alphas, as shown in table 12.1, which range from 0.60 to 0.75 for the four newly developed scale items— Value (0.75), Importance (0.60), Product (0.68), and Restaurant (0.70). Additionally, we test for discriminant validity of the four latent variables in the PLS model. A latent variable should share more variance with its assigned indicators than with any other latent variable (Boo et al. 2015). The square root of the AVE of each latent variable should be greater than the latent variable's highest correlation with any other latent variable. Acceptable reliability and discriminant validity were confirmed for the measures. Having established the soundness of the measures, this study subsequently used them to test the hypothesized relationships. As noted by Ringle, Wende, and Will (2005), once the measurement model is satisfactory, this study can proceed to evaluate the structural model.

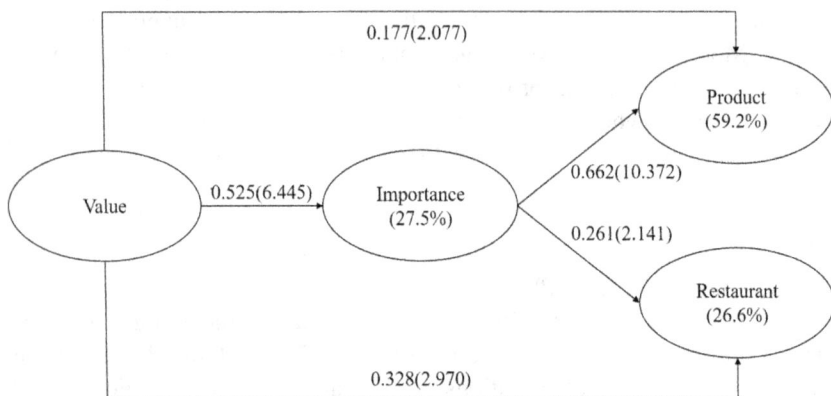

Figure 12.1 Results of Structural Equation Modeling.[a] Note[a]: Path coefficients and t-values (in parentheses) are marked near line arrow and coefficients of determination (R^2) are reported as percentage.

Direct Effects Tests

The explained variances (R^2 values) for NI importance, product, and restaurant are 27.5, 59.2, and 26.6, respectively. This study applied a bootstrapping procedure (200 subsamples; 247 cases) to assess the significance of the path coefficients (Joung, Choi, Lee, and Kim 2010). The measurement model for value and the path estimates and relative *t*-values of the structural model appear in figure 12.1. This study used the path coefficients to test our hypotheses.

> Hypothesis 1 postulates that higher levels of healthy-eating value will each have positive effects on food-related behaviors. Standard errors of the parameter estimates are obtained by bootstrapping the sample 5,000 times (Joung, Choi, Lee, and Kim 2010). The R^2 for the structural model predicting importance is 0.27, and parameter estimates for the drivers of food-related behaviors are significant ($p<0.05$).
>
> Hypothesis 2 posits that nutrition information importance affects travelers' intentions to visit restaurants which provided nutrition information.

Table 12.2 Structural Path Estimates

Independent Variable (IV)	Dependent Variable (DV)	Parameter Estimates	Standard Error	T-statistics
Value	Importance	0.525	0.081	6.445[a]
Value	Product	0.177	0.085	2.077[a]
Value	Restaurant	0.328	0.110	2.970[a]
Importance	Product	0.662	0.064	10.372[a]
Importance	Restaurant	0.261	0.122	2.141[a]

Note[a]: Parameter is significant at p < 0.05.

Mediation Effects Test

Hypotheses 3 theorize that NI importance moderates the relationship between healthy-eating value and travelers' food-related behaviors.

Hypothesis 4 predicts that NI importance will moderate the impact of healthy-eating value on food-related behaviors such that the effect is lower at higher levels of nutrition information importance. A significant estimate of parameter confirms that the relationship between healthy eating value and food-related behaviors is moderated by NI importance.

While confirming the traditional view of higher healthy-eating value leading to higher food-related behaviors, we extend this finding by identifying two key moderating variable (Importance) that affect this relationship between value and behaviors. Importance of nutrition information has a positive main effect on food-related behaviors. More specifically, the higher the level of NI importance drives the greater the food-related behaviors. Similarly, customers who exhibit higher levels of NI importance are likely to be more loyal.

Table 12.3   Mediation Tests

Hypotheses	Dependent Variable (DV)	a (Sa) Value → Importance	b (Sb) Importance → DV	C' (Value → DV; Mediator Controlled)
H3	Product	0.525[a] (0.0869)	0.662[a] (0.070)	0.339[a]
H4	Restaurant	0.525[a] (0.0869)	0.261[a] (0.109)	0.328[a]

Note[a]: Significant at p < 0.001; all paths are b coefficients. Sobel test statistic, 5.09124335; One-tailed probability, 0.00000018; Two-tailed probability, 0.00000036; Sobel test statistic, 2.22602691; One-tailed probability, 0.01300619; Two-tailed probability, 0.02601238.

DISCUSSIONS AND CONCLUSIONS

The aim of this study was to explore the importance of food tourism to Busan, South Korea, from domestic tourists' perspectives. The results show that perceived value is great importance for tourists' travel in Busan, which indicates that food tourism can be main role to Busan. In terms of the practical implications, this study enables the destination marketers to access a more accurate understanding of the importance of food tourism. Although this research makes a contribution to the food tourism development and research in Busan, there still are certain limitations that should be taken into account and that constitute potential lines of research for the future. Firstly, regarding the research instrument, questionnaire survey, as the only method, was adopted in the study. However, in order to achieve the credibility of the research and minimize personal or methodological biases, various methods are suggested to be implemented in the research design. Secondly, reviewing the profile of the respondents in the research, it is noted that the age and the education level might have an influence on the results of the study. Future studies should pay attention to balancing the number of respondents from different age groups to avoid this resulting deviation.

NOTE

1. This chapter was previously published with the same title in *Culinary Science & Hospitality Research*, *22*(1), 135–140.

REFERENCES

Ahn, J., Jun, K., & Kim, H. (2015). An exploration of the relationships among brand value, customer satisfaction and behavioral intention in fast food restaurant visitors. *Culinary Science and Hospitality Research*, *21*(5), 14–24.

An, H., Jeon, H., & Yang, T. (2009). A study on the customer behavior and recognition of Jeju regional cuisine: Focusing on customer satisfaction, revisit intention, and word of mouth among the tourists in Jeju. *The Korean Journal of Culinary Research*, *15*(2), 93–107.

Bessiere, J. (1998). Local development and heritage: Traditional food and cuisine as tourist attractions in rural areas. *Sociologia Ruralis*, *38*(1), 21–34.

Boo, Y., Noh, J., Kim, Y., Kim, S., & Rha, Y. (2015). Perception of privacy and sensitivity of personal information among university students. *Culinary Science and Hospitality Research*, *21*(5), 25–37.

Borra, S. (2006). Consumer perspectives on food labels. *American Journal of Clinical Nutrition*, *83*(5), 1235S.

Chang, R., Kivela, J., & Mak, A. (2010). Food preferences of Chinese tourists. *Annals of Tourism Research*, *37*(4), 989–1011.

Chang, R., Kivela, J., & Mak, A. (2011). Attributes that influence the evaluation of travel dining experience: When East meets West. *Tourism Management*, *32*(2), 307–316.

Crompton, J. (1979). Motivation for pleasure vacation. *Annals of Tourism Research*, *6*(4), 408–424.

Feather, N. (1990). Bridging the gap between values and actions: Recent applications of the expectancy-value model. In E. Higgins & R. Sorrentino (Eds.), *Handbook of Motivation and Cognition: Foundation of Social Behavior* (pp. 151–192). New York: Guilford.

Gedrich, K. (2003). Determinants of nutritional behavior: A multitude of levers for successful intervention. *Appetite*, *41*(3), 231–238.

Hair, J., Hult, G., Ringle, C., & Sarstedt, M. (2014). *A Primer on Partial Least Squares Structural Equation Modeling (PLS-SEM)*. Thousand Oaks, CA: Sage.

Hall, C., & Mitchell, R. (2000). We are what we eat: Tourism, culture and the globalisation and localisation of cuisine. *Tourism Culture and Communication, 2*(1), 29–37.

Henseler, J., Ringle, C., & Sinkovics, R. (2009). The use of partial least squares path modeling in international marketing. *Advances in International Marketing, 20,* 277–320.

Hwang, J., & Lorenzen, C. (2008). Effective nutrition labeling of restaurant menu and pricing of healthy menu. *Journal of Foodservice, 19*(5), 270–276.

Jang, S., & Woo, I. (2015). A study on consumer awareness, preference, and consumption behavior regarding local food: Focusing on Gyeongju area. *The Korean Journal of Culinary Research, 21*(2), 154–170.

Jennings, L. (2008). Menu-labeling mandates meet industry's resistance nationwide. *Nation's Restaurants, 42*(12), 1–41.

Joung, H., Choi, E., Lee, D., & Kim, H. (2010). Exploring internal marketing mix and its applications in the foodservice industry. *Culinary Science and Hospitality Research, 21*(5), 192–203.

Kim, H., Oh, C., & No, J. (2016). Can nutrition label recognition or usage affect nutrition intake according to age? *Nutrition, 32*(1), 56–60.

Kim, J. (2012). A study on the current status and activation of food tourism festivals: Centering around Gwangju, Jeonnam province. *The Korean Journal of Culinary Research, 18*(5), 129–145.

Kim, J., Lim, S., & Han, H. (2013). Investigating the impact of Busan convention-tour contents on image of Busan, expected value, and international- convention participation intention. *Journal of Tourism and Leisure Research, 25*(2), 213–230.

Kwon, K., Park, S., Lee, J., Kim, J., Yoo, K., & Lee, J. (2007). Prevalence of nutrition labeling and claims on processed, and packaged foods. *Korean Journal of Community Nutrition, 12,* 206–213.

Long, L. (2004). *Culinary Tourism.* Lexington, KY: University Press of Kentucky.

Quan, S., & Wang, N. (2004). Towards a structural model of the tourist experience: An illustration from food experience in tourism. *Tourism Management, 25*(3), 297–305.

Ringle, C., Wende, S., & Will, A. (2005). *Smart PLS 2.0 M3.* Hamburg: University of Hamburg.

World Tourism Organization. (2012). Global report on food tourism. Retrieved from https://www.e-unwto.org/doi/book/10.18111/9789284414819.

Chapter 13

Toward a Regional Level of Food Security in East Asia

Lessons from the 2007–2008 Rice Crisis

Dong-Yeob Kim

This[1] study was conducted to assess the current status of food security in East Asia and to shed light on regional cooperation as a viable option for the future of food security in the region. The study focuses on the specific case of the 2007–2008 global food crisis, and considers this crisis in the context of East Asian food security policies. Food security is one of the global issues that attracts continuous attention. The Food and Agriculture Organization (FAO) estimates that, in 2006, 16 percent of the population in Asia and the Pacific region, and 30 percent in sub-Saharan Africa, were undernourished (FAO 2009). Furthermore, in 2009, the United Nations (UN) called attention to the increasing number of hungry people surpassing one billion (UN 2010).

Food security, similar to issues of poverty and hunger, is often conceived as a problem at the individual or family level. However, food security was regarded as a national and regional issue during the global food crisis of the early 1970s, when the concept was first generated. Recently, the issue of food security has become a great concern of the global community. Indeed, reduction of hunger has been accepted as part of the world development agenda since the late 1990s, and the World Food Summit (WFS) of 1996 set a target of halving the number of undernourished people by 2015.

In East Asia, many countries identify food security with national food self-sufficiency, often pursuing it through substantial government intervention. While this may not always be economically efficient, they still keep this policy orientation because it has important political and strategic overtones. Most governments are unwilling to leave their food security matters to the vagaries of the international market. They have, therefore, pursued vigorous policies of agricultural development through a range of instruments, including public sector research and extension services, input subsidies, the provision of agricultural infrastructure, such as irrigation systems, and the operation of a buffer stock (Gill, Farrington, Anderson, Luttrell, and Conway 2003). However, an individual country's unilateral measures have their limitations, unless a country has enough resources to act self-sufficiently.

When it comes to deciding on a method for approaching food security, regional organizations have been closely discussed as a viable option. The FAO encourages regional cooperation to meet given targets of food security goals. Twelve Regional Economic Organizations (REOs), in collaboration with the FAO, have prepared the Regional Programs for Food Security (RPFS). The RPFS has three major components trade facilitation, harmonization of national agricultural policies, and support of national-specific programs (Bello 2005). The European Union (EU) represents a good example of regional cooperation for food security. Governments in Europe have a long history of intervening in agricultural markets in order to protect farm incomes, ensure food security, and stabilize prices. The integration of agricultural markets in the EU required from the outset that these functions were transferred to the EU level, and the Common Agricultural Policy (CAP) was thus borne (Matthews 2003). However, the model cannot be easily applied to other regional organizations due to different regional contexts and policies. It would be difficult, if not impossible, to create a regional CAP with which all member countries are satisfied. Such a wide-reaching policy would likely create conflicts of interests among member countries.

In the field of food security study, focus has shifted substantially between the 1970s and the twenty-first century. In the early period of the 1970s, scholars and policy makers were concerned about food production, primarily working to ensure that enough food was available. The green revolution was a notable achievement of such efforts. Subsequently, the focus of study shifted to a livelihood perspective by recognizing the fact that people were hungry not because of food shortages but because of a lack of resources to access it. Food safety is also a hot spot in the field of food security study. Today, food security has become an increasingly more complicated issue by involving newly emerging concerns such as free trade, energy, environment, and so forth (Falvey 2004; Maxwell et al. 2008; Ninno et al. 2007; Othman 2007; Pingali 2006).

Many scholars in this field subscribe to the idea of free trade and in the regional- and global-level approach to improving food security worldwide (Balisacan 2004; David 2003; Dawe 2001, 2002; Dawe, Moya, Casiwan, and Cabling 2008; Gill et al. 2003). They believe that since the problem is not insufficient production, free trade could promote effective distribution of resources and economic development to improve the livelihood of the poor. However, such a proposition has been challenged by a number of scholars, many of whom have pointed out the tendency of unequal distribution of benefits in a free market system. Their concern focuses on the poor in developing countries, who are most vulnerable to a food crisis. Those scholars, who are wary of relying on the free market to bolster access to food among the world's poor, base their perspective on the idea that access to food is a basic human right and should be guaranteed to every human being (Carr 2006; Dilley and Boudreau 2001; Shiva 2000). There is increasing literature that focuses on the role of regional cooperation in food security (Bello 2005; Brahmbhatt and Christiaensen 2008; Erjavec and Erjavec 2009; ESCAP 2009; Matthews 2003). Much of this literature argues that regional cooperation could meet national and regional specificities for food security concerns, and avoid the pitfalls embedded in relying on the global free market system.

By assessing the track record of the 2007–2008 rice crisis in East Asia, this study aims to tackle the following research queries. First, what is the food security status in East Asia? Second, what is the short-term and long-term threat for food security in the region? Third, what is the regional cooperation scheme for food security in East Asia? Fourth, what are the promises and pitfalls of regional cooperation for food security? It should be noted that among the various types of food, this study deals only with rice; rice was chosen because it is a common staple food in East Asia and traditionally treated as a main element of food security in the region. However, it is also true that the current changes in dietary preferences undermine the importance of rice and increase the importance of other types of food, especially wheat, meat, and vegetables.

In this study, the statistical data published by the FAO, the World Trade Organization (WTO), and the Association of Southeast Asian Nations (ASEAN) Secretariat were used to analyze the trends and status of food security in East Asia. As for individual countries' perceptions and stands on food security, this chapter made use of the outputs of the two NEAT (Network of East Asian Think-Tanks)[2] Working Group Meetings on Food Security, delegated by 13 ASEAN Plus Three member countries. These meetings were held on July 1, 2009, and July 9, 2010, in Tokyo. The author of this study participated in these meetings as a delegate.

This study consists of six sections. The first section provides a short introduction of the study with a brief review of related literature. The second section outlines a conceptualization that provides an understanding of food security. The conceptualization also served in the study as an analytical tool for the issues by providing operational definitions of important terms, although the terms were used for assessing rather than measuring the facts. The third section describes the status of food security in the East Asia region. The fourth section analyzes the 2007–2008 food crisis, as guided by the conceptualization. The fifth section focuses on the regional scheme for food security in East Asia as a regional mechanism to deal with the crisis. And the sixth and final section serves as a summary and conclusion of the study, where the limitation of this study and the necessary future studies in the field are identified.

UNDERSTANDING FOOD SECURITY

After the end of the Cold War, the traditional concept of security that focused on territorial integrity was redefined. Individual countries and the international community came to recognize that such values as human security, economic independence, cultural identity, social stability, and environmental and energy security were as important as territorial integrity. The concept of *comprehensive security* became a popular norm among scholars and policy makers. Against the backdrop of the new security concept, *human security* was defined as insuring *freedom from want* and *freedom from fear* for all people. The areas of concern are extensive, including economic security, food security, health security, environment security, personal security, community security, political security, and so forth (UNDP 1994). As an integral part of human security, the concept of food security emerged at the FAO World Food Conference in 1974. The World Food Summit of 1996 stated that "food security, at the individual, household, national, regional and global level is achieved when all people, at all times, have physical and economic access to sufficient, safe and nutritious food to meet their dietary needs and food preferences for an active and healthy life" (FAO 1996). This definition has been widely used.

Food security is conventionally assessed in terms of three components: food availability, food access, and food utilization (FAO 1996; Maxwell, Caldwell, and Langworthy 2008; Pinstrup-Anderson 2009). Food availability is the sum of domestic production, imports, and changes in national stock. It is related to the supply side of food security. Food access is a measure of people's entitlement to food, which is the amount they can produce, purchase, or receive. It is closely related to income, prices, subsidies, safety nets, and access to the market. Food utilization is the capacity of an individual to absorb and utilize the nutrients in the food he or she consumes. It is determined by practices, beliefs, eating habits, hygiene, sanitation, and the healthcare system (Gill et al. 2003, 6).[3] The level of accomplishment of these components heavily depends on the natural, socioeconomic, and international environments in which each nation is situated.

As illustrated in figure 13.1, food security is continuously exposed to short- and long-term threats. The short-term and temporary threat may come from natural calamities, policy changes, unseasonal weather patterns,

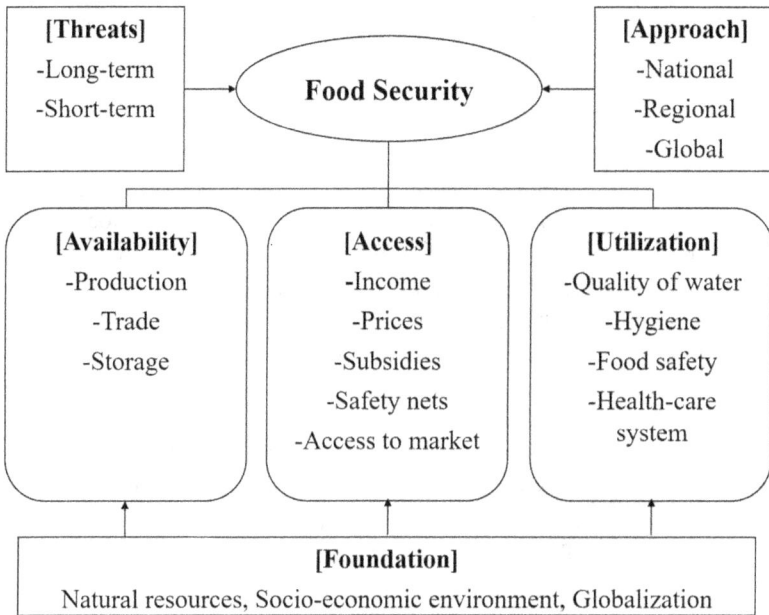

Figure 13.1   Understanding Food Security: A Conceptualization.

supply disruptions, and pest outbreaks. Recent studies suggest that rising energy and fertilizer prices and the falling dollar have contributed to perhaps one-third of the rise in world food prices. As an example, rising fuel costs directly increase the cost of operating agricultural machinery, irrigation systems, and transportation (Brahmbhatt and Christiaensen 2008; ESCAP 2009). Recently, the government policy of encouraging the production and use of bio fuels became a serious factor to affect food security.[4] Although the benefits of bio fuels have been acknowledged, their production poses new food security risks and challenges for the poor by causing an increase in food prices. The domestic prices of tradable goods are also influenced by movements in exchange rates. Since food stuffs become increasingly tradable, large exchange rate depreciation can have a severely adverse effect on food security, particularly when occurring over a short time span (Gill et al. 2003, 10).

On the other hand, the long-term and persistent threats to food security could be listed as low investment in agriculture, poverty, and the alternative use of grains, to name a few. The sharp rise of agricultural production costs, led by fuel and fertilizers, has substantially contributed to agriculture losing competitive ground compared to other industries. Recently, the demand to use over one-third of the world's grain production to feed animals has become a more pressing concern to food security.[5] Additional threats to long-term food security include population growth, diet transitions, and climate change, among others.

The short- and long-term threats tend to create a food insecurity situation. Food insecurity is indicated by the following three factors: shortages of supply, increased demand, and a volatile market. It is more specifically characterized as food shortages, food price increases, food hoarding, and food contamination. Food insecurity affects individual and family health, and quality of life overall, which, in turn, leads hungry people to a situation of frustration. Such individual frustration causes political, economic, and social instability in the affected nation. Such effects may spill over to neighboring countries and even onto the global level, thus destabilizing international relations.

In order to cope with food insecurity, three different levels of approach have been studied, which include national, regional, and global. Among these three, the global level of approach has demonstrated the least potential to accomplish the goal. The track record of this approach exhibits only humanitarian aid and the promotion of seamless free trade for food presented and promoted by international organizations without any substantive measures being taken. Consequently, the national and regional levels of approach are considered more seriously in their merits and shortcomings.

In the national level of approach for food security, two ideological discourses are under debate. One is *mercantilism* represented by protectionism, and the other is *liberalism* represented by the free market system (Erjavec and Erjavec 2009). The essence of mercantilism lies in domestic market regulation and border protection, or, when these are not possible, market price support coupled with direct payments.[6] Mercantilists maintain a policy orientation for food security geared toward self-sufficiency. On the other hand, liberalists believe that the globalized world offers unprecedented opportunities for growth through intensified competition. In order to realize the promise, unfettered free trade and the dismantling of state bureaucracy is required. Hence, liberalists tend to believe that the foreign market is a reliable source to ensure individual countries' food security.

These two opposing discourses have their own merits and pitfalls, and each government's policy preference depends on its particular situation. In the age of globalization, various international trade agreements are pushing the world in the direction of free trade. Yet price stabilization is not always consistent with free trade (Dawe 2001). Countries that depend on food imports to a great extent are more vulnerable to shocks arising in the global food market. Hence, many governments are still striving for food self-sufficiency.

Along the same line of argument, the regional level of approach for food security takes two different directions—*a community-oriented approach* and *a free trade approach.* The community-oriented approach is based on the ideology that food is a basic human need and its access should be treated as a basic human right rather than relying on economic logic (Falvey 2004). A strategy for this approach is to operate a food reserve system that runs for humanitarian purposes in the region. This is to ensure not only against unexpected natural calamities but also against the dangers posed by the volatility of food prices and supplies. The tendency toward greater commoditization of food and speculative investments makes the international market increasingly unreliable. By undermining the competitive market mechanism, however, this approach could result in losing the region's agricultural competitiveness in the world market. It might compromise the spirit and the efforts of the region's food producers to bring about more cost-effective means of production in order to win over world market competition. Proper measures to secure and promote a region's agricultural industry should be accompanied by this approach.

The free trade approach is based on the ideology that the liberalized market would create an optimal condition for food security. It would promote in farmers an innovative spirit in production, and provide consumers with the best possible food prices. Many governments subsidize the price of agricultural inputs such as fertilizers, pesticides, water, and electricity; such policy has imposed a fiscal burden on the government and distorted the market mechanism, not to mention garner increasing criticism from international trade partners. The free trade approach advocates that food should be subject to the same market forces as manufactured goods with minimum state intervention. However, the free market system usually produces winners and losers in the market, and the rich and powerful market players generally have a better chance of winning the competition. This scenario could create a sense of injustice among regional countries. Without proper measures to cope with such problems, the free trade approach could damage the spirit of regional cooperation.

The most appropriate approach to cope with a food insecurity situation depends on the causes, characteristics, and nature of the crisis. A short-term, national-level approach could take the form of a trade policy response either restricting exports or increasing imports to secure enough food for the nation's people. A long-term, national approach could involve strengthening food production capacity. Regional- and global-level approaches, on the other hand, should focus on making use of emergency reserves and promoting the free trade of food, which is believed to be effective not only for short-term relief but also for the long-term improvement of the livelihood of the poor by vitalizing the national economy. Each level of approach has its strengths and weaknesses. The national-level approach may appeal to the affected people most, but it might damage international relations since it tends to throw its problem on to others, which could make things worse at the international level. This is why the regional level of approach emerges as a viable option for food security.

FOOD SECURITY STATUS IN EAST ASIA

In East Asia, food security is often synonymous with self-sufficiency in rice supplies, since rice represents the most important staple food item in the region. In order to keep a certain level of rice production and rice reserves, governments usually undermine market mechanisms either by keeping domestic rice prices high or by subsidizing rice farmers. Such government policy aims to achieve the inherently conflicting objectives of ensuring low and stable prices for the benefit of consumers and sufficiently high and stable prices for the benefit of farmers (David 2003, 193). This policy orientation has continuously been criticized by the liberalist school of thought. Liberalists argue that such distortion of the market may not be a solution for food security in the long run because such measures distort producer incentives and undermine the operation of local markets. It is also a heavy burden for governments to bear at the international trade negotiation table, such as Free Trade Agreement (FTA) and the WTO, where they have to sacrifice other opportunities for trade benefits in order to protect the domestic rice market. In spite of all the contradictions, many governments in East Asia are still unwilling to put off the policy of protection in the domestic food market, specifically the rice market.

As far as rice self-sufficiency is concerned, most East Asian countries maintain a certain level of security due to the governments' consistent efforts to achieve this goal. However, some countries, like Brunei, Malaysia, and the Philippines, are not included in this group, as shown in table 13.1. As far as the availability of rice as a staple food is concerned, East Asia faces no serious problem. However, when the other two categories of food security are taken into account, problems and potential issues become more serious. The high rate of income inequality and the high proportion of people living below the poverty level make a significant number of the populace vulnerable to problems concerning food access. Some countries in the region face problems in utilization in terms of access to safe water and adequate sanitation. As for the overall criterion for measuring food security, the proportion of undernourishment indicates that many countries in the region could be considered to be in a food insecurity situation. As table 13.1 attests, a food security situation runs almost parallel with the level of national economic development. The poorest countries in the region, such as Cambodia and Laos, suffer most from a food security problem.

Table 13.1 Food Security Status of East Asian Countries

| | Food Security Criteria | | | | | | | |
| | Availability | | | Access | | Utilization | | |
Country	GDP Per Capita US$ (2008)	Proportion of Undernourishment (%), (2005–2007)[b]	Ratio of Production to Consumption by Rice, Milled (%), (2005–2007)	Gini of Income (%)[a]	National Poverty Level (%)	Access to Safe Water (%), (2008)	Access to Adequate Sanitation (%), (2008)	Proportion of Undernourishment (%), (2005–2007)[b]
Brunei	31,076	2.1	118.2	-	-	94.0	-	-
Cambodia	648	169.6	0.3	44.0 (2007)	30.1 (2007)	31.0	29.0	22.0
Indonesia	2,245	108.4	1.7	38.0 (2007)	16.7 (2004)	69.0	52.0	13.0
Laos	882	147.9	2.3	33.0 (2002)	35.5 (2003)	52.0	53.0	23.0
Malaysia	8,212	74.2	32.4	38.0 (2004)	-	94.0	96.0	-
Myanmar	-	200.7	0.1	-	32.0 (2005)	29.0	81.0	16.0
Philippines	1,844	87.7	15.1	44.0 (2006)	25.1 (1997)	74.0	76.0	15.0
Singapore	39,950	-	-	-	-	-	-	-
Thailand	4,043	264.7	0.0	42.0 (2004)	13.6 (1998)	87.0	96.0	16.
Viet Nam	943	154.4	0.0	38.0 (2006)	28.9 (2002)	88.0	75.0	11.0
China	3,414	101.2	0.9	-	2.8 (2004)	82.0	55.0	10.0
Japan	38,268	99.2	7.0	25.0 (1993)	-	97.0	100.0	-
Korea	19,162	107.6	0.5	32.0 (1998)	-	95.0	100.0	-

Source: FAO Food Security Indicators by Country (updated October 2010); World Bank data.
Note[a]: A value of 0 represents absolute equality, and a value of 100 absolute inequality.
Note[b]: In the international standard set by the FAO, a rate of undernourishment above 10% would signify food insecurity in a nation.

Individual countries in the region have their own problems to tackle in terms of food security. Rice exporters like Thailand and Vietnam are concerned about increasing production costs, climate change, and the fluctuation of international rice prices. But those countries that depend heavily on international markets, like Brunei, Malaysia, and the Philippines, suffer most from international price fluctuations. Once a nation has become dependent on cheap imported rice and has given up costly domestic production, it is not easy for it to recover the previous level of domestic production in a short span of time, as rice fields have generally already been converted to other purposes. On the other hand, comparatively well-off countries like Japan and Korea have their own share of pains in food security matters. They suffer huge economic losses in order to keep the excessive rice reserve created by production and imports. They are bound on the one hand by domestic pressure to preserve a certain level of rice production and on the other international pressure to open up their domestic rice market. The commercialization of the excessive rice stocks is also restricted by international agreements. For these countries, food safety issues are of more concern than other categories of food security.

Rice has been one of the few food items in relation to which East Asian countries have enjoyed competitiveness due to the favorable climate and labor-intensive type of farming. However, for most of other major food items, East Asian countries cannot compete with international players who enjoy much better conditions for food production (Gill et al. 2003; Pingali 2006). As a result, most East Asian countries are heavily dependent on the international market for other food items aside from rice. Furthermore, the region's traditional rice-based diet has become a more diversified and Westernized diet in which people consume greater quantities of livestock and wheat products; these are products that East Asian countries do not typically produce and in relation to which they cannot be competitive. Thus, East Asia has gradually been connected to the global food market to import necessary food items, and unduly influenced by the complicated economic and political factors of the other regions. The shift in diet suggests that the future of food security in the region could be more vulnerable and worse than the situation today.

2007–2008 RICE CRISIS

In mid-2008, the price of rice reached its highest level in thirty years. Not only the price of rice surged, but also that of major cereals like wheat and maize. The result of this surge in food prices was widespread anxiety over food accessibility and affordability worldwide (Tolentino 2009, September 23). However, it was proved that there was no physical shortage of rice in the world market at the time. In fact, overall world rice production had reached a record high in 2007 and hit a new high in 2008, while world rice stocks remained fairly steady at 17–18 percent of world consumption in those years. This crisis was different to the 1973–1975 food crisis. Although both cases were worsened by the protection policies of rice exporting countries,[7] a shortage of supply caused by a severe El Nino in 1972–1973, followed by major La Nina events in 1973–1974 and 1975–1976 provided the fundamental differences between the two cases (Dawe 2002).

The 2007–2008 rice crisis could be understood as an unfortunate convergence of short-and long-term threats to food security and the failure of policy to deal with them. As international rice prices were controlled by speculative impulse, an incorrect signal was sent to several major rice exporters such as Vietnam, Egypt, and Cambodia that a rice shortage would shortly materialize, and hence they began to restrict rice exports in order to keep reserves for their domestic markets. The spiraling situation was exacerbated by political posturing. The then-biggest rice exporter, Thailand, openly discussed the possibility of export restrictions, a measure they had not imposed in more than thirty years. A Thai government official also floated the idea of organizing a rice cartel called the Organization of Rice Exporting Countries (OREC). The real surge in prices, however, came in March 2008 when the Philippines, the world's largest importer of rice, signaled that it would import 2.1 million tons of rice, much more than the 1.6 million tons expected, and would be willing to pay a substantial price premium for the additional rice. The Philippines' attempt to increase its level of stocks during a time of volatile price fluctuations had an enormous impact on the world's rice prices (Tolentino 2009,

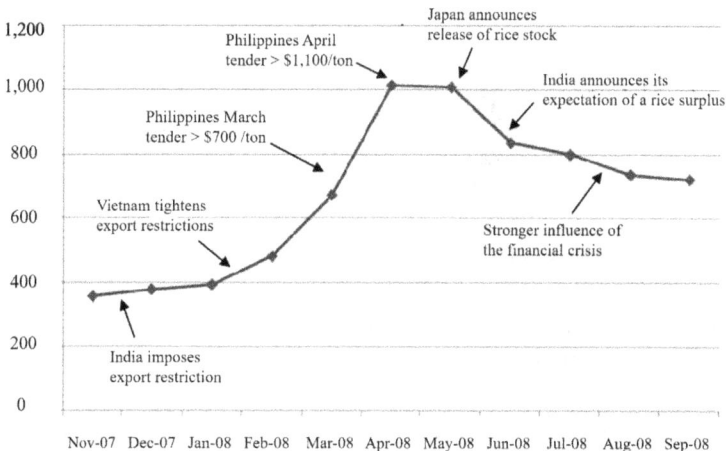

Figure 13.2   Trade and the Price of Rice 2007–2008. *Source*: Adapted from ESCAP (2009, 78).

September 23). Figure 13.2 demonstrates the dramatic incidents of the 2007–2008 rice crisis.

The exporting and importing countries' policy at the time was not entirely incomprehensible. On facing people's protests against expensive food in the domestic consumer market, the governments of rice exporting countries were obliged to take necessary action. The most immediate action was to restrict or ban exports in order to increase domestic supply as a means of cooling down domestic rice prices. As for the rice importing countries, governments needed to show their sincere effort to secure the sufficient amount of rice by whatever means in order to stabilize the domestic market. Such self-helping policies drove the international rice price to a record high in April 2008.

Since the crisis situation was not initiated by a real shortage of rice stock, the price surge shortly subdued as market confidence recovered. The panic only fully subsided after Japan announced the release of its rice stock; Japan had a rice stock of around 900,000 tons of U.S. medium-grain rice, and 600,000 tons of long-grain rice imported from Thailand and Vietnam, which was far in excess of domestic consumption needs. However, the re-export of the rice stock was restricted by agreement with the WTO, and by exporting countries like the United States, Thailand, and Vietnam. In mid-May of 2008, on demands from international society to take immediate action on the rice crisis, key members of the WTO and related parties held a behind-the-scenes discussion. They agreed that Japan's stockpiled rice could be released and re-exported to the crisis-affected countries. In actual terms, only 200,000 tons of the stock was sold to the Philippines (Brahmbhatt and Christiaensen 2008, 36).

Although the food crisis of 2007–2008 was over, the aftermath and implications were immense. As a result of the crisis, an additional 100 million people grew hungry during the period of 2006 to 2008.[8] The most heavily affected country was the Philippines, and the most hard hit were the country's poor. Most Filipinos felt the effect of the rising food prices in 2008, when rice prices reached 36.72 pesos per kilogram (about US$0.8) in July 2008. This was 22 percent higher than the average retail price for the first six months of the year, and 63 percent more than the average retail price for 2007. Escalating price tags on almost all food items in the Philippines have since made life more difficult for every citizen of the country, increasing the incidences and severity of poverty (Domoguen and Arban 2008). Not only Filipinos were affected, but so too were most of the people in the region who lived hand-to-mouth and depended on this basic food staple.

The 2007–2008 rice crisis made the countries in the region realize that under a crisis situation, individual countries would pursue self-helping policies regardless of the situation abroad. The experience strengthened the belief that the bedrock of any food security system would be built at the national level. The government of the Philippines launched a new rice production initiative entitled "Focusing on Increasing Provincial Productivity—Rice Self-Sufficiency Plan 2009–2013." The plan envisions a 100 percent self-sufficient rice economy by 2013 through improved rice productivity.

Given how steeply food prices increased and how fast they fell in 2007–2008, it is likely that the growing presence of financial investors in food commodity markets will make the prices overreact to new market information and deviate from fundamentals.[9] It is also reported that once the world economy recovers from the economic recession, both oil and food prices will probably start to rise again.[10] Even though a food crisis is felt most at the national level, the causes of the crisis are usually found in international situations. Thus, solutions depend more and more on international cooperation. There is an urgent need for international leadership to improve cooperation among major food exporting and importing countries to break the upward price spiral, at least for key staple foods like rice, exacerbated by self-fulfilling policies.

REGIONAL LEVEL OF COOPERATION
FOR FOOD SECURITY IN EAST ASIA

The issue of hunger is most precisely felt at the individual and family level. However, responsibility to solve the hunger problem is a concern of national government as well. As experienced in the 2007–2008 rice crisis, the main actors handling food security policy concerns were government bodies. However, it was proved that an individual country alone was not capable of solving the problem because the crisis hit most severely those countries who were not self-sufficient in relation to food. Individual countries were inclined to ensure food security for their own people, regardless of the impact on the international market. Such policy orientation caused the crisis to escalate even further. It is also worth noting that an individual country's self-help policies set back the will and efforts to build a regional community, for which enormous time and money had been invested during the past several decades in the Southeast Asian region.

On the other hand, food security has been treated as an important global issue. Many international organizations such as the FAO, World Food Programme (WFP), and even the World Bank and International Monetary Fund are keen on the food security issue. However, it has not been easy to come up with a viable mechanism to cope with it because of the complexity of the problem. The role of such organizations has usually been limited to humanitarian-aid programs by supporting individual countries' programs for vulnerable people. They have also promoted the seamless trade of food under the belief that the positive role of free trade can improve people's livelihoods.[11] During the crisis, even though many concerns and prescriptions were presented by various international organizations, no concrete measures emerged to ensure food security at the global level. As a result, the global-level projects, such as the Millennium Development Goals (MDGs), seem to be missions impossible or simply a form of lip service.

As for an alternative approach, relying on regional organizations has drawn attention from concerned parties. Since a regional organization is located in-between the national and the global levels, it could be in a better position to come up with a means for food security that is more capable than at the national level and more manageable than at the global level. Of course, the importance of each individual country's role as a bedrock of food security policy cannot be underestimated, and some issues such as climate change and global economic impacts on food security still need to be dealt with at the global level. RPFS in general are designed to implement key elements in the regional strategies, and usually consist of three components as noted by Matthews (2003): trade facilitation, harmonization of national agricultural policies, and support of national special programs for food security.

As summarized in table 13.2, regional food security schemes in East Asia have evolved. In Southeast Asia, ASEAN is a regional organization that has been in existence for more than forty years. Successful implementation of RPFS is not taken for granted at any regional organizations. In the area of food security, ASEAN adopted the Food Security Reserve Agreement on October 4, 1979, so-called the ASEAN Emergence Rice Reserve (AERR), to prevent food shortages resulting from emergency situations. However, not a single ASEAN member country ever tapped into the scheme. The regional rice crisis of 2007–2008 revealed the incapacity of ASEAN's food security scheme for the region. Bello (2005) identified some reasons for the incapacity of AERR: insignificant volume, no information system, weakness of the organization's board due to a small budget, time-consuming measures, and no rules for special prices when earmarked rice needs to be released in emergency.

Previously, an initiative was made by the Japanese government to establish the East Asia Emergency Rice Reserve (EAERR), which covered ASEAN plus three additional countries, namely Japan, China, and South Korea (ASEAN Plus Three).[12] The feasibility study on EAERR was endorsed in 2001, and approved by the second Meeting of ASEAN Ministers on Agriculture and Forestry (AMAF) Plus Three in October 2002. As the coordinator-country of the pilot project, Japan provided 40 million yen to finance the secretariat's expenses in 2004 and 2005. The EAERR is a regional cooperative standing

Table 13.2   East Asian Regional Food Security Scheme[a]

Since	Schemes	Members	Components
1979	AERR	ASEAN members	An implementation of the ASEAN Food Security Reserve Agreement (AFSR) signed by the ASEAN Ministers of Foreign Affairs in 1979 Establish an earmarked rice reserve, initially with 87,000 tons of rice reserve
2003	AFSIS	ASEAN Plus Three members	A scheme to strengthen food security in the region through the systematic collection, analysis, and dissemination of food security related information Focus on human resource development, information network development
2004	EAERR (pilot project)	ASEAN Plus Three members	A regional cooperation standing on humanitarian ground with professional business sense operation Mutual assistance system to provide necessary quantity of rice flexibly and effectively to rice-needy people in the region
2009	AIFSF/ SPA-FS	ASEAN members	A scheme to ensure long-term food security and to improve the livelihoods of farmers in the ASEAN region Consists of four components: Food Security and Emergency / Shortage Relief; Sustainable Food Trade Development; Integrated Food Security Information System; and Agricultural Innovation
2010	APTERR	ASEAN Plus Three members	A scheme to secure food security in an emergency caused by temporary and large-scale calamity Focus on sharing knowledge and expertise; building confidence to improve food security; helping to increase nutritional status of the people

Note[a]: AERR (ASEAN Emergency Rice Reserve); AFSIS (ASEAN Food Security Information System); EAERR (East Asian Emergency Rice Reserve); AIFSF/SPA-FS (ASEAN Integrated Food Security Framework/Strategic Plan of Action on Food Security); APTERR (ASEAN Plus Three Emergency Rice Reserve).

on humanitarian ground with a professional business-model operation. It is a mutual assistance system created to provide necessary quantities of rice, flexibly and effectively, to rice-needy people. Under the EAERR scheme, a number of achievements have been recorded.[13]

As a response to the 2007–2008 rice crisis, the special Senior Officers' Meeting (SOM) at the 29th AMAF on August 5–7, 2008, discussed the concept of the ASEAN Integrated Food Security (AIFS) Framework and the establishment of an ad hoc taskforce to develop detailed work, including a Strategic Plan of Action on Food Security (SPA-FS) in the ASEAN region. The direction to ensure food security in the region was elaborated at the

14th ASEAN Summit in March, 2009 by adopting the AIFS Framework and SPA-FS. Furthermore, the 12th ASEAN Plus Three Summit in October 2009 welcomed the efforts to transform EAERR into a permanent scheme under the name of ASEAN Plus Three Emergence Rice Reserve (APTERR). The 9th AMAF Plus Three Meeting in November 2009 endorsed the preparatory stage of APTERR, and this stage began on March 1, 2010. The finalized APTERR related document was adopted at the 10th AMAF Plus Three Meeting in October 2010.[14]

It seems that the 2007–2008 rice crisis forced ASEAN leaders to face the reality of their food security scheme in the region, and to pursue more reliable measures by expanding the cognitive regional boundary to East Asia. The new scheme that emerged for food security in the East Asian region has both promises and pitfalls. In order to subdue the pitfalls while materializing the promises, it is imperative to form a common ideology and goal to which all regional countries are willing to commit. As Bello (2005) noted, if regional cooperation is to be used as a venue for ensuring food security, the member countries must agree on what food security collectively means to them, and what food items are important to each of them and the region in general, so that regional cooperation under the auspices of a regional organization can be promoted.

As for regional approaches to food security, two directions contend for priority, *a community-oriented approach* and *a free trade approach*. Although the two approaches have different priorities, they do not necessarily work against each other. They could be complementary in the broader perspective of regional cooperation and integration. The food security issue is usually given priority over economic interests because it directly affects the very lives of the people. Should long-term food security be considered, the importance of economic effectiveness would be prominent. The basic condition needed to achieve food security is to maintain food availability at a comfortable level. However, the situation in the world today is not favorable for the agricultural industry to beat out other industries in terms of profit making. In these circumstances, the agricultural sector faces increasing pressure for structural adjustments and technological innovation in order to survive in competition with other industries.

On the other hand, structural adjustment and technological innovation in the agricultural sector, under a free market system, may create a problem in relation to food access. In fact, food access is the most serious problem for food security in East Asia. The issue of food access is closely connected with levels of economic development. In this globalizing world, regional cooperation and integration gain currency to cope with the *jungle game* of the world economy. Regional market integration would increase trade volume if it is coupled with a significant degree of trade liberalization, and if emphasis is put on reducing cost-creating trade barriers, which simply waste resources. Thus, it is believed that regional economic integration may be a precondition for, rather than an obstacle to, integrating developing countries into the world economy by minimizing the costs of market fragmentation (Matthews 2003).

In the area of food security, most East Asian countries have their own weakness, either a lack of competitiveness due to high production costs or lack of resources to promote their production. Given these weaknesses, pursuing an individual country's food self-sufficiency becomes more and more difficult. Thus, initiating and institutionalizing APTERR could be an important step toward regional cooperation for food security in East Asia. APTERR in principle is a community-oriented approach; it is a confidence-building measure among regional countries that are moving toward a regional community. Once the countries in the region have confidence in the regional level of their food security system as a reliable mechanism, the food security burden on member countries would be lessened, and policies aimed at self-sufficiency could be relaxed. Since sharing food implies the closeness of the members of the group, it would be a great initiative to lay the foundation for regional integration in East Asia.[15]

CONCLUSION

The food security status of East Asia, as assessed using the measure of rice, does not seem to be critical. Regional rice production is far beyond the regional consumption level. Although rice does not represent all aspects of food security, it is still the most important grain as a staple food and often considered as a standard item for food security. Food security issues have been taken into serious account not only at the individual country level, but also the regional and global level, since the 1970s. Nevertheless, until recently individual countries took full responsibility for their own food security problems. They felt obliged to count on self-sufficiency as the only option to ensure food security. However, food security threats became increasingly various and originated from unexpected sources, which individual countries found it difficult to tackle via a unilateral approach. Such issues as climate change, energy problems, and economic fluctuations make food security a more globalized issue rather than an individual country's domestic problem.

The 2007–2008 rice crisis in East Asia provided a number of lessons. Among others, the conventional approach to tackle food security problems through unilateral action could make the situation worse. This lesson was taken seriously, and the leaders of East Asian countries took the initiative to establish a capable regional mechanism to ensure food security. Various discussions and decisions have been made to substantiate the initiative. The Plus Three dialogue partners of ASEAN showed their seriousness by committing a substantial volume of earmarked rice reserves to APTERR.[16] This is a very encouraging move, not only for food security issues per se, but also for deepening the spirit of regional cooperation.

However, it is too early to rejoice over what has been accomplished so far because this is just one step forward in the march toward regional food security in East Asia. The capability and sustainability of the scheme is yet to be proved in terms of its progress and performance. The areas of food security concern are evolving continuously from food availability to food access, and today more countries are paying attention to food utilization and safety to ensure food quality. Each country has its own point of concern depending on where it is situated. Thus, it is not easy to incorporate all the different demands into one measure. Deciding on a gradual approach with a long-term perspective would be a wise way to begin. Moreover, the emerging cooperative mechanism for food security in East Asia could propel the ongoing effort toward East Asian regional integration and community building and thus reduce the current sense of gridlock surrounding this plan.

NOTES

1. This chapter was previously published with the same title in *Korean Political Science Review*, *45*(3), 65–86. The original work was supported by the National Research Foundation of Korea (NRF) Grant funded by the Korean Government (MEST) (NRF-2009-362-B00016).

2. Officially recognized at the ASEAN Plus Three Summit meeting (consists of ASEAN 10 countries and China, Japan and Republic of Korea), the Network of East Asian Think-Tanks (NEAT) is a mechanism for research and academic exchange, and a platform for the second-track diplomacy in the regional cooperation among ASEAN Plus Three countries in East Asia.

It aims at integrating the research resources in East Asia, promoting the academic exchanges and providing intellectual support for East Asian cooperation.

3. Food security has become an ever-more complex concept seeking locally specific causes of insecurity. The participants of the 6th East Asia Forum (EAF) in 2008 reiterated that food security should include accessibility, availability, quality, and safety of food.

4. By 2008 one-third of the US maize crop was diverted to biofuel production, encouraged by subsidies of $7 billion per year. Over 5 percent of global cereal production is allocated to biofuels, a rising proportion that has accounted for 30 percent of the increase in the price of corn in the period 2000–2007 (Oneworld UK 2008).

5. Economic development has increased the demand for food products such as wheat, milk and dairy products, and beef, rather than grain. As 7 kg of grain is

required to produce 1 kg of beef, increasing consumption of meat is directly related to more use of grain for feed, not for food (Gill et al. 2003, 33).

6. Agricultural products remain the most protected product group in any type of trade arrangements of the Organization for Economic Co-operation and Development (OECD) countries (ESCAP 2009).

7. Thailand's exports fell to just 10 percent of domestic production from 1973 to 1975, reaching its lowest point in the postwar period, and the country banned exports completely for a few months in 1973. Cambodia joined South Vietnam and completely exited the market, while for all practical purposes Myanmar had also opted out (Dawe 2002, 364–365).

8. Dr. Kayano, vice president of the International Fund for Agricultural Development (IFAD), stressed the fact during the 2nd IFAD-Philippines Partners Knowledge and Learning Market on Food Security, People's Wealth, which was held in the Philippines on October 28–29, 2008.

9. A World Bank study of the causes of the 2007–2008 food price hike concluded that index fund activity (one type of *speculative* activity) played a key role. Biofuels played some role too, but much less than initially thought. No evidence was found that alleged stronger demand by emerging economies had any effect on world prices (Baffess and Haniotis 2010).

10. According to the International Energy Agency, over the period 2008–2015 the price of crude oil will be, on average, $100 per barrel at constant 2007 prices, and rise to $120 in 2030 (ESCAP 2009, 56).

11. During the 2007–2008 rice crisis, the FAO and WFP, together with the Philippine government developed the "Rapid Food Production Enhancement Program," which aimed to improve the government's emergency response to soaring food prices. It was especially designed to support long-term plans of the government to improve paddy production, to contribute to government policy and its development efforts, and to improve the overall living conditions of rural people in all regions to facilitate policy dialogue in the agriculture sector (Muchhala and Molina 2008).

12. Since the process began in 1997, the ASEAN Plus Three cooperation has broadened and deepened in many areas of cooperation. See details in Stubbs (2002).

13. There are three tiers for release of rice stock in the time of emergency. Tier 1 is to release earmarked emergency rice reserves based on a supply-demand matching process between surplus and deficit member countries to meet emergency demand for rice under a commercial trade basis. Tier 2 is to release earmarked emergency rice reserves based on long-term loan agreements, or grant rice between supplying and recipient member countries. Tier 3 is to release stockpiled emergency rice reserves based on requests or an automatic trigger system. This is to meet acute and urgent emergency demand as a first emergency food-aid. There have been many cases of implementation of Tier 3 since 2006, specifically to Indonesia, the Philippines, Cambodia, and Myanmar. The cases of implementing Tier 1 were the realization of talk between Vietnam and the Philippines since 2005, and between Thailand and the Philippines in February 2008.

14. See details about APTERR at http://www.apterr.org/.

15. The issue of regional integration is closely connected with the process and result of regional food security cooperation. However, this study does not touch the issue but leaves it open for separate study in the future.

16. The 13 ASEAN Plus Three countries have agreed in principle to earmark rice stock amounting to 787,000 tons for the emergency reserve, with pledges of 87,000 tons from ASEAN member countries, 250,000 from Japan, 300,000 from China and 150,000 from the Republic of Korea (Rahil 2010, May 8).

REFERENCES

Baffess, J., & Tassos, H. (2010). Placing the 2006/08 commodity price boom into perspective. *Policy Research Working Paper, WPS 5371*. Retrieved from https://openknowledge.worldbank.org/handle/10986/3855.

Balisacan, A. (2004). Averting hunger and food insecurity in Asia. *Asian Journal of Agriculture and Development*, 1(1), 36–55.

Bello, A. (2005). Ensuring food security: A case for ASEAN integration. *Asian Journal of Agriculture and Development*, 2(1–2), 87–108.

Brahmbhatt, M., & Christiaensen, L. (2008). The run on rice. *World Policy Journal*, 25(2), 29–37. Retrieved from http://www.mitpressjournals.org.

Carr, E. (2006). Postmodern conceptualisations, Modernist applications: Rethinking the role of society in food security. *Food Policy*, 31, 14–29.

David, C. (2003). Agriculture. In A. Balisacan & H. Hill (Eds.), *The Philippine economy: Development, policies, and challenges* (pp. 175–218). Quezon City: Ateneo de Manila University Press.

Dawe, D. (2001). How far down the path to free trade? The importance of rice price stabilization in developing Asia. *Food Policy*, 26(2), 163–175.

Dawe, D. (2002). The changing structure of the world rice market, 1950-2000. *Food Policy*, 27(4), 355–370.

Dawe, D., Moya, P., Casiwan, C., & Cabling, J. (2008). Rice marketing systems in the Philippines and Thailand: Do large numbers of competitive traders ensure good performance? *Food Policy*, 33(5), 455–463.

Dilley, M., & Boudreau, T. (2001). Coming to terms with vulnerability: A critique of the food security definition. *Food Policy*, 26(3), 229–247.

Domoguen, R., & Arban, Y. (2008). The challenge of soaring food prices in the Philippines. Retrieved from http://www.ifad.org/newsletter/pi/24.htm.

Economic and Social Commission for Asia and the Pacific (ESCAP). (2009). *Sustainable Agriculture and Food Security in Asia and the Pacific*. Bangkok: United Nations Economic and Social Commission for Asia and the Pacific.

Erjavec, K., & Erjavec, E. (2009). Changing E.U. agricultural policy discourses? The discourse analysis of commissioner's speeches 2000-2007. *Food Policy*, 34(2), 218–226.

Falvey, L. (2004). Reconceiving food security and environmental protection. *Asian Journal of Agriculture and Development*, 1(2), 13–28.

Food and Agriculture Organization (FAO). (1996). Rome declaration on world food security. Retrieved from http://www.fao.org/3/w3613e/w3613e00.htm.

Food and Agriculture Organization (FAO). (2009). Food security statistics. Retrieved from http://www.fao.org/economic/ess/food-security-statistics/en/.

Gill, G., Farrington, J., Anderson, E., Luttrell, C., Conway, T., Saxena, N., & Slater, R. (2003). Food security and the millennium development goal on hunger in Asia. *Working Paper 231 of Overseas Development Institute*. London, UK.

Matthews, A. (2003). *Regional Integration and Food Security in Developing Countries*. Rome: Food and Agriculture Organization of the United Nations.

Maxwell, D., Caldwell, R., & Langworthy, M. (2008). Measuring food insecurity: Can an indicator based on localized coping behaviours be used to compare across contexts? *Food Policy, 33*(6), 533–540.

Muchhala, B., & Molina, N. (2008). Quick fixes or real solutions? The World Bank and IMF respond to the global food and fuel crises. Retrieved from https://foodsecurecanada.org/sites/foodsecurecanada.org/files/Quick_Fixes_or_Real_Solutions.pdf.

Ninno, C., Dorosh, P., & Subbarao, K. (2007). Food aid, domestic policy and food security: Contrasting experiences from South Asia and sub-Saharan Africa. *Food Policy, 32*(4), 413–435.

Oneworld UK. (2008). Food security guide. Retrieved from http://uk.oneworld.net/guides/food_ security#Biofuels.

Othman, N. (2007). Food safety in Southeast Asia: Challenges facing the region. *Asian Journal of Agriculture and Development, 4*(2), 83–92.

Pingali, P. (2006). Westernisation of Asian diets and the transformation of food systems: Implications for research and policy. *Food Policy, 32*(3), 281–298.

Pinstrup-Anderson, P. (2009). Food security: Definition and measurement. *Food Security, 1*(1), 5–7.

Rahil, S. (2010, May 8). Japan, East Asian nations closer to pact on emergency rice reserve. *Japan Times Online*. Retrieved from http://search.japantimes.co.jp/cgi-bin/nn20100508f3.html.

Shiva, V. (2000). *Stolen Harvest: The Hijacking of the Global Food Supply*. Cambridge: South End Press.

Stubbs, R. (2002). ASEAN PLUS THREE: Emerging East Asian Regionalism? *Asian Survey 42*(3), 440–455.

Tolentino, B. (2009, September 23). The G20 and persistent food insecurity. *The Asia Foundation*. Retrieved from http://asiafoundation.org/in-asia/2009/09/23/the-g20-and-persistent-food-insecurity/.

United Nations (UN). (2010). *The Millennium Development Goals Report 2010*. New York: United Nations.

United Nations Development Program (UNDP). (1994). *New Dimensions of Human Security*. New York: Oxford University Press.

Index

agency, 5, 91–94, 97, 109, 110n5
agricultural, 3–4, 7–8, 13–14, 18, 20,
    29–33, 39, 42–43, 47–58, 62–63,
    103, 112n39, 140, 148, 149n6,
    167–68, 231–32, 235, 237, 244, 246,
    249n6
agriculture, 4–5, 8, 21, 47–53, 55–56,
    58, 61–62, 73, 81, 125, 133, 139–40,
    149n6, 235, 249n11
agri-food, 5, 47–48, 53–55, 58, 61–62,
    140, 149
ancestor(s), 76, 126–27
Andong food, 6, 122, 125–27, 129
articulation, 133, 137, 147
authenticity, 215, 221
authority(-ies), 93–94, 124, 149n3, 165

Buddhism, 92, 95–96, 99, 100, 107,
    109, 110n7, 118, 122–24, 127
Buddhist, 5, 91–92, 94–101, 103–9,
    111n11, 111n16, 112n43, 112n49,
    117, 122–24, 127–28, 130, 193;
    cuisine, 6, 91–92, 95–100, 103–9,
    110n3, 122, 129; temple food, 5,
    91–94, 96, 98–101, 103, 108, 110n2,
    122, 125, 128

capital, 14, 15–17, 19, 25, 27–30, 92,
    95–96, 109, 162; cultural, 1; -ism,

46, 69, 106, 125; -ist, 6, 18, 42–43,
    121–22, 126–27, 129–30; -ize(d), 6,
    107, 109; -izing, 103, 107–8, 129
certification, 7, 54, 61, 63n7, 158–60,
    165, 167, 169, 170n7
Chōsen, 14, 16, 21, 29, 32nn7–8, 33.
    See also Joseon
coefficients, 24–25, 215, 226–27
colonial, 4, 13, 14, 16–17, 19–20, 22,
    24, 29–31, 45, 49, 69, 81, 93, 96,
    135; -ism, 1, 3, 135, 146; -ist, 3,
    150n7; Korea, 13–14, 30, 32n3,
    32n11; modernization, 14; post-, 5,
    85, 92, 94, 110n5; reclamation, 13,
    15, 21, 29. *See also* colonization
colonization, 14, 123, 142, 150
commodification, 79, 126, 148
commodity(-ies), 94, 103, 105–6, 108–
    9, 124, 127, 129, 187, 243
communication, 1–2, 134, 165, 169,
    182; food-, 149; studies, 1–2, 149
community, 4, 8, 39–40, 42–45,
    70–71, 76, 78, 106, 135, 144, 162,
    234, 248; agricultural, 42–43;
    global, 187, 231; imagined, 71;
    international, 57, 234; Muslim, 161,
    163; national, 70; -oriented, 236–37,
    246–47; regional, 243, 247; rural,
    50; traditional, 40

About the Editors and Contributors

Namsoo Chang is Professor Emeritus in the Department of Nutritional Science and Food Management at Ewha Womans University. She received her PhD from Rutgers University and worked as research nutritionist at Yale School of Medicine and Washington University School of Medicine. Chang has served as president of the Korean Nutrition Society and internationally on the WHO/FAO Expert Working Group on Vitamins/Minerals Risk Assessment and NIH/Office of Dietary Supplements Annual Bibliography Projects. She has published numerous scholarly papers in international archival journals in the field of vitamin nutrition and metabolism, delivered many invited lectures in international meetings and conferences, and published several books.

Hong Sik Cho is a professor in the Department of Political Science and International Relations at Soongsil University. He obtained his PhD in political science from Sciences Po Paris in 1993 with a dissertation titled "Europe Faces Japan: The EC's Policy towards Japan Cho" and has been teaching European politics and political economy at Soongsil University since 2006. His research interests are the politics of identity, the European regional integration, and the evolution of capitalism. His most recent books include *The Political Economy of Capitalist Civilization* (2020) and *The Networks of Civilization: A Panorama of European Culture* (2018), both published in Korean.

Haney Choi works as a senior medical information specialist at Medical Research and Operation Team of AbbVie Korea. She received her master's degree in nutritional epidemiology at Ewha Womans University. With expertise in the epidemiological studies and post-marketing surveillance, Choi is engaged in scientific communication with health care professionals to generate real-world evidence at the global pharmaceutical company.

Hye Won Chung is a professor of obstetrics and gynecology in the School of Medicine at Ewha Womans University. Her research focuses on reproductive endocrinology, environmental medicine, and mutiethnic cohort study. Chung is the president of the Korean Society of Gynecologic Endocrinology.

Ji-Yun Hwang is an associate professor of foodservice management and nutrition at Sangmyung University. She received her PhD in nutritional sciences at Cornell University. Her research focuses on theory- and evidence-based nutrition education, development of knowledge for interventions to improve nutrition of the underprivileged using epidemiology and qualitative methods, evaluation of effectiveness of nutrition programs and policies, and dietary factors related to chronic diseases. Hwang has authored more than 100 peer-reviewed papers. The significance of her research has been recognized by many awards, such as SNEB-KSCN Professional Award, Excellent Young Scientist Award from American Society for Nutrition, Frontier Award from Federation of Women's Science & Technology Associations, and three Outstanding Paper Awards.

Hee Sun Jeong is an associate professor of traditional culinary culture at Sookmyung Women's University. She has expertise in traditional food culture, changes in trends, royal cuisine, and menu development. Jeong has promoted and educated Korean cuisine in a wide variety of countries, including the United States, Australia, Iraq, Japan, Malaysia, Vietnam, and China. Through her recent research on K-food preferences, she seeks to establish a new direction of Korean food culture and develop new Korean menus across different countries, which would lead to efficient consultations with local governments and leadership training.

Jaehyeon Jeong is an assistant professor (lecturer) of communication at the University of Utah Asia Campus. He obtained his bachelor's degree in anthropology from Seoul National University, master's degrees in visual communication and in media, culture, and communication from Yonsei University and New York University, respectively, and PhD in mass media and communication from Temple University. His broad research program stands at the intersection of critical cultural studies, media industry studies, and global communication. Jeong has published multiple peer-reviewed journal articles, monographs, and online essays on Korean television, food and nationalism, and comics industry/culture, including *Korean Food Television and the Korean Nation* (2020), *Webtoons Go Viral?: The Globalization Processes of Korean Digital Comics*

(Korea Journal, 2020), *A Critique of Korean Cartoonist, Bongsung Park* (2019, published in Korean), and *Genre Hybridity as the Scheme of the Korean Comics Industry* (*International Journal of Comic Art*, 2017).

Nami Joo is a professor in the Department of Food and Nutrition at Sookmyung Women's University. Her primary research interest lies in the dietary life in Korea. Reflecting the shifting demographic structure of the Korean society, her recent works have examined the dietary life of multicultural families and the eating patterns of the elderly with a goal to find the healthiest viable eating pattern. Joo has also developed silver foods for seniors, which have been patented.

Dong-Yeob Kim is an associate professor of the Korea Institute for ASEAN Studies at Busan University of Foreign Studies. He obtained his PhD in political science from the University of the Philippines Diliman in 2003. His primary research areas include democracy and development in East Asia (specifically, the Philippines and South Korea) and ASEAN studies. Kim has served as vice president of the Korean Association of Southeast Asian Studies. Currently, he is the editor of *The Journal of Asian Studies* (Korean) and associate editor of *SUVANNABHUMI: Multi-disciplinary Journal of Southeast Asian Studies* (English). Kim has published a number of books, including *Transforming Western Democracy in Southeast Asia: The Case of Lanao del Sur, the Philippines* (2018), *ASEAN-Korea Relations: Twenty-five Years of Partnership and Friendship* (2015, coauthor), *Noli Me Tángere* (2015, translated to Korean), and *The Promise of ICTs in Asia: Key Trends and Issues* (2008, coedited), and articles both domestically and internationally.

Hak-Seon Kim is an associate professor in the School of Hospitality and Tourism Management at Kyungsung University. He completed his bachelor's degree and master's degree at Seoul National University and received his PhD in hospitality administration from Texas Tech University. Kim's research focuses on hospitality service management, consumer behavior, and tourism big data analysis. He is the founder of research center for Wellness & Tourism Big Data Analysis, which conducts a variety of research in the field of hospitality and tourism industry. His research team has won numerous awards at both domestic and international conferences. In addition, Kim has served as the vice-dean of External Affairs (2018 to spring 2020) and the dean of International Affairs (since fall 2020) at Kyungsung University. His teaching and research excellence have been recognized by multiple Faculty Awards at Kyungsung University.

Jeehee Kim is a PhD student in comparative literature at Yonsei University. Her broad research program stands at the intersection of cultural studies and literary analysis, and, more specifically, her research has involved exploring urban space, modernism, trauma, and contemporary art/literature. Kim's work on the narratives in contemporary Korean visual and literary arts was funded by the Global Ph.D. Fellowship Program in Korea. In addition, her recent research project, which examines the narrative of growth in the novels by Kim Seung Ok, has been supported by BK21 Plus project of the National Research Foundation of Korea Grant. In the study, Kim employs the concept of "soundscape" to investigate the uncanny detected in the voice of the narrator and the way that narrative represents the urban space through sound images and auditory experience.

Eun-Jin Lee is an affiliate professor of hotel confectionary and bakery at Kimpo University. She received her master's degree from the Graduate School of Hotel and Tourism at Kyung Hee University, and she is currently pursuing her doctoral degree at Sejong University. Lee has published multiple articles in peer-reviewed journals, including *The Korean Journal of Culinary Research* and *Culinary Science & Hospitality Research*. She has also (co)authored a number of practical books within the fields of foodservice management, confectionary and bakery, and Western culinary practice.

Jee Hye Lee is an assistant professor of food and nutrition at University of Ulsan. She received her bachelor's degree in Food and Nutrition (2004) from University of Ulsan; master's degree (2008) and PhD (2012) in food science, from University of Missouri. Her doctoral dissertation was on the microbiological and psychological perspectives of ethnic foods. Lee obtained the Korean Registered Dietitian (RD) Certification in 2004. She also worked as a director of Children's Food Management Support Center (Ulsan Jung-Gu) from 2014 to 2017. Lee is a recipient of the Best Paper Award at the annual Korean Dietetic Association conference.

Youngmin Lee is a cultural geographer teaching and working in the College of Education as well as in the Graduate School of Multi/Inter-cultural Studies and Asian Women's Studies at Ewha Womans University. He received his PhD in geography and anthropology from Louisiana State University. Lee's research explores the theoretical relations between culture and geography in the framework of post-isms, and the reconstruction of place and region according to global migration and tourism. He had worked as the President of Korean Urban Geographical Society and has involved with several government institutes as an advisor for the policies of place and culture.

Chaisung Lim is a professor of economics at Rikkyo University. He received his PhD from University of Tokyo in 2002. Lim has published numerous monographs and journal articles on the economic history of Northeast Asia, including *A Wartime Economy and Railroad Management* (2005), *History of Sino-Japanese War of the North China Railway Company* (2016), *Embodying Labor* (2019), and *Eating and Drinking Korea* (2019).

Seungsook Moon is a professor of sociology at Vassar College, where she has served as the chair of Sociology Department, the director of Asian Studies Program, and the resident director of London Program for Media and Culture. She is the author of *Militarized Modernity and Gendered Citizenship in South Korea* (2005) and a coeditor, coauthor, and contributor of *Over There: Living with the U.S. Military Empire from World War II to the Present* (2010). As a political and cultural sociologist and scholar of gender studies specializing in South Korea, Moon has published numerous articles and has been consulted by a variety of news media, including *CNN*, *The Economist*, *El Periodico* (Spain), *Korea Herald* (South Korea), *Weekendavisen* (Denmark), and *South China Morning Post* (Hong Kong).

Joong-Hwan Oh is a professor of sociology at Hunter College of the City University of New York. He received his BA in sociology from Pusan National University (South Korea) and his MA and PhD in sociology from the University of South Carolina. He teaches a wide range of courses, including urban sociology, the sociology of online communities, Asians in the United States, and peopling in New York City, at Hunter College. His research expertise lies in immigration, urban communities, online social networks, racial and ethnic inequalities, and East Asia. Oh is the author of *Examining the Use of Online Social Networks by Korean Graduate Students: Navigating Intercultural Academic Experiences* (2019) and *Immigration and Social Capital in the Age of Social Media: Messages of the American Social Institutions on a Korean-American Women's Online Community* (2016). His works have also appeared in more than twenty peer-reviewed journals, including *International Migration Review*, *Urban Studies*, *New Media & Society*, *Social Science & Medicine*, *American Journal of Economics and Sociology*, and *Sociological Inquiry*.

Hyunseo Park is a PhD student in the Department of Geography, Environment, and Spatial Sciences at Michigan State University. She obtained her master's degrees in Geography from Saint Mary's University (Canada) and Ewha Womans University (South Korea), at the latter of which she completed her bachelor's degree in Social Studies. Park's research interest revolves around geographical understandings of food from a multidimensional perspective and its relation to health and well-being. Her master's thesis in Korea investigated how competing narratives about halal food had been articulated within social discourses of healthy diet and religious extremism as well as its impacts on Muslim immigrants and the halal food market in Korea. Since her research in Canada, she has examined the accessibility to health-promoting resources such as primary healthcare and ethnic food retailers among Korean Canadians. Her current research focuses on neighborhood environments that affect social and geographical inequalities in health and well-being among immigrants and ethnic minorities across different places.

Youngil Park is an instructor at Sookmyung Women's University, where she received her PhD in Food and Nutrition in 2016. Her research areas include food service, food development, functional food, dietary culture, and cooking method. Park has published multiple articles in Korean peer-reviewed journals, such as *Nutrition Research and Practice*, *Journal of the East Asian Society of Dietary Life*, *The Korean Journal of Food and Nutrition*, and *Journal of the Korean Dietetic Association*.

Joung-Min Son is an affiliate professor of Foodservice Management at Yeongsan University. She received her doctoral degree at Kyungsung University, where she studied the quality of service of Japanese restaurants. Son has published multiple peer-reviewed journal articles within the fields of foodservice management, culinary science, and tourism management. In addition to her academic contribution, she had worked as a chef at a variety of high-end hotels in Korea, such as Commodore Hotel, the Westin Chosun Busan, and Homers Hotel. Son has also serviced as a referee of Craftsman Cook of Japanese Food and Craftsman Cook of Blowfish.

Wonkyu Song is a deputy director of Research Institute for Agriculture and Peasant Policies established by the Korean Peasants League and the Korean Women Peasant Association. He received a PhD in agri-food economics from Konkuk University Glocal Campus. He is an editorial board member of *The Journal of Rural Society* (Korea) and coauthor of *Food and Agriculture in South Korea—Past, Present, and Alternative of Korean Agrifood System*. His research focuses on food sovereignty and alternative agri-food movements of non-state actors, such as peasant organizations and alternative food networks.

Soh-yon Yi is an adjunct faculty of Korean modern literature at Sogang University and Hongik University. She is the author of *Staring Overlapping Eyes* (2005) and a co-translator of *The Cambridge Introduction to Narrative* (2010). As a literary critic and scholar of narratology and mass media studies, she has published numerous articles in peer-reviewed journals and taught on Korean postwar fictions, TV dramas, and movies.

Byeong-Seon Yoon is a professor of the Division of International Business and Economics at Konkuk University Glocal Campus and the representative of Korea Forum of UN Declaration on the rights of peasants. His main research fields are political economy of modern agri-food system and alternative movements. Yoon is the author of *Who Is Threatening Our Dinner Table?: The Power of Transnational Agribusiness* (2006) and first author of *The Struggle for Food Sovereignty in South Korea* (2013).